D1204981

FTCE Exceptional Stu Education K-12

Teacher Certification Exam
Sharon A Wynne, MS.

XAMonline, Inc.

Boston

XAMonline, Inc.
21 Orient Avenue
Melrose, MA 02176
Toll Free 1-800-509-4128
Email: info@xamonline.com
Web www.xamonline.com
Fax: 1-617-583-5552

Library of Congress Cataloging-in-Publication Data

Wynne, Sharon A.
    Exceptional Education Ed. K-12: Teacher Certification / Sharon A. Wynne
    ISBN 978-1-60787-473-7
    1. Exceptional Education Ed. K-12.   2. Study Guides.   3. FTCE
    4. Teachers' Certification & Licensure.   5. Careers

Disclaimer:
The opinions expressed in this publication are the sole works of XAMonline and were created independently from the National Education Association, Educational Testing Service, or any State Department of Education, National Evaluation Systems or other testing affiliates.

Between the time of publication and printing, state specific standards as well as testing formats and website information may change and these changes may not be included in part or in whole within this product. Sample test questions are developed by XAMonline and reflect content similar to that on real tests; however, they are not former tests. XAMonline assembles content that aligns with state standards but makes no claims nor guarantees teacher candidates a passing score. Numerical scores are determined by testing companies such as NES or ETS and then are compared with individual state standards. A passing score varies from state to state.

Printed in the United States of America

FTCE: Exceptional Education Ed. K-12
ISBN: 978-1-60787-473-7

TABLE OF CONTENTS

About the Florida Teacher Competency Exam (FTCE)

The following information was taken directly from the Florida Department of Education website and is current at the time of the creation of this publication.

Florida law requires that teachers demonstrate mastery of basic skills, professional knowledge, and content area of specialization (Exceptional Student Education K-12). Testing requirements for teacher candidates seeking certification are described in Section 1012.56, Florida Statutes (FS), and in 6A-4.0021, Florida Administrative Code (FAC). The content areas of specialization exams are generally given in the morning, with arrival at 8:30 A.M. and departure at about noon. Actual testing time is 2 and 1/2 hours. The passing score for certification in Exceptional Student Education K-12 is 69%. A standard scaled score of at least 200 is considered a 'passing' score.

Graduates of Florida state-approved teacher preparation programs **who have passed all three portions of the Florida Teacher Certification Examination (FTCE)** will qualify for a Professional Florida Educator's Certificate.

If the above statement describes you, then begin the "Steps to Certification" by going to www.fldoe.org. You will apply for a Florida Professional Certificate in your program area. Be sure that your application package includes an official score report reflecting passing scores on all portions of the FTCE **if taken prior to July 2002**. All scores earned after July 1, 2002, are submitted electronically.

After your application for certification is on file, the Bureau will issue you an **Official Statement of Status of Eligibility**. This statement will indicate your individualized testing requirements. After your application has been received and is on file, you may contact the Bureau by phone at: Toll free in Florida: (800) 445-6739 or check the application status at www.fldoe.org/edcert.

Examination Dates

Examination dates occur throughout the year. Tests can be taken by appointment, Monday through Saturday, at various testing locations. Pearson VUE and other testing locations can be found on the following website: http://www.fl.nesinc.com/FL_TestDates.asp

Score reports for multiple choice tests are released within four weeks of the test date. An unofficial score report is provided at the test site as well, unless the test was being redeveloped or revised at the time of competition.

For the latest information regarding test registration, pass/fail status, viewing and downloading the registration bulletin, and information on computer-based testing, please visit the University of South Florida's (USF) FTCE/FELE Web site.

For all phone inquiries, please contact the FTCE/FELE office at (813) 974-2400. Or write to

FTCE/FELE
P.O. Box 17900
Tampa, FL 33682-7900

Registration for FTCE

Electronic registration can be completed twenty-four hours a day, seven days a week, at the following web address: http://www.fl.nesinc.com/FL_Register.asp

A *current, completed, and correct* application for FTCE *MUST BE RECEIVED* at the FTCE Tampa address by the deadlines listed in the latest Registration Bulletin and on this Web site.

If you are mailing your application with ample delivery time before the on-time or late registration deadline, use the preaddressed envelope that is attached inside the Registration Bulletin or send the application to the address listed below.

FTCE/FELE
P.O. Box 17900
Tampa, FL 33682-7900

If you need to deliver the application in person or have an overnight carrier service deliver it (e.g., FedEx, DHL) to ensure it arrives by the on-time registration deadline or late deadline, use the address listed below.

FTCE/FELE
10421 University Center Drive
Suite 300C
Tampa, FL 33612

It is to an applicant's advantage to submit application materials as early as possible. Applications can be ordered through the University of South Florida's FTCE/FELE Web site; bulletins and applications can also be requested by calling (813) 974-2400.

Applicants should check the University of South Florida's FTCE/FELE Web site and the FTCE Bulletin for updated information regarding changes in tests and application procedures.

Applications and registration bulletins are also available from the following locations:

- Florida school district offices
- Education departments at Florida colleges and universities

Fees and Payment Methods for the FTCE

An application is not considered complete without the appropriate fee. As of April 2009, there is a $25.00 fee for each of the tests (General Knowledge, Professional Education, and subject areas). During late registration, there is a $15.00 charge *for each test, in addition to the regular fee.*

Supplemental Administration Fees: An additional charge of $100.00 is added to the required test fees. Refer to the FTCE Registration Bulletin for additional information. As of 2014, the first testing attempt fee is $200, and the retake fee is $220.

General Information

As an alternative to paper-and-pencil tests, several computer-based tests will be made available. The tests will be offered at flexible times and at certain locations throughout the year, including several Pearson VUE testing centers and university computer labs. The computer-based tests are equivalent to the paper-and-pencil tests in length and difficulty. All of the tests contain only multiple-choice questions. Examinees will be able to preview the questions as well as review and change their answers while taking the test. Unofficial score reports will appear on the computer monitor at the conclusion of each test. Official score reports will be mailed approximately 2 weeks after the test.

INTRODUCTION

This one-volume study guide was designed for professionals preparing to take a teacher competency test in special education or in any field in which the principles of special education are a part of the test content. Objectives specific to the field of special education were obtained from state departments of education, federal territories, and dependencies across the nation. Educators preparing to take tests in the various areas of special education should find the manual helpful, as the objectives and the scope of the discussions concerning each objective cover a wide range of topics in the field.

The study guide offers many benefits to the person who requires a qualifying score on a competency test in special education. A large number of source materials must be covered in order to study the conceptual knowledge reflected by the objectives listed in each state study guide. These objectives encompass the major content of the special education field. The term "objective" may be called "competency" in some states, such as in Florida. These terms are synonymous and refer to an item of professional knowledge the applicant must master.

Many prominent textbooks used by teacher training programs nationwide were researched for the content of this book. Other important resources (e.g. books, journal articles, and media) were included in the discussions about the objectives. The compilation of this research alleviates the hardship imposed on a teacher who attempts to accumulate, as one individual preparing for an examination, the vast body of professional material. This one-volume study guide highlights the current knowledge and accepted concepts of the field of special education, thus gathering this material in one tome.

The book is organized in order of competency, followed by major topical sections according to each competency. These topics often correspond with course titles and textbooks in pre-service teacher training programs. The objectives and discussions about them comprise the main content within each section. Specific references have been given for charts and quoted materials, which were included to enhance understanding of conceptual discussions. Complete reference citations can be located in the reference listings in the back of this test guide. Specialized terms are defined in the body of the text as they arise. The definitions are stated in the contextual usage of special education.

Finally, questions specific to the discussion of each objective have been included to help determine if the reader understands the material. Correctness of responses to questions can be checked in the Answer Key section. Test questions are written as teaching mechanisms and appear in the style and format to cover those used on tests by the state.

Though this manual is comprehensive, it in no way purports to contain all the research and applied techniques in every area of exceptionality. Research generates new applications, and continuing in-service education is a requirement for all special education professionals. This manual gives the reader a one-volume summary of the fundamentals known and practiced at the time of writing.

Great Study and Testing Tips!

What to study in order to prepare for the subject assessments is the focus of this study guide but equally important is *how* you study.

You can increase your chances of truly mastering the information by taking some simple but effective steps.

Study Tips:

1. *Some foods aid the learning process.* Foods such as milk, nuts, seeds, rice, and oats help your study efforts by releasing natural memory enhancers called CCKs (*cholecystokinin*) composed of *tryptophan, choline,* and *phenylalanine.* All of these chemicals enhance the activity of neurotransmitters associated with memory. Before studying, try a light, protein-rich meal of eggs, turkey, or fish. All of these foods release the memory-enhancing chemicals. The better the connections, the more you comprehend.

Likewise, before you take a test, stick to a light snack comprised of energy boosting and relaxing foods. A glass of milk, a piece of fruit, or some peanuts all release various memory-boosting chemicals and help you to focus on the subject at hand.

2. *Learn to take great notes.* A by-product of our modern culture is that we have grown accustomed to getting our information in short doses (i.e., TV news sound bites or *USA Today*-style newspaper articles.)

Consequently, we've trained ourselves to assimilate information better in *neat little packages.* If your notes are scrawled all over the paper, it fragments the flow of the information. Strive for clarity. Newspapers use a standardized format to achieve clarity. Your notes can be much clearer through use of proper formatting.

A very effective format is called the *"Cornell Method."* Take a sheet of loose-leaf lined notebook paper and draw a line all the way down the paper about 1-2" from the left-hand edge. Draw another line across the width of the paper about 1-2" up from the bottom. Repeat this process on the reverse side of the page.

Look at the highly effective result. You have ample room for notes, a left hand margin for special emphasis items or inserting supplementary data from the textbook, a large area at the bottom for a brief summary, and a little rectangular space for anything you want.

3. *Get the concept, then the details.* Too often we focus on the details and don't gather an understanding of the overall concept. However, if you simply memorize only dates, places, or names, you may miss the whole point of the subject.

A key way to understand things is to put them in your own words. If you are working from a textbook, automatically summarize each paragraph in your mind. If you are outlining text, don't simply copy the author's words.

Rephrase them in your own words. You remember your own thoughts and words much better than someone else's, and subconsciously tend to associate the important details to the core concepts.

4. *Ask Why?* Pull apart written material paragraph by paragraph and don't forget the captions under the illustrations.

Example: If the heading is "Stream Erosion", flip it around to read "Why do streams erode?" Then answer the question.

If you train your mind to think in a series of questions and answers, not only will you learn more, but it also helps to lessen the test anxiety because you are used to answering questions.

5. *Read for reinforcement and future needs.* Even if you only have 10 minutes, put your notes or a book in your hand. Your mind is similar to a computer; you must input data in order to process it. *By reading, you are creating the neural connections for future retrieval.* The more times you read something, the more you reinforce the learning of ideas.

Even if you don't fully understand something on the first pass, *your mind stores much of the material for later recall.*

6. *You must relax to learn, so go into exile.* Our bodies respond to an inner clock called biorhythms. Burning the midnight oil works well for some people, but not everyone.
If possible, set aside a particular place to study that is free of distractions. Shut off the television, cell phone and electronic devices, and exile your friends and family during your study period.

If you are bothered by silence, try background music. Light classical music at a low volume has been shown to be particularly effective in aiding concentration. Music that evokes pleasant emotions without lyrics is highly recommended. Try just about anything by Mozart. It relaxes you.

7. *Use arrows, not highlighters.* At best, it's difficult to read a page full of yellow, pink, blue, and green streaks. the mess of colors obscure the message. A quick note, an underline, or an arrow pointing to a particular passage are much clearer than clusters of highlighted words.

8. *Budget your study time.* Although you shouldn't ignore any of the material, *allocate your available study time in the same ratio that topics may appear on the test.*

Testing Tips:

1. *Get smart, play dumb.* Don't read anything into the question. Don't make an assumption that the test writer is looking for something other than what is asked. Stick to the question as written and don't read into it.

2. *Read the question and all the choices twice before answering.* You may miss something by not carefully reading, and then re-reading, both the question and the answers.

If you don't have a clue as to the right answer, leave it blank the first time through. Go on to the other questions, as they may provide a clue to how to answer the skipped questions.

If, later on, you still can't answer the skipped ones . . . ***Guess.***

The only penalty for guessing is that you *might* get it wrong. Only one thing is certain; if you don't put anything down, you *will* get it wrong!

3. *Turn the question into a statement.* Look at the way the questions are worded. The syntax of the question usually provides a clue. Does it seem more familiar as a statement rather than as a question? Does it sound strange?
By turning a question into a statement, you may be able to spot whether an answer sounds right, and it may also trigger memories of material you have read.

4. *Look for hidden clues.* It's actually very difficult to compose multiple-foil (choice) questions without giving away part of the answer in the options presented.

In most multiple-choice questions you can often easily eliminate one or two of the potential answers. This leaves you with only two real possibilities. Your odds become 'fifty-fifty' for very little work.

5. ***Trust your instincts.*** For every fact that you read, you subconsciously retain a portion of the knowledge. On questions that you aren't really certain about, go with your basic instincts. **Your first impression on how to answer a question is usually correct.**

6. ***Mark your answers directly on the test booklet.*** Don't bother trying to fill in the optical scan sheet on the first pass through the test. *Just be very careful not to miss-mark your answers when you eventually transcribe them to the scan sheet.*

7. ***Watch the clock***! You have a set amount of time to answer the questions. Don't get bogged down trying to answer a single question at the expense of ten questions you can more readily answer.

Good Luck!

COMPETENCY 1.0   KNOWLEDGE OF FOUNDATIONS OF EXCEPTIONAL STUDENT EDUCATION

Skill 1.1   Identify state and federal legislation and case law that have affected the education of students with disabilities.

Background: The U.S. Constitution does not specify protection for education. However, all states provide education, and thus individuals are guaranteed protection and due process under the 14th Amendment. The basic source of law for special education is the Individuals with Disabilities Education Act (IDEA) and its accompanying regulations. IDEA represents the latest phase in the philosophy of educating children with disabilities. Initially, children with disabilities often did not go to school. When they did, they were segregated into special classes in order to avoid disrupting the regular class. Their education usually consisted of simple academics, and later, training for manual jobs.

By the mid-1900s, advocates for handicapped children argued that segregation was inherently unequal. By the time of P.L. 94-142, about half of the estimated 8 million handicapped children in the U.S. were either not being appropriately served in school or were excluded from schooling altogether. There were a disproportionate number of minority children placed in special programs. Identification and placement practices and procedures were inconsistent, and parental involvement was generally not encouraged. After segregation on the basis of race was declared unconstitutional in *Brown v, Board of Education*, parents and other advocates filed similar lawsuits on behalf of children with handicaps. The culmination of their efforts was P.L. 94-142. This section is a brief summary of that law and other major legislation which affect the manner in which special education services are delivered to children with disabilities.

Significant Legislation with an Impact on Exceptional Student Education

Brown v. Board of Education, 1954: While this case specifically addressed the inequality of "separate but equal" facilities on the basis of race, the concept that segregation was inherently unequal—even if facilities were provided—was later applied to handicapping conditions.

Diana v. the State Board of Education, 1970: This case resulted in the decision that all children must be tested in their native language.

Wyatt v. Stickney, 1971: This case established the right to adequate treatment (education) for institutionalized persons with intellectual disabilities.

1

Pennsylvania Association for Retarded Citizens (PARC) v. Commonwealth of Pennsylvania, 1972: Special Education was guaranteed to children with intellectual disabilities. The victory in this case sparked other court cases for children with other disabilities.

Mills v. Board of Education of the District of Columbia, 1972: The right to special education was extended to all children with disabilities, not just intellectually disabled children. Judgments in PARC and Mills paved the way for P.L. 94-142.

Public Law 93-112 (Rehabilitation Amendments of 1973): The first comprehensive federal statute to address specifically the rights of disabled youth. It prohibited illegal discrimination in education, employment, or housing on the basis of a disability.

Section 504, Rehabilitation Act of 1973: Section 504 expands an older law by extending its protection to other areas that receive federal assistance, such as education. Protected individuals must (a) have a physical or mental impairment that substantially limits one or more major life activities, such as self-care, walking, seeing, breathing, working, or learning; (b) have a record of such an impairment; or (c) be regarded as having such an impairment. A disability in itself is not sufficient grounds for a complaint of discrimination. The person must be otherwise qualified, or able to meet, the requirements of the program in question.

Public Law 93-380 (Education Amendments of 1974): Public Law 94-142 is the funding portion of this act. It required states to provide full educational opportunities for children with disabilities. It addressed identification, fair evaluation, alternative placements, due process procedures, and free, appropriate public education.

Public Law 94-142 (Education for all Handicapped Children Act), 1975: This law provided for a free, appropriate public education for all children with disabilities, defined special education and related services, and imposed rigid guidelines on the provisions of those services. (Refer to Objectives 2 and 3 in this section). It paralleled the provision for a free and appropriate public education in Section in 504 of Public Law 94-142 and extended these services to preschool children with disabilities (ages 3-5) through provisions to preschool incentive grants.

The philosophy behind these pieces of legislation, and their subsequent reauthorization and renaming as IDEA in 1990, is that education is to be provided to all children aged 6-18 who meet eligibility requirements. All children are assumed capable of benefiting from education. For children with severe or profound handicaps, "education" may be interpreted to include training in basic self-help skills and vocational training, as well as academics.

The principles of IDEA also incorporate the concept of "normalization." Within this concept, persons with disabilities are allowed access to everyday patterns and conditions of life that are as close as possible or equal to their non-disabled peers. There are seven fundamental provisions of IDEA.

1. **Free Appropriate Public Education (FAPE).**
2. **Notification and procedural rights for parents.**
3. **Identification and services to all children**
4. **Necessary related services**
5. **Individualized assessments**
6. **Individualized Education Plans**
7. **Least Restrictive Environment (LRE)**

These provisions are discussed in detail in Competency 1.2.

Goss v. Lopez, 1975: This case ruled that the state could not deny a student education without following due process. While this decision is not based on a special education issue, the process of school suspension and expulsion is obviously critical in assuring an appropriate public education to children with disabilities.

Public Law 95-56 (Gifted and Talented Children's Act), 1978: This case defined the gifted and talented population, and focused upon this exceptional category, which was not included in Public Law 94-142.

Larry P. v. Riles, 1979: This case ordered the reevaluation of black students enrolled in classes for educable mental retardation (EMR) and enjoined the California State Department of Education from the use of intelligence tests in subsequent EMR placement decisions.

Parents in Action on Special Education (PASE) v. Hannon, 1980: This case ruled that IQ tests are necessarily biased against ethnic and racial subcultures.

Board of Education v. Rowley, 1982: Amy Rowley was a deaf elementary school student whose parents rejected their school district's proposal to provide a tutor and speech therapist services to supplement their daughter's instruction in the regular classroom. Her parents insisted on an interpreter even though Amy was making satisfactory social, academic, and educational progress without one. In deciding in favor of the school district, the Supreme Court ruled that school districts must provide those services that permit a student with disabilities to benefit from instruction. Essentially, the court ruled that the states are obligated to provide a "basic floor of opportunity" that is reasonable to allow the child to benefit from social education.

Public Law 98-199 (Education of the Handicapped Act [EHA] Amendments), 1983: Public Law 94-142 was amended to provide added emphasis on parental education and preschool, secondary, and post-secondary programs for children and youth with disabilities.

Irving Independent School District v. Tatro, 1984: EHA and **IDEA** list health services as one of the "related services" that schools are mandated to provide to exceptional students. Amber Tatro, who had spina bifida, required the insertion of a catheter on a regular schedule in order to empty her bladder. The issue was specifically over the classification of clean, intermittent catheterization (CIC) as a medical service (not covered under IDEA) or a "related health service" which would be covered. In this instance, the catheterization was not declared a medical service, but a "related service" necessary for the student to have in order to benefit from special education. The school district was obliged to provide the service. The Tatro case has implications for students with other medical impairments who may need services to allow them to attend classes at the school.

Smith v. Robinson, 1984: This 1984 case concerned reimbursement of attorney's fees for parents who win litigation under IDEA. At the time of this case, IDEA did not provide for such reimbursement. Following this ruling, Congress passed a law awarding attorneys' fees to parents who win their litigation.

Public Law 99-372 (Handicapped Children's Protection Act of 1985): This law allowed parents who are unsuccessful in due process hearings or reviews to seek recovery of attorneys' fees.

P.L. 99-457, 1986 (Revisions of EHA): Beginning with the 1991-1992 school year, special education programs were required for children ages 3-5, with most states offering outreach programs to identify children with special needs from birth to age 3. In place of, or in addition to, an annual IEP, the entire family's needs are addressed by an Individual Family Service Plan (IFSP), which is reviewed with the family every six months.

Public Law 99-457 (Education of the Handicapped Act Amendments of 1986): It reauthorized existing EHA, amended Public Law 94-142 to include financial incentives for states to educate children 3 to 5 years old by the 1990-1991 school year, and established incentive grants to promote programs serving infants with disabilities (birth to 2 years of age).

Public Law 99-506 (Rehabilitation Act Amendments of 1986): It authorized formula grant funds for the development of supported employment demonstration projects.

School Board of Nassau County v. Arline, 1987: This case established that contagious diseases are a disability under Section 504 of the Rehabilitation Act and that people with them are protected from discrimination if otherwise qualified (actual risk to health and safety to others make persons unqualified).

Honig v. Doe, 1988: Essentially, students may not be denied education or exclusion from school when their misbehavior is related to their handicap. The "stay put" provision of IDEA allows students to remain in their current educational setting pending the outcome of administrative or judicial hearings. In the case of behavior that is a danger to the student or to others, the court allows school districts to apply their normal procedures for dealing with dangerous behavior, such as time-out, loss of privileges, detention, or study carrels. Where the student has presented an immediate threat to others, that student maybe temporarily suspended for up to 10 school days to give the school and the parents time to review the IEP and discuss possible alternatives to the current placement.

Public Law 101-336 (American with Disabilities Act ADA), 1990: This law was patterned after Section 504 of the Rehabilitation Act of 1973 and gives civil rights protection to individuals with disabilities in private sector employment, all public services, public accommodations, transportation, and telecommunications. It bars discrimination in employment, transportation, public accommodations, and telecommunications in all aspects of life, not just those receiving federal funding. Title ll and Title lll are applicable to special education because they cover the private sector, such as private schools, and require access to public accommodations. New and remodeled public buildings, transportation vehicles, and telephone systems now must be accessible to the handicapped. ADA also protects individuals with contagious diseases, such as AIDS, from discrimination.

In 1990, the U.S. House of Representatives opened for citizen comment the issue of a separate exceptionality category for students with attention deficit disorders. The issue was tabled without legislative action.

Public Law 101-476 (Individuals with Disabilities Education Act/IDEA), 1990:: Reauthorized and renamed existing EHA. This amendment to EHA changed the term "handicapped" to "disability," expanded related services, and required individual education programs (IEPs) to contain transitional goals and objectives for adolescents (ages 16 and above, special situations).

Florence County School Dist Four v. Shannon Carter, 1993: This case established that when a school district does not provide FAPE for a student with a disability, the parents may seek reimbursement for private schooling. This decision has encouraged districts to be more inclusive of students with autism who receive ABA/Lovaas therapy.

IDEA 97 reauthorization: This amendment retains the major provisions of previous federal laws and also includes modifications to the law. Some of the changes include: participation of students with disabilities in statewide assessment programs with accommodations when required; changes to the IEP with emphasis on students with disabilities participating in the general curriculum and regular education teachers taking part in developing the IEP; lowering the age to begin focusing on transition service needs from 16 to 14; the guarantee that no student with a disability is deprived of continuing educational services because of behavior.

No Child Left Behind Act (NCLB), 2002: No Child Left Behind, Public Law 107-110, was signed on January 8, 2002. It addresses accountability of school personnel for student achievement with the expectation that every child will demonstrate proficiency in reading, math, and science. The first full wave of accountability will be in 12 years when children who attended school under NCLB graduate, but the process to meet that accountability has already begun. In fact, as students progress through the school system, testing will show if an individual teacher has effectively met the needs of his/her students. Through testing, each student's adequate yearly progress, or lack thereof, will be tracked.

NCLB affects regular and special education students, gifted students and slow learners, and children of every ethnicity, culture, and environment. NCLB is a document that encompasses every American educator and student.

Educators are affected as follows: Elementary teachers of grades K-3 are responsible for teaching, reading, and using different science-based approaches as needed. Elementary teachers of upper grades will teach reading, math, and science. Middle and high school teachers will teach to new, higher standards. Sometimes, they will have the task of playing catch up with students who did not have adequate education in earlier grades.

Special educators are responsible for teaching students to a level of proficiency comparable to that of their non-disabled peers. This will raise the bar of academic expectations throughout the grades. For some students with disabilities, the criteria for getting a diploma will be more difficult. Although a small percentage of students with disabilities will need alternate assessments, they will still need to meet grade appropriate goals.

In order for special education teachers to meet the professional criteria of this act, they must be *highly qualified* - that is, certified or licensed in their area of special education, and show proof of a specific level of professional development in the core subjects that they teach. As special education teachers receive specific education in the core subjects they teach, they will be better prepared to teach to the same level of learning standards as the general education teacher.

M.L. v. Federal Way School District (WA) in the Ninth Circuit Court of Appeals, 2004: This case ruled that absence of a regular education teacher on an IEP team was a serious procedural error.

IDEA 2004 reauthorization: The second revision of IDEA occurred in 2004. IDEA was reauthorized as the Individuals with Disabilities Education Improvement Act of 2004 (IDEIA 2004) and is commonly referred to as IDEA 2004. IDEA 2004 was effective July 1, 2005.

The intention was to improve IDEA by adding the understanding that special education students need preparation for further study beyond the high school setting by teaching compensatory methods. Accordingly, IDEA 2004 provided a close tie to PL 89-10, the Elementary and Special Education Act of 1965, and stated that students with special needs should have maximum access to the general curriculum. This was defined as the amount for an individual student to reach his/her fullest potential. Full inclusion was stated not to be the only option by which to achieve this and specified that skills should be taught to help students compensate later in life in cases where inclusion was not the best setting.

IDEA 2004 added a new requirement for special education teachers on the secondary level, enforcing NCLBs "Highly Qualified" requirements in the subject area of their curriculum. The rewording in this part of IDEA states that they shall be "no less qualified" than teachers in the core areas.

Free and Appropriate Public Education (FAPE) was revised by mandating that students have maximum access to appropriate general education. Additionally, LRE placement for those students with disabilities must have the same school placement rights as those students who are not disabled. IDEA 2004 recognizes that due to the nature of some disabilities, appropriate education may vary in the amount of participation/placement in the general education setting. For some students, FAPE will mean a choice as to the type of educational institution they attend (private school for example), any of which must provide the special education services deemed necessary for the student through the IEP.

The definition of *assistive technology devices* was amended to exclude devices that are surgically implanted (i.e., cochlear implants) and clarified that students with assistive technology devices shall not be prevented from having special education services. Assistive technology devices may need to be monitored by school personnel, but schools are not responsible for the surgical implantation or replacement of such devices.

"*Child with a disability,*" the term used for children ages 3-9 with a developmental delay, now has been changed to allow for the inclusion of Tourette's Syndrome.

IDEA 2004 recognized that all states must follow the National Instructional Materials Accessibility Standards, which state that students who need materials in a certain form will get those at the same time their non-disabled peers receive their materials. Teacher recognition of this standard is important.

Changes in Requirements for Evaluations

The time allowance between the request for an initial evaluation and the determination of whether or not a disability is present has been changed to state that the finding/determination must occur within 60 calendar days of the request. This is a significant change as previously it was interpreted to mean 60 school days. Parental consent is also required for evaluations and prior to the start of special education services.

No single assessment or measurement tool may now be used to determine special education qualification. Assessments and measurements used should be in a *language and form* that will give the most accurate picture of the child's abilities.

IDEA 2004 recognized that there exists a disproportionate representation of minorities and bilingual students and that pre-service interventions that are scientifically *based on early reading programs, positive behavioral interventions and support, and early intervening services* may prevent some of those children from needing special education services. This understanding has led to a child not being considered to have a disability if he/she has not had appropriate education in math or reading, nor shall a child be considered to have a disability if the reason for his/her delays is that English is a second language.

When determining a specific learning disability, the criteria may or may not use a discrepancy between *achievement and intellectual ability,* but may also consider whether or not the child responds to scientific, research-based intervention. In general, children who may not have been found eligible for special education (via testing) but are known to need services (via functioning, excluding lack of instruction) are still eligible for special education services. This change now allows input for evaluations to include state and local testing, classroom observation, academic achievement, and related developmental needs.

Changes in Requirements for IEPs

Individualized Education Plans (IEPS) continue to have multiple sections. One section, *present levels,* now addresses *academic achievement and functional performance.* Annual IEP goals must now address the same areas.

IEP goals should be aligned to state standards; thus, short-term objectives are not required on every IEP. Students with IEPs must not only participate in regular education programs to the fullest extent possible, they must also show progress in those programs. This means that goals should be written to reflect academic progress.

For students who must participate in alternate assessment, there must be alignment to *alternate achievement standards.* Significant change has also been made in the definition of the IEP team, as it now includes *not less than 1* teacher from each of the areas of special education and regular education be present.

IDEA 2004 recognized that the amount of required paperwork placed upon teachers of students with disabilities should be reduced, if possible. For this reason, a pilot program has been developed in which some states will participate using multi-year IEPs. Individual student inclusion in this program will require consent by both the school and the parent.

Florida Exceptional Children Education Laws: Florida's laws regarding the instruction of Exceptional students (Fla. Stat. § 1003.57) reflect the national IDEA rulings. In addition, they specify that each school district must be in compliance with state law and provide not only instruction, but also the professional services for diagnosis and evaluation of student needs. Florida law requires that the student be served in regular school facilities if at all possible and that the facilities and services must be modified to meet the needs of the students. Segregation into self-contained classrooms is allowed only when evidence exists that the student cannot succeed in a regular class.

On January 21, 2009, the State Board of Education adopted Rule 6A-6.03018, Florida Administrative Code (F.A.C.), Exceptional Student Education Eligibility for Students with Specific Learning Disabilities (SLD). This rule became effective March 23, 2009. It reflects changes in IDEA and also provides detailed guidance on definitions, diagnosis, and services for students with specific learning disabilities. Detailed information on Florida special education laws can be found at: *http://www.fldoe.org/ese/pdf/1b-stats.pdf*

The 2013 Florida Legislature passed Senate Bill 1108, which impacted many statutes related to special education. It changed 1002.20, Florida Statutes, K-12 student and parental rights. School district staff may not object to or discourage a parent, when he or she wants to bring an adult with them to attend a meeting. At the end of a meeting, all attendees must sign a form which states whether any school district staff member has prohibited, discouraged, or attempted to discourage parents from inviting a person to a meeting. Meetings can include eligibility determination meetings, IEP or IFSP meetings, 504 development meetings, transitional meetings, or any meetings pertaining to educational placement.

This bill also changed Section 1003.57 pertaining to exceptional students' instruction. It defined ESE centers, or special day schools, as being separate public schools in which nondisabled peers are not to attend. Definitions were also refined for regular, resources, and separate class placements, and inclusion. The same section also stated all school districts must complete a BPIE (Best Practices in Inclusive Education) assessment every three years. All short and long term improvement efforts must be documented.

Furthermore, Section 1012.585 prompted changes pertaining to the renewal of professional certificates, beginning July 1, 2014. An applicant for renewal of a professional certificate is required to earn one additional college credit or equivalent in-service points in teaching students with disabilities. Applicants must have at least six additional semester hours of college credits (or equivalent in-service points) in order to renew the certificate.

Parental power and consent has increased, per Section 1003.5715, because there are new parent consent forms which districts must use for decreeing specific actions included in a student's IEP. School districts cannot proceed with sending a student to an ESE center without parent consent, unless the school documents reasonable efforts in which the parent failed to respond to the school, or via a due process hearing. And except for a change of placement resulting from disciplinary action(s), if a school determines there is a need to change a student's IEP in regard to such actions, then an IEP meeting has to be held.

Under Section 1003.572, public and private instructional personnel, such as behavioral analysts, speech and language pathologists, occupational therapists, and social workers, are to collaborate and enhance but not replace the school district's responsibilities under IDEA. Private instructional personnel who are hired by parents to work with public school personnel must be permitted to observe, collaborate, and provide services to students in the educational settings if: the public and private personnel and principal consent to a time and place, and the private personnel meets state requirements (1012.32 or 1012.321).

Section 1008.212 states that am IEP team may determine that specific conditions prevent a student with a disability from physically demonstrating mastery of skills that have been acquired and measured by statewide assessments. If that is the case, there can be an end-of-the-year assessment or another type of assessment can be used; this extraordinary exemption is granted from the administration of the assessment. Granting extraordinary exemption to a student may include such criteria as the presence of a learning, emotional, behavioral, or significant cognitive disability, or the receipt of services via homebound or a hospital-based program. An IEP team, which must include the parent, may submit a written request for extraordinary exemption at any time during a school year, but no later than 60 days before the current year's assessment administration.

Further information regarding the new bill can be directly obtained from the Florida Department of Education, on http://www.fldoe.org/ese/

Florida State, MAFS/LAFS and the 'Common Core State Standards'

According to the Florida Department of Education, Bureau of Standards and Instructional Support (http://www.fldoe.org/bii/curriculum/sss/), both the *Mathematics Florida Standards (MAFS)* and *Language Arts Florida Standards (LAFS)* were approved by the Florida State Board of Education on February 18, 2014. Three public meetings were held in 2013 in different locations in the state, where attendees could communicate any commentary regarding the standards. There were also web-based sources of outreach via websites and emails, and based on the results of the public commentary, in January of 2014, the Department recommended that changes be made to the original Common Core State Standards which were originally adopted in July 2010. The finalized *MAFS* and *LAFS* are to be fully implemented across the grades in the 2014-15 school year.

The standards are available to view as PDF formats on the following links:
LAFS standards: http://www.fldoe.org/core/fileparse.php/5390/urlt/0081014lafs.pdf
MAFS standards: http://www.fldoe.org/core/fileparse.php/5390/urlt/0081015mathfs.pdf

Skill 1.2 **Identify appropriate practices based on legal and ethical standards (e.g., due process, procedural safeguards, confidentiality, access to general education, least restrictive environment, transition planning, and free appropriate public education).**

1. Free Appropriate Public Education (FAPE):   Special education and related services must: (1) be provided at public expense; (2) meet the standards of the state educational agency; (3) include preschool, elementary, and/or secondary education in the state involved and; (4) be provided in conformity with each student's individualized education program, if the program is developed to meet requirements of the law.

2. Notification and procedural rights for parents: These include:
- Right to examine records and obtain independent evaluations.
- Right to receive a clearly-written notice that states the results of the school's evaluation of their child and whether the child meets eligibility requirements for placement or continuation of special services.
- Parents who disagree with the school's decision may request a **due process** hearing and a **judicial hearing** if they do not receive satisfaction through due process.

3. Identification and services to all children: States must conduct public outreach programs to seek out and identify children who may need services.

4. Necessary related services: Developmental, corrective, and other support services that make it possible for a student to benefit from special education services must be provided. These may include speech, recreation, or physical therapy.

5. Individualized assessments: Evaluations and tests must be nondiscriminatory and individualized.

6. Individualized Education Plans: Each student receiving special education services must have an **individualized education plan** developed at a meeting that is attended by a qualified representative of the local education agency (LEA). Others who should attend would be the proposed special education teachers, mainstream teachers, parents, and, when appropriate, the student.

7. Least Restrictive Environment (LRE): There is no simple definition of LRE. LRE differs with each child's needs. LRE means that the student is placed in an environment that is not dangerous or overly controlling or intrusive. The student should be given opportunities to experience what other peers of similar mental or chronological age are doing. Finally, LRE should be the environment that is the most integrated and normalized for the student's strengths and weaknesses. LRE for one child may be a regular classroom with support services, while LRE for another may be a self-contained classroom in a special school.

Essentially, the LRE strives to allow all students access to an inclusive environment when deemed possible, regardless of ability. A student's participation in the least restrictive placement is highly individualized and dependent upon a student's needs.

A continuum of educational services must be made available by the LEA. Children must be placed in their least restrictive environment and, insofar as possible, with regular classmates. Deno (1970) describes a seven tier cascade system for such services.

Figure 1-2 Cascade System of Special Education Services

Level 1	Regular classroom, including students with disabilities able to learn with regular class accommodations, with or without medical and counseling services
Level 2	Regular classroom with supportive services (i.e. consultation, inclusion)
Level 3	Regular class with part-time special class (i.e. itinerant services, resource room)
Level 4	Full-time special class (i.e. self-contained)
Level 5	Special stations (i.e. special schools)
Level 6	Homebound
Level 7	Residential (i.e. hospital, institution)

Placement decisions must be made based upon the student's IEP, and the stipulated goals and objectives must be reviewed and rewritten on an annual basis. Thus, progress

13

revisions may suggest the need for a change in placement to a less (or more) restrictive environment.

All individuals with disabilities should participate in academic and non-academic (i.e., extracurricular) services to the maximum extent appropriate, considering the individual needs of the child. If skills (e.g., self-help, social, physical education) need to be acquired by a child with disabilities in order to participate successfully in these services or activities, then the skills should be included as goals or objectives in the student's IEP.

Due Process

"Due process is a set of procedures designed to ensure the fairness of educational decisions and the accountability of both professionals and parents in making these decisions" (Kirk and Gallagher, 1986, p. 24). These procedures serve as a mechanism by which the child and his family can voice their opinions or concerns if dissents arise. Due process safeguards exist in all matters pertaining to identification, evaluation, and educational placement.

Due process occurs in two realms - substantive and procedural. Substantive due process is the content of the law (e.g., appropriate placement for special education students). Procedural due process is the form through which substantive due process is carried out (i.e. parental permission for testing). Public Law 101-476 contains many items of both substantive and procedural due process.

1. A due process hearing may be initiated by parents or the LEA as an impartial forum for challenging decisions about identification, evaluation, or placement. Either party may present evidence, cross-examine witnesses, obtain a record of the hearing, and be advised by counsel or by individuals having expertise in the education of individuals with disabilities. Findings may be appealed to the state education agency (SEA), and if still dissatisfied, either party may bring civil action in a state of federal district court. Hearing timelines are set by legislation.

2. Parents may obtain an independent evaluation if there is disagreement about the education evaluation performed by the LEA. The results of such an evaluation: (1) must be considered in any decision made with respect to the provision of a free, appropriate public education for the child, and (2) may be presented as evidence at a hearing. Furthermore, the parents may request this evaluation at public expense: (1) if a hearing officer requests an independent educational evaluation or (2) if the decision from a due process hearing is that the LEA's evaluation was inappropriate. If the

final decision holds that the evaluation performed is appropriate, the parent still has the right to an independent educational evaluation, but not at public expense.

3. Written notice must be provided to parents prior to a proposal or refusal to initiate or make a change in the child's identification, evaluation, or educational placement. This notice must include the following:

   a. A listing of parental due process safeguards.
   b. A description and a rationale for the chosen action.
   c. A detailed listing of components (e.g., tests, records, reports) that were the basis for the decision.
   d. Assurance that the language and content of notices were understood by the parents.

4. Parental consent must be obtained before evaluation procedures can occur unless there is a state law specifying otherwise.

5. Sometimes parents or guardians cannot be identified to function in the due process role. When this occurs, a suitable person must be assigned to act as a surrogate. This is done by the LEA in full accordance with legislation.

Transition

Transition is defined as a movement from one stage or setting to another, either vertically or horizontally. Transition plans are developed for students with disabilities to help bridge the gap from school to work. Transition for special education students also includes moving to another school, a new classroom, or going to the next grade. Transition occurs frequently for students of all ages, but the main and arguably largest transition is from school life to the adult world. Transitioning into mainstream society involves in-depth preparation which can begin as early as age 14, though it often is discussed in an IEP meeting, with the student present, by age 16.

Vocational Training in Special Education

Vocational training in special education has typically focused upon the exceptionality area of intellectual disabilities. Special guidance and training services have more recently been directed toward students with learning disabilities, emotional behavior disorders, physical disabilities, visual impairments, and hearing impairments. Whenever possible, individuals with disabilities are mainstreamed with non-disabled students in vocational training programs. Special sites provide training for those persons with more severe disabilities who are unable to be successfully taught in an integrated setting. Specially trained vocational counselors monitor and supervise student work sites.

Regardless of the disabling condition, aptitude testing is considered an important component in vocational training for students in a mild or moderate setting. This assessment is necessary in order to identify areas of interest and capability. Attitudes and work habits are deemed important by many prospective employers, so these competencies are included in the training.

Training Provisions for individuals with severe intellectual disabilities have been expanded. They include special programs for school-aged children and secondary-level adolescents, along with sheltered workshop programs for adults. Instruction focuses upon self-help skills, social-interpersonal skills, motor skills, rudimentary academic skills, simple occupational skills, and lifetime leisure and recreational skills. In addition, secondary-level programs offer on-the-job supervision, and sheltered workshop programs provide work supervision and pay a small wage for contract labor. Some persons with moderate to severe intellectual disabilities can be trained for employment in supervised unskilled occupations while others are only able to perform chores and other simple tasks in sheltered workshops.

Career Education

Curricular aspects of career education include the phases of (1) career awareness (diversity of available jobs); (2) career exploration (skills needed for occupational groups); and (3) career preparation (specific training and preparation required for the world of work). The concept of career education (1) extended this training into all levels of public school education (i.e., elementary through high school); (2) emphasized the importance of acquiring skills in the areas of daily living and personal-social interaction, as well as occupational training and preparation; and (3) focused upon integrating these skills into numerous areas of academic and vocational curricula. In general, career education attempts to prepare the individual for all facets of life.

Zero Reject

The principle of zero reject requires that *all* children with disabilities be provided with a free, appropriate public education. This legal requirement was made for all school-age children, as for those in the 3 to 5 and 18 to 21 age groups, unless a state law or a court order makes an exception to the extended age ranges.

A documented report is filed annually by each local education agency (LEA) reporting all attempts to locate, identify, and evaluate children with disabilities residing within jurisdiction. Priorities identified in the legislation for the delivery of services and appropriation of federal funds are: (1) children with disabilities not receiving any education, and (2) children with the most severe disabilities receiving an inappropriate education.

Ethically, zero reject exists to guard against both total and functional exclusion. "*Total exclusion* refers to past situations in which children with disabilities have been denied access to any educational services at all. *Functional exclusion* occurs in cases in which educational services have been provided, but they have been inappropriate to the needs of the student with a disability." (Turnbull, Strickland, & Brantley, 1978, p. 4).

The Family Educational Rights and Privacy Act (1974), also known as the Buckley Amendment, assures confidentiality of student records. Parents are afforded the right to examine, review, and request changes in information deemed inaccurate and also to stipulate persons who might access their child's records.

The development and approval of educational policy is another means for involving parents. Membership on advisory boards, participation at public hearings, and review of local and state special education plans are examples of ways in which parents might participate in the formulation of policy and later monitoring of these guidelines.

Nondiscriminatory Evaluation

A complete individual evaluation must be made in order to determine a student's eligibility for special education services. The use of evaluation material, as well as functional procedures, is outlined in legislation and must meet specific standards.

Testing instruments must be administered in the child's native language or other mode of communication. Furthermore, tests must be validated for the specific purpose for which they are intended and tailored to assess specific areas of educational needs, as well as all areas related to the suspected disability. Evaluation must be made by a multidisciplinary team, and no single procedure may be used as the sole criterion for determining placement or an appropriate educational program.

Skill 1. 3   Demonstrate knowledge of the required policies and processes of individual educational plans, family support plans, and transition plans

Individualized Education Programs (IEPs)

The IEP is the very document which encompasses all current and future goals for an individual child. It is the basis of the IEP meeting and all goal-setting when the team and parents meet to discuss a child's strengths and weaknesses. It is important to understand how much the law affects the required components of the IEP. Educators must keep themselves apprised of the changes and amendments to laws, such as IDEA and Florida Special Education Law, and how these changes can modify the essential elements to the IEP and the required manner in which it must be completed. At present, the following elements are required in an IEP:

1. The student's present level of academic performance, functional performance and a statement of how the disability affects the student's involvement as well as progress in the general education curriculum. Preschool children must have a statement explaining how the disability affects the child's participation in appropriate activities.

2. A statement of annual goals or anticipated attainments.

3. Short-term objectives are no longer required on every IEP. Students with severe disabilities or those taking an alternate assessment may need short-term objectives, which lead to the attainment of annual goals.

4. A statement of when the parents will be notified of their child's progress, which must be at least as often as the regular education student.

5. Modifications or accommodations for participation in statewide or citywide assessments, or if it is determined that the child cannot participate, why the assessment is inappropriate for the child and how the child will be assessed.

6. Specific educational services, assistive technology, and related services to be provided and those who will provide them.

7. Evaluate criteria and timeliness for determining whether instructional objectives have been achieved.

8. Projected dates for initiating services, along with their anticipated frequency, location, and duration.

9. The extent to which the child will not participate in the regular education program.

10. Transitional needs for students age 14. This should include, when appropriate, interagency responsibilities and links for possible future assistance.

Recent Changes in the Way IEPs Must Be Written

IDEA 2004's Indicator 13 is changing the way IEPs are written across the country. The federal government is requiring changes in IEPs to create an easier way to collect statistics on student success at reaching post school goals. Also, a transition services plan must be firmly in place, with realistic post-secondary goals. The annual IEP goals must correlate with the student's transition needs, and there should be a focus on education, training, employment, and independent living skills, as well as community-oriented participation. While many of the requirements stated below have been used for years, compliance is now being measured by the items listed below.

Present Levels of Performance

Student voice must be included in each Present Level of Performance. This means that Academic, Social, Physical, Management, etc. must include one student voice statement either in the strengths or needs or both. For example:

> John reads fluently on a 3rd grade level. He is able to add and subtract two digit numbers. He has difficulty with grouping and multiplying. *John states that he would rather read than do math.*

Student voice can express either his/her strengths, preferences, and/or interests. When the child begins to do vocational assessments, student voice should be related to transition to post-school activities of his/her choice. In addition, Present Levels of Performance must indicate why a student's post adult goals are realistic, or why they are not.

Post-Secondary Goals

Post-Secondary Goals must be measurable. This means they must be stated with the word "will." Using this verb tense enhances the student's self-fulfilling prophecy in a positive light.

Wrong—Bill wants to become a doctor.
Correct—Bill will become a doctor.

Goals

IEP goals are the core of the IEP. All goals must be directly correlated to student needs. This means that if a need is stated in the present levels, it must have a goal. These goals should, when possible, have benchmarks denoting possible levels of achievement. The ending or outcome of a goal ultimately is 'mastery' of the goal. Once a goal is achieved or 'mastered,' it can be replaced with a new goal which may arise as the child progresses developmentally or academically. Goals must be stated in an objective, measureable manner. Clarity is of the utmost importance, so all parties/stakeholders understand what is being stated for the student's sake.

Course of Study

The student's course of study includes a statement of the transition service needs. This could be a statement that the student is on track for a High School Diploma or an IEP Diploma. This also could entail goals pertaining to a work study, internship, life skills program, or self-advocacy plan.

Recommended Programs and Services

The intended special education program, such as a substantially separate classroom or a resource room pull-out, must be on the IEP. The stated program must align with the needs of the student given in the Present Levels of Performance. The Needs in the Present Levels of Performance must justify the program. A Speech/Language service must be justified by a statement of needs in that area.

Post-school Activities

IEPs must include a statement of post-school activities including:

- Instruction
- Related Services
- Community experiences
- The development of employment and other post adult living objectives, when appropriate.
- Acquisition of daily living skills
- Functional vocational evaluation

All six areas must be addressed on the IEP. However, the IEP can include a statement that "the student has no needs in a particular area *at this time.*"

Statement of Responsibilities

A clear indication of coordination between school district activities and participating agencies must be stated on the IEP. This must be done listing the job title of each person providing the service.

Individualized Family Service Plan (IFSP) and Transition Plan

According to Part C of IDEA, children ages 0-2 who are in need of special services must have an Individualized Family Service Plan (IFSP). The IFSP is a plan that documents and guides the early intervention process for children with disabilities and their families.

According to IDEA, the IFSP shall be in writing and contain the following:

1. A statement of the infant's or toddler's present levels of physical development, cognitive development, communication development, social or emotional development, and adaptive development, based on objective criteria.

2. A statement of the family's resources, priorities, and concerns relating to enhancing the development of the family's infant or toddler with a disability.

3. A statement of the measurable results or outcomes expected to be achieved for the infant or toddler and the family, including pre-literacy and language skills, as developmentally appropriate for the child, and the criteria, procedures, and timelines used to determine the degree to which progress toward achieving the results or outcomes is being made and whether modifications or revisions of the results or outcomes or services are necessary.

4. A statement of specific early intervention services based on peer-reviewed research, to the extent practicable, necessary to meet the unique needs of the infant or toddler and the family, including the frequency, intensity, and method of delivering services.

5. A statement of the natural environments in which early intervention services will appropriately be provided, including a justification of the extent, if any, to which the services will not be provided in a natural environment.

6. The projected dates for initiation of services and the anticipated length, duration, and frequency of the services.

7. The identification of the service coordinator from the profession most immediately relevant to the infant's or toddler's or family's needs (or who is otherwise qualified to carry out all applicable responsibilities under this part) who will be responsible for the implementation of the plan and coordination with other agencies and persons, including transition services.

8. The steps to be taken to support the transition of the toddler with a disability to preschool or other appropriate services

According to IDEA, a transition plan is a group of activities designed with an outcome-oriented process, which promote movement from school to post-school activities. The plan can begin as early as 14, but no later than 16. It should include the responsibilities of agencies and individuals used to link the student to the post-school activities. Competency 7 deals with transition issues in detail.

Skill 1.4 **Identify the classification systems and eligibility criteria under the current Individuals with Disabilities Education Improvement Act**

According to the American Psychological Association (2016), the Individuals with Disabilities Education Act (IDEA) ensures that all children with disabilities are entitled to a free appropriate public education to meet the individual needs of each child and ultimately prepare them for further education, employment, and independent living.

Before the IDEA was implemented, over four million children with disabilities were denied legitimate access to public education. Some children experienced a level of segregation and were potentially denied admittance into a school, refused services, and/or placed in a different area of the building.

IDEA has four sections: A, B, C, and D.
Part A of IDEA is the summary and foundation of the Act. This section defines all of the terms used in the body of the Act and insists on the formation of the Office of Special Education Programs. This office is responsible for administering all terms of IDEA (IDEA, 1997).

Part B of IDEA explains the educational guidelines for children 3-21 years of age. IDEA gives financial support for state and local school districts, but school districts have to comply with six standards in accordance with the IDEA, as sourced by the American Psychological Association (2016):

- Every child is entitled to a free and appropriate public education (FAPE).
- When a school professional believes that a student between the ages of 3 and 21 may have a disability that has substantial impact on the student's learning or behavior, the student is entitled to an evaluation in all areas related to the suspected disability.
- Creation of an Individualized Education Plan (IEP). The purpose of the IEP is to lay out a series of specific actions and steps through which educational providers, parents and the student themselves may reach the child's stated goals.
- The education and services for children with disabilities must be provided in the least restrictive environment, and, if possible, those children be placed in a "typical" education setting with non-disabled students.
- Input of the child and their parents must be taken into account in the education process.
- When a parent feels that an IEP is inappropriate for their child, or that their child is not receiving needed services, they have the right under IDEA to challenge their child's treatment (due process).

Part C of IDEA gives guidelines regarding the funding and services for children from birth through 2 years old. Families are entitled to several early childhood services, including but not limited to appropriate, timely, and multidisciplinary identification and intervention services. Families receive an Individualized family Service Plan (IFSP). This plan explains the resources available and the concerns of the family and describes the goals of the child, the services to be provided to the child, and steps for eventual transitioning of the child into formal education.

Part D explains national activities to improve the education for children with disabilities. This includes grants to improve education and transitional services. There are also resources to support students, such as programs, projects, and activities.

As noted by the American Psychological Association (2016), in 2010, the U.S. Department of Education published a report acknowledging the 35th anniversary of IDEA. The report highlighted many of the achievements gained because of this legislation, including the increase in college enrollment.

Source: American Psychological Association (2016)

http://www.apa.org/about/gr/issues/disability/idea.aspx

Definitions of Disabilities under IDEA 2004

Classification	Characteristics
Autism Spectrum Disorder	There are persistent social communication deficits and insufficient social interaction(s) in multiple contexts, by history or by the following, according to the DSM-V (2013): I. Deficit in social-emotional reciprocity II. Deficit in nonverbal communication used for social interaction III. Deficit in developing, maintaining, and understanding relationships. Severity is based upon social communication impairments and restricted repetitive patterns of behavior.
Deaf	Deafness is a hearing impairment that is so severe that the child is impaired in processing linguistic information through hearing, with or without amplification, that adversely affects a child's educational performance.
Deaf-blind	Deaf-blind is the concomitant hearing and visual impairments, the combination of which causes such severe communication and other developmental and educational needs that they cannot be accommodated in special education programs solely for children with deafness or children with blindness.
Emotional	Schizophrenia, and conditions in which one or more of these

Disturbance	characteristics is exhibited over a long period of time and to a marked degree, encompasses emotional disturbance: (a) inability to learn not explained by intellectual, sensory, or health factors, (b) inability to build or maintain satisfactory interpersonal relationships, (c) inappropriate types of behavior or feelings, (d) general pervasive unhappiness or depression, (e) tendency to develop physical symptoms or fears associated with personal or school problems.
Hearing Impairment	This is an impairment in hearing, whether permanent or fluctuating, that adversely affects a child's educational performance but that is not included under the definition of deafness in this section.
Intellectual Disability	Intellectual disability is indicative of a significant–subaverage general intellectual functioning, existing concurrently with deficits in adaptive behavior and manifested during the developmental period, which adversely affects a child's educational performance.
Multiple Disabilities	These are concomitant impairments (such as intellectual disability-blindness, intellectual disability-orthopedic impairment, etc.), the combination of which causes such severe educational needs that a student cannot be accommodated in special education programs solely for one of the impairments. The term does not include deaf-blindness.
Orthopedic Impairment	Orthopedic impairments adversely affects a child's educational performance; these impairments may include impairments caused by a congenital anomaly (e.g., clubfoot, absence of some member, etc.), impairments caused by disease (e.g., poliomyelitis, bone tuberculosis, etc.), and impairments from other causes (e.g., cerebral palsy, amputations, and fractures or burns that cause contractures).
Other Health Impairment	OHI is defined by having limited strength, vitality, or alertness, including a heightened alertness to environmental stimuli, that results in limited alertness with respect to the educational environment, that: I. Is due to chronic or acute health problems such as asthma, attention deficit disorder or attention deficit hyperactivity disorder, diabetes, epilepsy, a heart condition, hemophilia, lead poisoning, leukemia, nephritis, rheumatic fever, sickle cell anemia, or Tourette's syndrome; and

	II. Adversely affects a child's educational performance.
Specific Learning Disability	This term means a disorder in one or more of the basic psychological processes involved in understanding or in using language, spoken or written, that may manifest itself in an imperfect ability to listen, think, speak, read, write, spell, or do mathematical calculations, including conditions such as perceptual disabilities, brain injury, minimal brain dysfunction, dyslexia, and developmental aphasia. **Disorders not included**: The term does not include learning problems that are primarily the result of visual, hearing, or motor disabilities, of intellectual disabilities, of emotional disturbance, or of environmental, cultural, or economic disadvantage.
Speech or Language Impairment	A speech or language impairment is a communication disorder, such as stuttering, impaired articulation, a language impairment, or a voice impairment, that adversely affects a child's educational performance.
Traumatic Brain Injury	TBI is an acquired injury to the brain caused by an external physical force resulting in total or partial functional disability or psychosocial impairment, or both, that adversely affects a child's educational performance. The term applies to open or closed head injuries resulting in impairments in one or more areas, such as cognition, language, memory, attention, reasoning, abstract thinking, judgment, problem-solving, sensory, perceptual, and motor abilities, psychosocial behavior, physical functions, information processing, and speech. The term does not apply to brain injuries that are congenital or degenerative, or to brain injuries induced by birth trauma.
Visual Impairment including Blindness	Visual impairments include an impairment in vision that, even with correction, adversely affects a child's educational performance. The term includes both partial sight and blindness.

It should be noted that there is no specific classification for gifted children under IDEA, though 'giftedness' can occur in conjunction with a classification, or with a learning disability, and these children may be considered 'twice exceptional' students. Nevertheless, funding and services for gifted programs are left up to the individual states and school districts. In many states, there is very little budgetary conversation held with respect to 'giftedness.' In fact, many states do not allot much budget to the needs of gifted children at all. Therefore, the number of districts providing services and the scope of gifted programs varies vastly among states and school districts, and even individual schools.

Skill 1.5   Compare the development and characteristics (e.g., language, cognitive/academic, social/emotional, and physical/motor) of children with disabilities to the development and characteristics of children without disabilities

Social and Emotional Development Issues

Normality in child behavior is influenced by society's attitudes, religious, and cultural beliefs about what is normal for children (e.g., the motto for the Victorian era was "Children should be seen and not heard"). However, in general, criteria for what is considered "normal" in a particular group involve consideration of questions such as these:

- *Is the behavior age appropriate?* An occasional tantrum may be expected for a toddler, but is not typical for a high school student.
- *Is the behavior pathological in itself?* Drug or alcohol use would be harmful to children, regardless of how many engage in it.
- *How persistent is the problem?* A kindergarten student initially may be afraid to go to school. However, if the fear continues into first or second grade, then the problem would be considered persistent.
- *How severe is the behavior?* Self-injurious, cruel, and extremely destructive behaviors would be examples of behaviors that require intervention.
- *How often does the behavior occur?* An occasional tantrum in a young child or a brief mood of depression in an adolescent would not be considered problematic. However, if the behavior occurs frequently, it would not be characteristic of normal child development.
- *Do several problem behaviors occur as a group?* Clusters of behaviors, especially severe behaviors that occur together, may be indicative of a serious problem, such as schizophrenia.

Certain stages of child development have their own sets of problems, and it should be kept in mind that short-term undesirable behaviors can and will occur over these stages. Child development is also a continuum, and children may manifest these problem behaviors somewhat earlier or later than their peers.

Problem Behaviors Associated with Childhood Stages of Development
(See Gelfand et al., p. 120)

Toddler (1-3)	Preschool (3-5)	Elementary (6-10)	Early Adolescence	Adolescent (15-18)
Temper tantrums	Temper tantrums	Temper tantrums	Temper tantrums	--
Refuses to do things when asked	Refuses to do things when asked	--	--	--
Demands constant attention	Demands constant attention	--	--	--
Over activity	Over activity	Over activity	--	--
Specific fears	Specific fears	--	--	--
--	Oversensitivity	Oversensitivity	--	--
Inattentive	--	--	--	--
--	Lying	Lying	--	--
--	--	Jealousy	Jealousy	--
--	Negativism	--	--	--
--	--	School achievement problems	School achievement problems	School achievement problems
--	--	Excessive reserve	Excessive reserve	--
--	--	--	Moodiness	--
--	--	--	--	Substance abuse
--	--	--	--	Truancy or skipping school
--	--	--	--	Minor law violations (i.e. stealing, trespassing)
--	--	--	--	Sexual misconduct

About 15-20% of the school-aged population between 6 and 17 years old receive special education services. The categories of learning disabilities and emotional disturbance are the most prevalent. Exceptional students are very much like their peers without disabilities. The main difference is that they have an intellectual, emotional, behavioral, or physical deficit that significantly interferes with their ability to benefit from education.

Common Characteristics of Emotionally Disturbed Children

Children with emotional disturbances or behavioral disorders are not always easy to identify. It is easy to identify the acting-out child who is constantly fighting, who cannot stay on task for more than a few minutes, or who shouts obscenities when angry. But it is not always easy to identify the child who internalizes his or her problems, or who may appear to be the "model" student but suffers from depression, shyness, or fears. Unless the problem becomes severe enough to impact school performance, the internalizing child may go for long periods without being identified or served.

Studies show children with behavioral and emotional disorders share some general characteristics:

Lower Academic Performance: While it is true that some emotionally disturbed children have above average IQ scores, the majority are behind their peers in measures of intelligence and school achievement. Even a child with normal levels of intelligence and ability may perform poorly if the emotional or behavioral disturbance interferes with academic performance or learning. In addition, many students with emotional difficulties score in the "slow learner" or "mildly intellectually disabled" range on IQ tests, averaging about 90. Many have learning problems that exacerbate their acting out or "giving-up" behavior. As the child enters secondary school, the gap between the child and his/her non-disabled peers widens until the child may be as many as 2 to 4 years behind in reading and/or math skills by high school. Children with severe degrees of impairment may be difficult to evaluate.

Social Skills Deficits: Students with social deficits may be uncooperative, selfish in dealing with others, unaware of what to do in social situations, or ignorant of the consequences of their actions. This may be a combination of lack of prior training, lack of opportunities to interact, and dysfunctional value systems and beliefs learned from their family. However, it can also be the result of an emotional or behavioral disability that interferes with acquisition of normal social skills.

Classroom Behaviors: Emotionally disturbed children can exhibit behavior that is highly disruptive to the classroom setting. Emotionally disturbed children are often out of their seat or running around the room, hitting, fighting, or disturbing their classmates, stealing or destroying property, defiant and noncompliant, and/or verbally disruptive. They do not follow directions and often do not complete assignments.

Aggressive Behaviors: Aggressive children often fight or instigate their peers to strike back at them. Aggressiveness may also take the form of vandalism or destruction of property. Aggressive children also engage in verbal abuse.

Delinquency: As emotionally disturbed, acting-out children enter adolescence, they may become involved in socialized aggression (i.e., gang membership) and delinquency. Delinquency is a legal, rather than medical, term that describes truancy and actions that would be criminal if they were committed by adults. Of course, not every delinquent is classified as emotionally disturbed, but children with behavioral and emotional disorders are especially at risk for becoming delinquent because of their problems at school (the primary place for socializing with peers), deficits in social skills that may make them unpopular at school, and/or dysfunctional homes.

Withdrawn Behaviors: Children who manifest withdrawn behaviors may consistently act in an immature fashion or prefer younger children to play with. They may daydream or complain of being sick in order to "escape" to the clinic, cry, cling to the teacher, ignore others' attempts to interact, or suffer from fears or depression.

Schizophrenia and Psychotic Behaviors: Children with these conditions may have bizarre delusions, hallucinations, incoherent thoughts, and disconnected thinking. Schizophrenia typically manifests itself between the ages of 15 and 45, and the younger the onset, the more severe the disorder. These behaviors usually require intensive treatment beyond the scope of the regular classroom setting.

COGNITIVE DEVELOPMENT ISSUES

Beginning with pre-operational thought processes and moving to concrete operational thoughts, children go through patterns of learning. Eventually they begin to acquire the mental ability to think about and solve problems in their heads because they can manipulate objects and ideas symbolically. Even children who can use such symbols as words and numbers to represent objects and relations need concrete reference points. Children must be encouraged to use and develop the thinking skills that they possess in solving problems that interest them. The content of the curriculum must be relevant, engaging, and meaningful to the students.

The teacher of students with special needs must have a general knowledge of cognitive development. Although children with special needs have a cognitive development rate that may be different than other children, a teacher needs to be aware of the activities of each stage as part of the basis to determine what should be taught and when.

The following information about cognitive development was taken from the Cincinnati Children's Hospital Medical Center at www.cincinattichildrens.org Some common features indicating a progression from more simple to more complex cognitive development include the following:

Children (ages 6-12)

- Begin to develop the ability to think in concrete ways. Concrete operations are operations performed in the presence of the object and events that are to be used.
- Examples: how to combine (addition), separate (subtract or divide), order (alphabetize and sort and categorize), and transform (change items such as 25 pennies=1 quarter) objects and actions

Adolescents (ages 12-18)

- Adolescents begin to develop more complex thinking skills, including abstract thinking, the ability to reason from known principles (form own new ideas or questions), the ability to consider many points of view according to varying criteria (compare or debate ideas or opinions), and the ability to think about the process of thinking.

Cognitive Developmental Changes During Adolescence

During adolescence (between 12 and 18 years of age), the developing teenager acquires the ability to think systematically about all logical relationships within a problem. The transition from concrete thinking to formal logical operations occurs over time. Every adolescent progresses at varying rates in developing the ability to think in more complex ways. Each adolescent develops his or her own view of the world. Some adolescents may be able to apply logical operations to school work long before they are able to apply them to personal dilemmas. When emotional issues arise, they often interfere with an adolescent's ability to think in more complex ways. The ability to consider possibilities, as well as facts, may influence decision making in either positive or negative ways.

Some common features indicating a progression from more simple to more complex cognitive development can be seen in early, middle, and late adolescence.

Early Adolescence

During early adolescence, the use of more complex thinking is focused on personal decision making in school and home environments, including the following:

- Begins to demonstrate use of formal logical operations in school work.
- Begins to question authority and society standards.
- Begins to form and verbalize thoughts and views on a variety of topics, usually more related to his or her own life, such as
    - Which sports are better to play.
    - Which groups are better to be included in.
    - What personal appearances are desirable or attractive.
    - What parental rules should be changed.

Middle Adolescence

With some experience in using more complex thinking processes, the focus of middle adolescence often expands to include more philosophical and futuristic concerns, including the following:

- Often questions more extensively.
- Often analyzes more extensively.
- Thinks about and begins to form a code of ethics.
- Thinks about different possibilities and begins to develop own identity.
- Thinks about and begins to systematically consider possible future goals.
- Thinks about and begins to make his or her own plans.
- Begins to think long term.
- Systematic thinking begins to influence relationships with others.

Late Adolescence

During late adolescence, complex thinking processes are used to focus on less self-centered concepts and personal decision making, including the following:

- Develops idealistic views on specific topics or concerns.
- Debates and develops intolerance of opposing views.
- Begins to focus thinking on making career decisions.
- Begins to focus thinking on emerging role in adult society.
- Has increased thoughts about such global concepts as justice, history, politics, and patriotism.

Common Characteristics of Developmental Disabilities

"Developmental disability" is a term used to describe lifelong disabilities caused by mental and/or physical impairments that are seen in childhood or infancy. These disabilities usually impact cognitive development most heavily. The term most often refers to disabilities that affect at least three of the following areas of daily life:

- learning
- self-care
- self-direction
- mobility
- capacity for independent living and economic self-sufficiency
- receptive and expressive language

Common developmental disabilities include intellectual disability, autism, or genetic and chromosomal disorders such as Down syndrome and Fragile X syndrome.

Autism Spectrum Disorders: Autism Spectrum Disorders appear very early in childhood. Although current research is looking at both genetic and environmental factors, no definitive causes have been identified. Autism disorders are associated with both affective disorders and language impairment. Six common features of autism are:

- **Apparent sensory deficit-** The child may appear not to see or hear or react to a stimulus, then react in an extreme fashion to a seemingly insignificant stimuli.
- **Severe affect isolation-** The child does not respond to the usual signs of affection such as smiles and hugs.
- **Self-stimulation-** Stereotyped behavior takes the form of repeated or ritualistic actions that make no sense to others, such as hand flapping, rocking, staring at objects, or humming the same sounds for hours at a time.
- **Tantrums and self-injurious behavior (SIB)-** Autistic children may bite themselves, pull their hair, bang their heads, or hit themselves. They can throw severe tantrums and direct aggression and destructive behavior toward others.
- **Echolalia-** This is also known as "parrot talk." The autistic child may repeat what is played on television, for example, or respond to others by repeating what was said to him. Alternatively, he may simply not speak at all.
- **Severe deficits in behavior and self-care skills-** Autistic children may behave like children much younger than themselves.

In 1981, the condition of autism was moved from the exceptionality category of seriously emotionally disturbed to that of other health impaired by virtue of a change in language in the original definitions under Public Law 94-142 ("Education of Handicapped Children." *Federal Register,* 1977). With IDEA, in 1990, autism was made into a separate exceptionality category.

Mental Retardation or Intellectual Disabilities: "Mental retardation" is the term historically applied to overall developmental delays and disabilities in all academic and cognitive areas. Children with this condition generally display significantly below average intellectual functionality on all cognitive measures, as well as deficits in at least two adaptive skills. The precise degree of cognitive impairment will have a profound effect on the choice of educational programming. Characteristics with regard to the degree of cognitive impairment fall into four categories:

Mild (IQ of 50-55 to 70)
This level is sometimes referred to as "generalized learning disability"

- Delays in most areas (e.g., communication, motor, academic)
- Often not distinguished from normal children until of school age.
- Can acquire both academic and vocational skills; can become self-supporting

Moderate (IQ of 35-40 to 50-55)

- Only fair motor development; clumsy
- Poor social awareness
- Can be taught to communicate
- Can profit from training in social and vocational skills; needs supervision, but can perform semiskilled labor as an adult

Severe (IQ of 20-25 to 35-40)

- Poor motor development
- Minimal speech and communication
- Minimal ability to profit from training in health and self-help skills: may contribute to self-maintenance under constant supervision as an adult

Profound (IQ below 20-25)

- Gross disability, both mental and sensor-motor
- Little or no development of basic communication skills
- Dependency on others to maintain basic life functions
- Lifetime of complete supervision (institution, home, nursing home)

Learning Disabilities

The term "Learning Disability" refers to a wide range of disabilities found in students whose overall cognitive levels are for the most part within the normal range. These students often show a significant discrepancy between their overall cognitive functioning (normal) and one or more specific cognitive areas. Characteristics common to children with normal cognitive ability and one or more learning disabilities include:

- hyperactivity: a rate of motor activity higher than normal
- perceptual difficulties: visual, auditory, and haptic perceptual problems
- perceptual-motor impairments: poor integration of visual and motor systems, often affecting fine motor coordination
- disorders of memory and thinking: memory deficits, trouble with problem-solving and/or concept formation and association, poor awareness of own metacognitive skills (learning strategies)
- impulsiveness: acts before considering consequences, poor impulse control, often followed by remorselessness
- academic problems in reading, math, writing or spelling; significant discrepancies in ability levels

Children with mild learning, intellectual, and behavioral disabilities: In many cases, children with learning or cognitive disabilities will have relatively mild disabilities that are not immediately obvious. Teachers need to be alert to the symptoms of early learning disabilities. Some of the characteristics of students with mild learning and behavioral disabilities are as follows:

- Lack of interest in schoolwork
- preference for concrete rather than abstract lessons
- weak listening skills
- low achievement
- limited verbal and/or writing skills
- respond better to active rather than passive learning tasks
- have areas of talent or ability often overlooked by teachers
- prefer to receive special help in regular classroom
- higher dropout rate than regular education students
- achieve in accordance with teacher expectations
- require modification in classroom instruction
- easily distracted

PHYSICAL DEVELOPMENT, INCLUDING MOTOR AND SENSORY FACTORS

The teacher must be aware of the physical stages of development and how the child's physical growth and development affect learning. Factors determined by the physical stage of development include the ability to sit and attend, the need for activity, the relationship between physical skills and self-esteem, and the degree to which physical involvement in an activity (as opposed to being able to understand an abstract concept) affects learning.

Children with physical impairments possess a variety of disabling conditions. Although significant differences exist among these conditions, so do similarities. Each condition usually affects one particular system of the body—the cardiopulmonary system (blood vessels, heart, and lungs) or the musculoskeletal system (spinal cord, brain nerves). Some conditions develop during pregnancy, birth, or infancy because of known or unknown factors that may affect the fetus or newborn infant. Other conditions occur later because of injury (trauma), disease, or factors not fully understood.

In addition to motor disorders, individuals with physical disabilities may have such multi-disabling conditions as concomitant hearing impairments, visual impairments, perceptual disorders, speech defects, behavior disorders or mental handicaps, performance deficits, or deficits in emotional responsiveness.

The following are some characteristics that may present in individuals with physical disabilities and other health impairments:

1. Lack of physical stamina; fatigue.
2. Chronic illness; poor endurance.
3. Deficient motor skills; normal movement may be prevented.
4. Physical limitations or impeded motor development; a prosthesis or an orthotic may be required.
5. Limited mobility and exploration of one's environment.
6. Limited self-care abilities.
7. Progressive weakening and degeneration of muscles.
8. Frequent speech and language defects; communication may be prevented; echolalia may be present.
9. Pain and discomfort throughout the body.
10. Emotional (psychological) problems that require treatment.
11. Need for social adjustments; may display maladaptive social behavior.

12. Need for long-term medical treatment, which may become a financial burden on the family.
13. Embarrassing side effects from certain diseases or treatment.
14. Erratic or poor attendance patterns, which lead to the child missing many skills and the parent or caregiver missing days of work.

Communication and language development are discussed in detail in Competency 5.

Sensory Factors

Sensory systems which students may experience difficulties with include tactile (touch), vestibular (balance), proprioception (body awareness), visual (sight), auditory (hearing), gustatory (taste), and olfactory (smell). Senses provide the body about the environment and immediate surroundings.

Common Factors Affecting Identification of Disabilities

Gender: Many more boys than girls are identified as having emotional and behavioral problems, especially hyperactivity and attention deficit disorder, autism, childhood psychosis, and problems with under-control (i.e., aggression and socialized aggression). Girls, on the other hand, have more problems with over-control (i.e., withdrawal and phobias). Boys are much more prevalent than girls in problems with intellectual disability and language and learning disabilities.

Age Characteristics: When they enter adolescence, girls tend to experience affective or emotional disorders, such as anorexia, depression, bulimia, and anxiety, at twice the rate of boys, which mirrors the adult prevalence pattern.

Family Characteristics: Having a child with an emotional or behavioral disorder does not automatically mean that the family is dysfunctional. However, there are family factors that create or contribute to the development of behavior disorders and emotional disturbance, including:

- Abuse and neglect
- Lack of appropriate supervision
- Lax, punitive, and/or lack of discipline
- High rates of negative types of interaction among family members
- Lack of parental concern and interest
- Negative adult role models
- Lack of proper health care and/or nutrition

- Disruption in the family

Identifying such underlying causes can be useful in determining appropriate interventions and treatments.

Skill 1.6   Interpret curriculum information and assessment data for IEP and child study team members

As the due process procedure is followed, a series of major decisions are made by multidisciplinary teams. Team members include teachers (regular and special education), building and district administrators, school psychologists, school social workers, parents, medical experts, and sometimes the child being reviewed.

Identification

Identification of a student's learning problem occurs when comparisons are made within the general population about a student's academic progress. In addition to comparing a student's progress with that of others in the same grade or at the same age, comparisons can be made *within* the student's own abilities. Significant discrepancies between various abilities can be signs of a learning disability. Emotional and behavioral difficulties also impact academic progress.

Although academic success can vary from subject to subject for any child, consistent patterns of failure, and a widening gap between performance and ability can be signs that further investigation and intervention may be necessary. Classroom assessments combined with overall intelligence and achievement tests can help isolate problems.

Similarly, all children and youths exhibit behaviors and emotional states that deviate from the norm at times. But, overall, it is the intensity of the behavior, the degree to which it is shown, and the length of time that it persists that is significant. Behavior rating scales, checklists, inventories, and sociograms can be used to determine whether an aberrant behavior is occurring and to what extent.

Students with disabilities are identifiable by academic and social behaviors that deviate significantly from those of their classmates. The longer it takes to identify these students, the further they fall behind their peers in school.

Once a student is identified as being at-risk academically or socially, remedial interventions are attempted within the regular classroom. Federal legislation requires that sincere efforts be made to help the child learn in the regular classroom.

Whether a child can be serviced in a mainstream classroom depends upon many factors. Some forms of specialized instruction or small group environments cannot be met in a mainstream classroom. Other accommodations can be provided in regular education and in such instances the student can stay in the regular education setting. In addition, certain behaviors and social skills are necessary for success in the regular education setting and students who do not have these skills may not be able to stay in the mainstream setting. Salend and Lutz (1984) have pinpointed and explained a set of social behaviors that are prerequisites for success in the regular education classroom. In addition to the other assessments, the team needs information on the whether the child has the social skills to be successful in the regular education setting.

Assembling all this information and interpreting it for those making decisions about the child's educational programming is essential to the success of the child.

Child Study Team

The child study team (CST) is a school-level group comprised of members of the school community qualified to assess a child's eligibility for special services. The child study team provides pre-referral analysis of a child's perceived academic or functional challenges and determines eligibility for specialized intervention.

According to the Florida State Board of Education, the CST may include, but is not limited to, the school's guidance counselor, exceptional student basic education teacher, Title 1 reading teacher, reading coach, speech/language pathologist, principal, gifted education teacher, and the child's parents or guardians. The CST's oversight allows schools to meet the legal requirement that due diligence be performed before a student is officially declared eligible for exceptional student education services.
The CST coordinates and participates in this due diligence through a process similar to the following:

- When teachers or parents develop concerns about a child's academic or functional development, they may take their concerns to the school counselor, who is a typically a member of the CST. Counselors contact parents for permission to perform screening assessments of the child's skills. Meanwhile, teachers compile examples of the child's pre-intervention work, including documenting their observations of the child's social and classroom performance, their attempts to assist the child, and the results of those attempts. Parent contact and engagement, if not already obtained, are essential at this stage.

- The child study team meets for the first time without parents. The group reviews the pre-referral documentation and the child's complete school record and documents any additional insights gained. Members then brainstorm appropriate interventions and may recommend specific screening evaluations to confirm or rule out the child's eligibility for exceptional educational services.

This process is outlined in the model on the next page.

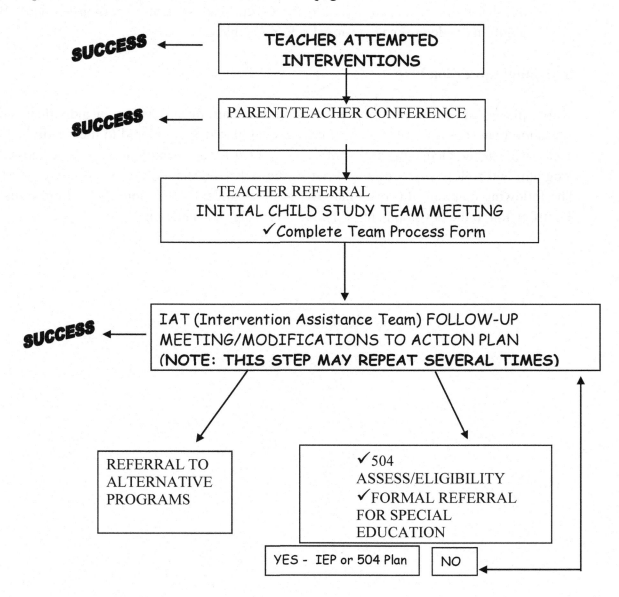

From: Georgia Department of Education

- During a prearranged period of time, recommended screening assessments are carried out and their results documented. The child's teachers and other service providers attempt the CST's recommended interventions and, again, document the results.
- At the end of this period, the CST meets again, this time extending an invitation to parents. The group reviews the results of the screening assessments, any other relevant test results, and the results of pedagogical interventions. The team then decides if the student is eligible for exceptional student education services. If eligibility is determined, a formal referral is made.

Individual Education Plan

Before placement can occur, the multidisciplinary team must develop an individualized education plan (IEP), a child-centered educational plan that is tailored to meet individual needs. IEPs acknowledge each student's requirement for a specially designed educational program, and follow strict rules laid out in the IDEA legislation (see Competency 1.3). The following diagram illustrates the flow of the a student's IEP 'journey' – from initial identification to the development of the IEP to regular reevaluation.

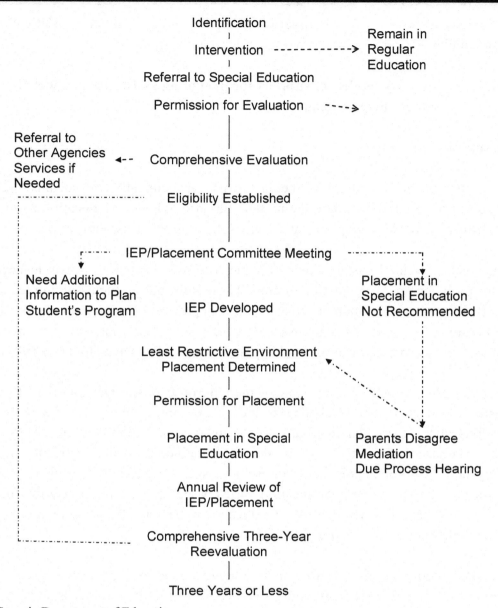

From: Georgia Department of Education

Three purposes are identified by Polloway, Patton, Payne, and Payne (1989):

1. IEPs outline instructional programs. They provide specific instructional direction, which eliminates any pulling together of marginally related instructional exercises.
2. IEPs function as the basis for evaluation.
3. IEPs facilitate communication among staff members, teachers, and parents, and to some extent, teachers and students.

Development of the IEP follows initial identification, evaluation, and classification. The educational plan is evaluated and rewritten at least annually.

Skill 1.7   Identify models of support for providing assistance in general education curricula

Intervention

Once a student is identified as being at-risk academically or socially, remedial interventions are attempted within the regular classroom. Federal legislation requires that sincere efforts be made to help the child learn in the regular classroom.

In some states, school-based teams of educators are formed to solve learning and behavior problems in the regular classroom. These informal problem-solving teams have a variety of names that include concepts of support (school support teams, student support teams), assistance (teacher assistant teams, school assistance teams, or building assistance teams), and appraisal (school appraisal teams - Pugach & Johnson 1989).

Regardless of what the teams are called, their purpose is similar. Chalfant, Pysh, and Moultrie (1979) state that teacher assistance teams are created to make professional suggestions about curricular alternatives and instructional modifications. These teams may be composed of a variety of participants, including regular education teachers, building administrators, guidance counselors, special education teachers, and the student's parent(s). The team composition varies based on the type of referral, the needs of the student, and the availability of educational personnel and state requirements. (Georgia department of Education 1986)

Instructional modifications are used in an attempt to accommodate the student in the regular classroom. Effective instruction is geared toward individual needs and recognizes differences in how students learn. Modifications are tailored to individual student needs. Some strategies for modifying regular classroom instruction, shown in Table 1-1, are effective with at-risk students with disabilities, as well as students without learning or behavior problems.

Table 1-1 Strategies for Modifying Classroom Instruction

Strategy 1	Provide active learning experiences to teach concepts. Student motivation is increased when students can manipulate, weigh, measure, read, or write using materials and skills that relate to their daily lives.

Strategy 2   Provide ample opportunities for guided practice of new skills. Frequent feedback on performance is essential to overcome the student's feelings of inadequacy. Peer tutoring and cooperative projects provide non-threatening practice opportunities. Individual student conferences, curriculum-based tests, and small group discussions are three useful methods for checking progress.

Strategy 3   Provide multi-sensory learning experiences. Students with learning problems sometimes have sensory processing difficulties; for instance, an auditory discrimination problem may cause misunderstandings about teacher expectations. Lessons and directions that include visual, auditory, tactile, and kinesthetic modes are preferable to a single sensory approach.

Strategy 4   Present information in a manner that is relevant to the student. Particular attention to this strategy is needed when there is a cultural or economic gap between the lives of teachers and students. Relate instruction to a youngster's daily experience and interests.

Strategy 5   Provide students with concrete illustrations of their progress. Students with learning problems need frequent reinforcement for their efforts. Charts, graphs, and check sheets provide tangible markers of student achievement.

Referral

Referral is the process through which a teacher, a parent, or some other person formally requests an evaluation of a student to determine eligibility for special education services. The decision to refer a student may be influenced by: (1) student characteristics, such as the abilities, behaviors, or skills that students exhibit (or lack of them); (2) individual differences among teachers in their beliefs, expectations, or skill in dealing with specific kinds of problems; (3) expectations for assistance with a student who is exhibiting academic or behavioral learning problems; (4) availability of specific kinds of strategies and materials; (5) parents' demand for referral or opposition to referral; and (6) institutional factors which may facilitate or constrain teachers in making referral decisions. Fewer students are referred when school districts have complex procedures for referral, psychological assessments are backlogged for months, special education classes are filled to capacity, or principals and other administrators do not fully recognize the importance of special services.

It is important that referral procedures be clearly understood and coordinated among all school personnel. All educators need to be able to identify characteristics typically exhibited by special needs students. Also, the restrictiveness of special service settings must be known and the appropriateness of each clearly understood. The more restrictive special education programs tend to group students with similar disabilities for instruction. Lastly, the specialized services afforded through equipment, materials, teaching approaches, and specific teacher-student relations should be clearly understood.

Evaluation

If instructional modifications in the regular classroom have not proven successful, a student may be referred for multidisciplinary evaluation. The evaluation is comprehensive and includes norm and criterion-referenced tests (e.g., IQ and diagnostic tests), curriculum-based assessment, systematic teacher observation (e.g., behavior frequency checklist), samples of student work, and parent interviews. The results of the evaluation are twofold: to determined eligibility for special education services and to identify a student's strengths and weaknesses in order to plan an individual education program.

The wording in federal law is very explicit about the manner in which evaluations must be conducted and about the existence of due process procedures that protect against bias and discrimination.

Provisions in the law include the following:

1. The testing of children in their native or primary language unless it is clearly not feasible to do so.
2. The use of evaluation procedures selected and administered to prevent cultural or ethnic discrimination.
3. The use of assessment tools validated for the purpose for which they are being used (e.g., achievement levels, IQ scores, adaptive skills).
4. Assessment by a multidisciplinary team utilizing several pieces of information to formulate a placement decision.

Furthermore, parental involvement must occur in the development of the child's educational program. According to the law:

Parents must:

1. Be notified before initial evaluation or any change in placement by a written notice in their primary language describing the proposed school action, the reasons for it, and the available educational opportunities.
2. Consent, in writing, before the child is initially evaluated.

Parents may:

1. Request an independent educational evaluation if they feel the school's evaluation is inappropriate.
2. Request an evaluation at public expense if a due process hearing decision finds that the public agency's evaluation was inappropriate.
3. Participate on the committee that considers the evaluation, placement, and programming of the student.

All students referred for evaluation for special education should have on file the results of a relatively current vision and hearing screening. This will determine the adequacy of sensory acuity and ensure that learning problems are not due to a vision and/or hearing problem.

Once a student has been evaluated, and their special needs identified, there are several models that can be used to address these needs. The "cascade of services' outlined in Competency 1.2 gives an overview of several common models of intervention and assistance. Competency 5.7 describes other common methods of organizing intervention and services.

Skill 1.8 Identify the purposes and functions of professional and advocacy organizations relevant to educating students with disabilities

Parent and Professional Advocacy Activities and Parent Organizations

There have always been exceptional children with special needs, but special education services have not always been in existence to provide for these needs. Private schools and state institutions were primary sources of education for individuals with intellectual disabilities in earlier years. The 9th and 10th amendments to the U.S. Constitution leave education as an unstated power, and therefore vested in the states. As was the practice in Europe, government funds in America were first appropriated to experimental schools to determine whether students with disabilities could be educated. During the mid-twentieth century, legislators and governors in control of funds were faced with evidence of the need and the efficacy of special education programs, but refused to expend funds adequately, thus creating the ultimate need for federal guidelines in PL 94-142 to mandate flow-through money. Concurrently, due process rights and procedures were outlined, based on litigation and legislation enacted by parents of children with disabilities, parent organizations, and professional advocacy groups. "Public support in the form of legislation and appropriation of funds has been achieved and sustained only by the most arduous and persevering efforts of individuals who advocate for exceptional children." (Hallahan & Kauffman, 1986 p. 26).

Parents, professionals, and other members of advocacy groups and organizations finally succeeded in bringing astounding data about the population of youth with disabilities in our country to the attention of legislators. Among the findings revealed, Congress noted that: (1) there were more than eight million children with disabilities in the United States, and more than half were not receiving an appropriate education; (2) more than one million children with disabilities were excluded from the educational system, and many other children with disabilities were enrolled in regular education classes where they were not benefiting from the educational services provided because of their undetected conditions; and (3) due to inadequate educational services within the public school systems, families were forced to seek services outside the public realm. Years of advocacy effort resulted in the current laws and court decisions mandating special education at a federal level.

Since the advent of IDEA legislation, there has been a proliferation of organizations and support groups designed to assist schools, parents, and exceptional students in meeting their special needs. The professional associations representing the spectrum of services for individuals with disabilities are listed here:

Organization	Members	Mission
Alexander Graham Bell Association for the Deaf and Hard of Hearing 3417 Volta Place, N.W. Washington, D.C. 20007 Phone: (202) 337-5220 Fax: (202) 337-8314 Email: info@agbell.org http://listeningandspokenlanguage.org/	Teachers of the deaf, speech-language pathologists, audiologists, physicians, hearing aid dealers	To promote the teaching of speech, lip reading, and use of residual hearing to persons who are deaf; encourage research; and work to further better education of persons who are deaf.
Alliance for Technology Access 1119 Old Humboldt Road Jackson, TN 38305 Phone (800) 914-3017 Fax (731) 554-5283 TTY (731) 554-5284 Email:atainfo@ataccess.org http://www.Ataccess.org	People with disabilities, family members, and professionals in related fields, and organizations with work in their own communities and ways to support the mission.	To increase the use of technology by children and adults with disabilities and functional limitations.
American Council of the Blind 2200 Wilson Boulevard Suite 650 Arlington, VA 22201-3354 Phone: (202) 467-5081 (800) 424-8666 Fax: (703) 465-5085 Email: info@acb.org http://Acb.org	People with visual impairments or blindness, family members, and professionals, and people who want to become leaders or members of ACB chapters in their own communities.	To improve the well-being of all blind and visually impaired people by: serving as a representative national organization of blind people and conducting a public education program to promote greater understanding of blindness and the capabilities of blind people.
American Council on Rural Special Education (ACRES) West Virginia University 509 Allen Hall, Box 6122 Morgantown, WV 26506 Phone: (304) 293-3450 Email: acres-sped@mail.wvu.edu http://acres-sped.org	Open to anyone interested in supporting their mission	To provide leadership and support that will enhance services for individuals with exceptional needs, their families, and the professionals who work with them, and for the rural communities in which they live

Organization	Members	Mission
American Psychological Association 750 First Street, NE, Washington, DC 20002-4242 Phone: (800) 374-2721 Fax: (202) 336-5500 TTY: (202) 336-6123 http://www.apa.org	Psychologists and Professors of Psychology	Scientific and professional society working to improve mental health services and to advocate for legislation and programs that will promote mental health; facilitate research and professional development.
American Society for Deaf Children 800 Florida Avenue NE Washington, CD 20002 Phone: (800) 942-2732 Email: asdc@deafchildren.org http://www.deafchildren.org	Open to all who support the mission of the association	To provide support, encouragement and information to families raising children who are deaf or hard of hearing.
American Speech-Language-Hearing Association 2200 Research Boulevard Rockville, MD 20850 Phone: (301) 296-5700 http://www.asha.org	Specialists in speech-language pathology and audiology	To advocate for provision of speech-language and hearing services in school and clinic settings; advocate for legislation relative to the profession; and work to promote effective services and development of the profession.
The Arc of the United States 1825 K Street NW, Suite 1200 Washington, DC 20002 Phone: (800) 433-5255 http://www.thearc.org	Parents, professionals, and others interested in individuals with intellectual disabilities	Work on local, state, and national levels to promote treatment, research, public understanding, and legislation for persons with intellectual disabilities; provide counseling for parents of students with intellectual disabilities.
Asperger Syndrome Education Network (ASPEN) 9 Aspen Circle Edison, NJ 08820 Phone: (732) 321-0880 http://www.aspennj.org		Provides families and individuals whose lives are affected by Autism Spectrum Disorders and Nonverbal Learning Disabilities with education, support and advocacy.

Organization	Members	Mission
Association for Children and Adults with Learning Disabilities 4900 Girard Road Pittsburgh, PA 15227 Phone: (412) 81-2253 http://www.acldonline.org	Parents of children with learning disabilities and interested professionals	Advance the education and general well-being of children with adequate intelligence who have learning disabilities arising from perceptual, conceptual, or subtle coordinative problems, sometimes accompanied by behavior difficulties.
Attention Deficit Disorder Association 15000 Commerce Pkwy Suite C Mount Laurel, NJ 08054 Phone: (856) 439-9099 FAX:　(856) 439-0525 Email: membership@add.org http://www.add.org	Open to all who support the mission of ADDA	Provide information, resources and networking to adults with AD/HD and to the professionals who work with them.
Autism Society of America 4340 East-West Hwy, Suite 350 Bethesda, MD 20814 Phone: (800) 328-8476 http://www.autism-society.org	Open to all who support the mission of ASA	To increase public awareness about autism and the day-to-day issues faced by individuals with autism, their families and the professionals with whom they interact. The Society and its chapters share a common mission of providing information and education, and supporting research and advocating for programs and services for the autism community.
Brain Injury Association of America 8201 Greensboro Drive Suite 611 McLean, VA 22102 Phone: (703) 761-0750 http://www.biausa.org	Open to all	Provide information, education and support to assist the 5.3 million Americans currently living with traumatic brain injury and their families.

Organization	Members	Mission
Formerly Child and Adolescent Bipolar Association (CABF), Now The Balanced Mind Parent Network 730 N. Franklin Street Suite 501 Chicago, IL 60654-7225 Phone: (847) 492-8510 http://www.bpkids.org	Physicians, scientific researchers, and allied professionals who provide services to children and adolescents with bipolar disorder or depression, as well as parents and students.	Educate families, professionals, and the public about pediatric bipolar disorder; connects families with resources and support; advocates for and empowers affected families; and supports research on pediatric bipolar disorder and its cure.
Children and Adults with Attention Deficit/ Hyperactive Disorder (CHADD) 4601 Presidents Drive Suite 300 Lanham, MD 20706 Phone: (301) 306-7070 Fax: (301) 306-7090 http://www.chadd.org	Open to all	Provide resources and encouragement to parents, educators and professionals on a grassroots level through CHADD chapters.
Council for Exceptional Children (CEC) 2900 Crystal Drive, Suite 1000 Arlington, VA 22202 Phone: (888) 232-7733 TTY: (866) 915-5000 FAX: (703) 264-9494 http://www.cec.sped.org	Teachers, administrators, teacher educators, and related service personnel	Advocate for services for individuals with disabilities and gifted individuals. A professional organization that addresses service, training, and research relative to exceptional persons.
Council for Educational Diagnostic Services 2900 Crystal Drive, Suite 1000 Arlington, VA 22202 Phone: (888) 232-7733 http://community.cec.sped.org/ CEDS/home/	Members of the Council for Exceptional Children who are school psychologists, educational diagnosticians, [and] social workers who are involved in diagnosing educational difficulties	Promote the most appropriate education of children and youth through appraisal, diagnosis, educational intervention, implementation, and evaluation of a prescribed educational program. Work to facilitate the professional development of those who assess students. Work to further development of better diagnostic techniques and procedures.

Organization	Members	Mission
Council of Administrators of Special Education 101 Katelyn Circle, Suite E Warner Robins, GA 31088 Phone: (478) 333-6892 Fax: (478) 333-2453 Email: lpurcell@casecec.org http://www.casecec.org	Members of the Council for Exceptional Children who are administrators, directors, coordinators, or supervisors of programs, schools, or classes for exceptional children; college faculty who train administrators	Promote professional leadership; provide opportunities for the study of problems common to its members; communicate through discussion and publications information that will facilitate improved services for children with exceptional needs.
Division for Communicative Disabilities and Deafness 2900 Crystal Drive, Suite 1000 Arlington, VA 22202 http://www.dcdd.us	Members of the Council for Exceptional Children who are speech-language pathologists, audiologists, teachers of children with communication disorders, or educators of professionals who plan to work with children who have communication disorders	Promote the education of children with communication disorders. Promote professional growth and research.
Division for Early Childhood 3415 S. Sepulveda Blvd. Suite 1100, Unit 1127 Los Angeles, CA 90034 Phone: (310) 428-7209 Fax: (855) 678-1989 Email: dec@dec-sped.org http://www.dec-sped.org	Members of the Council for Exceptional Children who teach preschool children and infants or educate teachers to work with young children	Promote effective education for young children and infants. Promote professional development of those who work with young children and infants. Promote legislation and research.

Organization	Members	Mission
Division for Physical, and Health and Multiple Disabilities 2900 Crystal Drive, Suite 1000 Arlington, VA 22202 Phone: (888) 232-7733 http://community.cec.sped.org/DPHMD/Home/	Members of the Council for Exceptional Children who work with individuals who have physical disabilities or educate professionals to work with those individuals	Promote closer relationships among educators of students who have physical impairments or are homebound. Facilitate research and encourage development of new ideas, practices, and techniques through professional meetings, workshops, and publications.
Division on Visual Impairments 2900 Crystal Drive, Suite 1000 Arlington, VA 22202 http://www.cecdvi.org	Members of the Council for Exceptional Children who work with individuals who have visual disabilities or educate professionals to work with those individuals	Work to advance the education and training of individuals with visual impairments. Work to bring about better understanding of educational, emotional, or other problems associated with visual impairment. Facilitate research and development of new techniques or ideas in education and training of individuals with visual problems.
Division on Career Development and Transition 2900 Crystal Drive, Suite 1000 Arlington, VA 22202 http://www.dcdt.org	Members of the Council for Exceptional Children who teach or in other ways work toward career development and vocational education of exceptional children	Promote and encourage professional growth of all those concerned with career development and vocational education. Promote research, legislation, information dissemination, and technical assistance relevant to career development and vocational education.
Epilepsy Foundation of America (EFA) 8301 Professional Place Landover, MD 20785 Phone: (800) 332-1000 Fax: (301) 577-2684 http://www.epilepsyfoundation.org	A non-membership organization	Work to ensure that people with seizures are able to participate in all life experiences; and to prevent, control and cure epilepsy through research, education, advocacy and services.

Organization	Members	Mission
Family Center on Technology and Disability (FCTD) 1825 Connecticut Avenue, NW 7th Floor Washington, DC 20009 Phone: (202) 884-8068 Fax: (202) 884-8441 Email: fctd@fhi360.org http://www.fctd.info	Nonmember association	Designed to support organizations and programs that work with families of children and youth with disabilities.
Hands and Voices P.O. Box 3093 Denver CO 80237 Phone: (866) 422-0422 http://www.handsandvoices.org	Families, professionals, other organizations, pre-service students, and deaf and hard of hearing adults who are all working towards ensuring successful outcomes for children who are deaf and hard of hearing.	Support families and their children who are deaf or hard of hearing, as well as the professionals who serve them.
The International Dyslexia Association 40 York Road, 4th floor Baltimore, Maryland 21204 Phone: (410) 296-0232 Fax: (410) 321-5069 http://www.interdys.org	Anyone interested in IDA and its mission can become a member	Provide information and referral services, research, advocacy and direct services to professionals in the field of learning disabilities.
Learning Disabilities Association of America (LDA) 4156 Library Road Pittsburgh, PA 15234 Phone: (412) 341-1515 Fax: (412) 344-0224 http://www.ldanatl.org	Anyone interested in LDA and its mission can become a member	Provide cutting edge information on learning disabilities, practical solutions, and a comprehensive network of resources. Provides support to people with learning disabilities, their families, teachers and other professionals.

Organization	Members	Mission
National Association of Special Education Teachers (NASET) 1250 Connecticut Avenue, N.W. Suite 200 Washington D.C. 20036 Phone and Fax: 800-754-4421 Email: contactus@naset.org	All special education teachers in America; provides individual or group/district membership	The mission is to render all possible support and assistance to professionals who teach children with special needs. **NASET** promotes innovation in special education research, practice, and policy in order to foster exceptional teaching for exceptional children.
National Association of the Deaf (NAD) 8630 Fenton Street, Suite 820, Silver Spring, MD Phone: (209) 210-3819 TTY: (301) 587-1789, , FAX: (301) 587-1791 http://nad.org	Anyone interested in NAD and its mission can become a member	Promote, protect, and preserve the rights and quality of life of deaf and hard of hearing individuals in the United States of America.
National Mental Health Services Administration 1 Choke Cherry Road Rockville, MD 20857 Phone: (877) SAMSA-7 www.samhsa.gov	Government Agency	Developed for users of mental health services and their families, the general public, policy makers, providers, and the media.
TASH (Formerly The Association for Persons with Severe Handicaps) 1001 Connecticut Avenue, NW, Suite 235 Washington, DC 20036 Phone: (202) 540-9020 Fax: (202) 540-9019 http:// www.tash.org	Anyone interested in TASH and its mission can become a member	Create change and build capacity so that all people, no matter their perceived level of disability, are included in all aspects of society.

Organization	Members	Mission
US Department of Education Office of Special Education and Rehabilitative Services 400 Maryland Avenue, SW Washington, D.C. 20202 Phone: (800) USA-LEARN http://www.ed.gov/about/offices/list/osers/index.html	Government Resource	Committed to improving results and outcomes for people with disabilities of all ages.
Wrights Law http://wrightslaw.com	Non-membership organization	Provide parent advocacy training and updates on the law throughout the country.
National Association for the Education of Young Children 1313 L St. N.W. Suite 500, Washington DC 20005 Phone: (800) 424-2460 http://www.naeyc.org		Promote service and action on behalf of the needs and rights of young children, with emphasis on provision of educational services and resources.
National Easter Seal Society 233 South Wacker Drive, Suite 2400 Chicago, IL 60606 Phone: (800) 221-6827 TTY: (312) 726-1494 http://www.easterseals.com	State units (49) and local societies (951); no individual members	Establish and run programs for individuals with physical impairments, usually including diagnostic services, speech therapy, preschool services, physical therapy, and occupational therapy.

COMPETENCY 2.0   KNOWLEDGE OF ASSESSMENT AND EVALUATION

Skill 2.1   **Identify the purposes of assessment (e.g., early identification, screening, interventions, eligibility, diagnosis, identification of relevant instructional content, monitoring the effectiveness of instruction) across disciplines**

All children enrolled in our educational system will experience testing throughout their schooling, whether it is preschool sensory screenings, teacher-made quizzes, or annual standardized assessments. Many special needs students are initially identified using these tests and later selected for further assessment. Testing supplies new parameters of information from the time that a student is first suspected of having an educational disability, through placement, intervention, and monitoring of progress.

The Individuals with Disabilities Education Act (Public Law 101-476) and its revisions make definite statements about appropriate evaluation of students for identification, placement, and program purposes. The full, individualized assessment procedure, using instruments validated to test disability areas by those serving on the multidisciplinary team, must be fully understood in order to operate within the mandates of the law and to ultimately make important decisions about a child. Assessment in special education is continuous and occurs on a regular basis. It is part of the diagnostic treatment process through which teachers continually asses the student, plan instruction, implement the planned instruction, and then reassess so that instruction might be modified.

The competencies in this section address the variety of assessment instruments: standardized, criterion-referenced, curriculum-based, and teacher-made. Teachers in the field of special education should possess sufficient knowledge to be able to determine quantitative dimensions, such as the validity and reliability of tests, to recognize sound test content, and to choose appropriate tests for specific purposes. They must be well trained in the administration, scoring, and interpretation of a wide variety of evaluative instruments. Furthermore, they need to know how to use the assessment data in IEP development, instructional planning, and program decision-making. Knowledge of methods used to assess academic and social behavior is yet another requirement for the special education teacher.

Assessment plays a vital role in the initial diagnosis, the decision to place, the planning of program goals and objectives, and the ongoing diagnostic evaluation of the exceptional student. The limitations of assessment are also addressed, especially as they relate to test bias, cultural and linguistic concerns, and student identification. Evaluation by a multidisciplinary team is the means by which eligibility for special education services in determined. Public Law 94-142 is very explicit about the manner in which evaluations may be done by local school districts, and due process safeguards exist to protect against bias and discrimination.

Assessment is the gathering of information in order to make decisions. In exceptional student education, assessment is used to make decisions about:

- Screening and initial identification of children who may need services
- Diagnosis of specific learning disabilities
- Selection and evaluation of teaching strategies and programs
- Determination of the child's present level of performance
- Classification and program placement
- Development of goals, objectives, and evaluation for the IEP
- Eligibility for a program
- Monitoring of progress and continuation of a program
- Effectiveness of instructional programs and strategies
- Effectiveness of behavioral interventions
- Accommodations needed for mandated or classroom testing

Early intervention screenings and assessments for young children are highly valuable; students with learning and developmental problems can be detected at an early age, even prior to entering school. This will alleviate some of the problems a student may encounter upon entering kindergarten. The early identification and intervention of suspected disabilities gives a child a head start on understanding and grappling deficits which have surfaced prior to entering school.

Criteria for eligibility is discussed among the multidisciplinary team members once assessment data has been gathered; this is true for both students who have been identified via early intervention screenings as well as students who were identified later in the school setting. The team asks if there is a significant gap that exists between a student's ability and their actual achievement (i.e. significant difference in IQ score and equivalent reading score). The team also identifies if there are other existent factors which may hinder a student's ability (i.e. poverty, poor school attendance). Processing skills are also evaluated comprehensibly; they analyze the student's characteristics (i.e. attention and memory).

Skill 2.2 **Identify the legal requirements and ethical principles regarding the assessment of students with disabilities (e.g., confidentiality, adherence to test protocols, and appropriateness of assessment for student needs)**

Skills 1.1 and 1.2 provide a detailed look at legal requirements in assessment and delivery of services to exceptional students. This section will briefly highlight the most critical legal and ethical issues to be considered when assessing students with disabilities.

IDEA legislation requires that assessment and evaluation be both individualized and nondiscriminatory. While there are many assessment resources available for individualizing assessment, it can be difficult to find *nondiscriminatory* assessments when the student is from a cultural or language background other than that of mainstream America, where typical standardized tests were normed. Many intelligence and achievement tests have been found to have bias against certain racial and ethnic cultures.

Bias in testing occurs when the information within the test or the information required to respond to a multiple choice question or constructed response (essay question) on the test is information that is not available to test takers who come from a different cultural, ethnic, linguistic, or socio-economic background than the majority of the test takers. Since they have not had the same prior linguistic, social, or cultural experiences as the majority of test takers, these test takers are at a disadvantage. No matter what their actual mastery of the material taught by the teacher, they cannot address the "biased" questions. Generally, other "non-biased" questions are given to them, and eventually the biased questions are removed from the examination.

An example of such bias would be reading comprehension questions about the fairy tale of the gingerbread boy. These questions may be simple and accessible for most American children. However, children who are recent arrivals from a different culture in which the story of the gingerbread boy was not known would be at a serious disadvantage. In that situation alternative questions consistent with the students' background would need to be constructed. Teachers and administrators are required by law to assure that the tests and assessments used are nondiscriminatory. More on this topic can be found in Skill 2.6.

Assessing students with disabilities presents additional issues of possible bias that may not be immediately obvious. Bias also occurs if the test purports to measure one skill, but the manner in which it measures that skill depends on *another* skill that is limited in children with certain disabilities. For example, an open response question requiring written output to demonstrate comprehension of an inference about cause and effect is biased against students with writing disabilities. These students might fully understand the inferential cause and effect relationship, but be unable to write well enough to demonstrate that comprehension. Therefore, this test question would also be discriminatory and invalid for that population. In order to make *appropriate* decisions about assessment, the teacher or team must be very clear on exactly *what they want to assess* and whether the instrument or method they choose actually assesses *that* variable.

IDEA legislation also requires that **no single assessment or measurement tool may be used to determine** eligibility or placement. This is a critical assessment principle and one that is often overlooked. It is easy to look at the results of one assessment and jump to conclusions about a student's ability or needs. To get an accurate picture of a child's needs, however, it is necessary to use a variety of measures, and the law requires that educators do so.

IDEA legislation requires that assessment be in *a language and a form* that will give the most accurate picture of a child's abilities or disabilities. Clearly this principle has implications for ESL students, and IDEA does require that testing be in the child's preferred language. However, the requirement that it be in the most appropriate *form* is also significant. Since students with disabilities are often limited on one or another mode of expression or reception of information, a form of response that is fully accessible to the child must also be found. Adherence to test protocols must be followed. The requirement of nondiscriminatory assessment also means that the assessments used must be validated for the specific purpose for which they will be used. Concepts of validity are discussed in Skill 2.4.

Appropriate assessment of a student's needs can include informal assessments, formal assessments, classroom observations, psychoeducational evaluations, curriculum-based measurements, portfolios, and more. Some Florida state-based assessments include the FCAT 2.0 and the Florida EOC (End of Course) assessments. Types of assessments are described in detail in Skill 2.3.

Finally, as in all educational endeavors, confidentiality is a critical requirement. The Family Educational Rights and Privacy Act of 1974 states that all assessment and discussion of assessment is to be considered strictly confidential and shared only with those immediately involved in decision making and delivery of services to students. Parents have the right to review any and all assessments and their written approval is needed before assessment information can be shared with anyone else (e.g., counselors, outside medical or treatment sources, etc.).

Skill 2.3   Identify measurement concepts, characteristics, and uses of norm-referenced, criterion-referenced, and performance-based assessments for students with disabilities

In order to understand, select, and interpret assessments for students with disabilities, it is necessary to understand certain basic measurement and assessment concepts.

Types of Assessment

Assessment types can be categorized in a number of ways, most commonly in terms of *what* is being assessed, *how* the assessment is constructed, or how it is to *be used*. It is important to understand these differences so as to be able to correctly interpret assessment results.

Formal vs. Informal: This variable focuses on how the assessment is constructed or scored. *Formal* assessments are assessments such as standardized tests or textbook quizzes; objective tests that include primarily questions for which there is only one correct, easily identifiable answer. These can be commercial or teacher-made assessments, given to either groups or individuals. *Informal* assessments have less objective measures, and may include anecdotes or observations that may or may not be quantified, as well as interviews, casual questioning during a task, etc. Informal evaluation strategies rely upon the knowledge and judgment of the professional and are an integral part of the evaluation. An advantage of using informal assessments is the ease of design and administration and the usefulness of information the teacher can gain about the student's strengths and weaknesses. An example might be watching a student sort objects to see what attribute is most important to the student, or questioning a student to see what he or she found confusing about a task.

Some assessment techniques can be found in both formal and informal tools. For example, observation may incorporate structured observation instruments as well as other informal procedures, including professional judgment. When evaluating a child's developmental level, a professional may use a formal adaptive rating scale while simultaneously using professional judgment to assess the child's motivation and behavior during the evaluation process.

Standardized Tests are formal tests that are administered to either groups or individuals in a specifically prescribed manner, with strict rules to keep procedures, scoring, and interpretation of results uniform in all cases. Such tests allow comparisons to be made across populations, ages or grades, or over time for a particular student. Intelligence tests and most diagnostic tests are standardized tests.

Norm-Referenced vs. Criterion Referenced: This distinction is based on the standard to which the student's performance is being compared.

Norm-Referenced tests establish a ranking and compare the student's performance to an established norm, usually for age or grade peers. **What** the student knows is of less importance than **how similar** the student's performance is to a specific group. Norm-referenced tests use normative data for scoring which include performance standards by age, gender, or ethnic group. Norm-Referenced tests are, by definition, standardized. Examples include intelligence tests and many achievement tests, such as are the CTBS, WISC-R, and Stanford-Binet. Norm-referenced tests are often used in determining eligibility for special needs services.

Criterion Referenced tests measure a student's knowledge of specific content, usually related to classroom instruction or curriculum standards. The student's performance is compared to a set of **criteria** or a pre-established standard of information the student is expected to know. On these tests, **what** the student knows is more important than **how he or she compares** to other students. Examples include math quizzes at the end of a chapter, or some state mandated tests of specific content. Criterion referenced tests are used to determine whether a student has mastered required skills. They are often referred to as curriculum based assessments.

Group vs. Individual Assessments: This variable simply refers to the manner of presentation, whether given to a group of students or on a one to one basis. Group assessments can be formal or informal, standardized or not, criterion or norm-referenced. Individual assessments can be found in all these types as well.

Authentic or Performance-Based Assessments are designed to be as close to real life as possible so they are relevant and meaningful to the student's life. They can be formal or informal, depending upon how they are constructed. Rather than an artificially constructed multiple choice test, the student is assessed on actual performance related to a practical example of the use of a skill. An example of an authentic test item would be calculating a 20 percent sales discount on a popular clothing item after the student has studied math percentages. Other performance-based assessments might require the student to make or construct something based upon principles taught in a lesson, or demonstrate practical knowledge in something other than a pencil and paper mode.

Rating Scales and Checklists are generally self-appraisal instruments completed by the student or observation-based instruments completed by teacher or parents. The focus is frequently on behavior or affective areas such as interest, motivation, attention or depression. These tests can be formal or informal and some can be standardized and norm-referenced. Examples of norm-referenced tests of this type would be ADHD rating scales or the Behavior Assessment System for Children.

Momentary Time Sampling—This is a technique used for measuring behaviors of a group of individuals or several behaviors from the same individual. Time samples are usually brief, and may be conducted at fixed or variable intervals. The advantage of using variable intervals is increased reliability, as the students will not be able to predict when the time sample will be taken.

Multiple Baseline Design—This may be used to test the effectiveness of an intervention in a skill performance or to determine if the intervention accounted for the observed changes in a target behavior. First, the initial baseline data is collected, followed by the data during the intervention period. To get the second baseline, the intervention is removed for a period of time, and data is collected again. The intervention is then reapplied, and data is collected on the target behavior.

An example of a multiple baseline design might be ignoring a child who calls out in class without raising his hand. Initially, the baseline could involve counting the number of times the child calls out before applying interventions. During the time the teacher ignores the child's call-outs, data is collected. For the second baseline, the teacher would resume the response to the child's call-outs in the way she did before ignoring them. The child's call-outs would probably increase again if ignoring actually accounted for the decrease. If the teacher reapplies the ignoring strategy, the child's call-outs would probably decrease again.

Multiple baseline designs may also be used with single-subject experiments where:

1. The same behavior is measured for several students at the same time. An example would be observing off-task or out-of-seat behavior among three students in a classroom.

2. Several behaviors may be measured for one student. The teacher may be observing call-outs, off-task, and out-of-seat behavior for a particular child during an observation period.

3. Several settings are observed to see if the same behaviors are occurring across settings. A student's aggressive behavior toward his classmates may be observed at recess, in class, going to or from class, and in the cafeteria.

Individualizing Informal Assessments

Although standardized testing will often be used for program placement and eligibility issues, informal, individually administered tests can be very useful in providing detailed qualitative information for diagnosis and instructional design. When administering an informal individual test, the tester has the opportunity to observe the individual's responses and to determine how such things as problem solving are accomplished.

Within limits, the tester is able to control the pace and tempo of the testing session and to rephrase and probe responses in order to elicit the individual's best performance. If the child becomes tired, the examiner can break between sub tests or end the test; if he loses his place on the test, the tester can help him to regain it; if he dawdles or loses interest, the tester can encourage or redirect him. If the child lacks self-confidence, the examiner can reinforce his efforts. In short, such informal individual tests allow the examiner to encourage best efforts and to observe how a student uses his skills to answer questions. Thus, informal individual tests provide for the gathering of both quantitative and qualitative information. Standardized tests, whether administered individually or to a group, do not allow such flexibility. The examiner cannot rephrase questions, or probe or prompt responses.

IDEA requires that a variety of assessment tools and strategies be utilized when conducting assessments. Before utilizing a formal or informal tool, the practitioner should make sure that the tool is the most appropriate one that can be used for that particular student. If it is norm-referenced, it should be scored on a group to which the student belongs. Many assessment tools can be used across disabilities. Dependent upon the disability in question, such as blindness, autism, or hearing impairment, some assessment tools will give more information than others or will need modifications.

The choice between standardized and informal testing should be primarily determined by purpose and efficiency. When testing for program evaluation, screening, and some types of program planning (such as tracking), standardized tests are appropriate.

When planning individual programs, specific lesson plans, and instructional interventions, more informal and individually administered tests can be useful. When a student is being evaluated for placement in a special education program, all areas related to the suspected disability must be assessed. Individual tests should be administered when there is a reason to question the validity of results of group tests or when an in-depth evaluation of the test taker's performance is needed.

Special consideration may need to be given to a particular student who possesses limitations that require accommodations to make a test or assessment accessible to the student. If a student cannot read the instructions or content (e.g., math reasoning test), or is unable to perform the type of response required, the test results reflect measured inability to read or write, rather than skill or ability in the area of the test content. Children with learning disabilities or physical impediments may know the answers but be unable to deliver them orally.

Skill 2.4 **Interpret, analyze, and apply the results of norm-referenced, criterion-referenced, and performance-based assessments for students with disabilities**

Concepts of Validity and Reliability in Testing

Regardless of what type of assessment is used, it is important to use tests that are both valid and reliable. These terms have a very specific meaning for assessment.

Validity is how well a test measures what it is supposed to measure. A test is valid insofar as it measures what it is supposed to measure. Many standardized tests have published measures of validity. However, teachers need to remember that the test is only valid *for their class if it measures what THEY want to measure.* A test can be "valid" in one setting, for a particular set of measurements, and invalid in another setting because the teacher wants to measure something else. An "expert's" statement that a test is valid is only relevant if it tests what the teacher wants assessed, is appropriate for THAT teacher's students, and meets any special needs of the student population. Obviously, any bias (discussed in the previous section) found in the test would make it impossible to draw conclusions from the results.

Reliability is the consistency of the test. This is measured by whether the test will indicate the same score for the child who takes it twice or who takes two halves of it or two comparable versions of it.

Norm-Referenced Tests

Results of norm-referenced tests are given in derived scores, which compare the student's raw score to the performance of a specified group of subjects. Criteria for the selection of the group may be based on characteristics such as age, sex, or geographic area. The test results of such assessments must always be interpreted in light of what type of tasks the individual was required to perform and the group to which the student's scores are being compared. One of the most common errors in interpretation of norm-referenced tests is using a test that is not appropriately normed for the student being assessed. A test normed on American third graders from inner city schools would not, for example, be appropriately normed for recent immigrants living in rural America. Geographic and socioeconomic variables can impact the appropriate norm group, as can culture, language, age, and time period (e.g., a test normed in the 1930's would not be as appropriate as one normed more recently).

Although many of the assessment tools used in for eligibility and placement decisions are chosen by the school system, the teacher must be careful not to inappropriately interpret scores from such tests. It is the teacher's responsibility to be familiar with the norm group to which the student is being compared. This information will be in the literature provided with instruction manuals for norm referenced tests. Some the most commonly used derived scores are provided below.

Age and Grade Equivalents

Age and grade equivalent scores are considered developmental scores because they attempt to convert the student's raw score into an average performance of a particular age or grade group.

Age equivalents are expressed in years and months, i.e. 7-3. In the standardization procedure, a mean is calculated for all individuals of the particular age who took the test. If the mean or median number of correct responses for children 7 years and 3 months was 80, then an individual whose raw score was 80 would be assigned an age equivalent of 7 years and 3 months.

Grade equivalents are written as years and scholastic months. For example, 6.2 would read sixth grade, second month.

Age and grade equivalents often seem practical and easy to understand, particularly when talking to parents. Such scores are in widespread use in the education field, in large part because the concept of a grade equivalent is intuitively comfortable to those without testing expertise, such as parents and the student.

However, these scores are so often misinterpreted by parents and teachers alike that the International Reading Association (IRA) has issued a statement (1981) strongly urging teachers and schools NOT to use them. More recently, in 2007, ASHA had an article posted by Emily Maloney and Linda Larrivee, which also supported such caution when using or considering age and grade equivalents, because the scores can be limiting. The PDF article can be accessed on:

http://www.asha.org/uploadedfiles/asha/publications/cicsd/2007flimitationsofageequivale
ntscores.pdf

If they are used, the teacher must be *very* careful to explain what they do and **do not** mean. If, for example, 3rd grade Johnny's parents are told his grade equivalency on a reading test was 6.4, they are likely to think he is reading on a 6th grade level. The teacher will need to explain that the results mean Johnny got a score similar to the score a typical 6th grader would get on this **3rd grade** material. However, since the test material was NOT 6th grade material, this does not mean Johnny could read 6th grade material. It was 3rd grade material and Johnny did very well on it, as well as a 6th grader would.

This sort of confusion on the part of parents (and even some teachers) is why the IRA prefers the score not be used. In addition, Venn (2004) points out additional difficulties. Research shows that the accuracy and reliability of age and grade equivalencies decrease as the students age.

Finally, age and grade equivalencies are not expressed in equal units and equivalencies from *different tests are not comparable*, so a child's grade equivalency on one test cannot be compared to his or her grade score on another. Venn also notes that the American Psychological Association, in 1999, advocated the elimination of age and grade scores completely for all these reasons.

Quartiles, Deciles, and Percentiles

These scores indicate the percentage of scores that fall below the individual's raw score. Quartiles divide the score into four equal parts; the first quartile is the point at which 25% of the scores fall below the full score. Deciles divide the distribution into ten equal parts; the seventh decile would mark the point below which 70% of the scores fall. Percentiles are the most frequently used, however. A percentile rank of 45 would indicate that the person's raw score was at the point below which 45% of the other scores fell.

Interpreting these scores of parents and others outside of the testing field must be done with care. Percentiles can be confusing because parents are accustomed to looking at percentage correct for grading purposes. They may look at a score showing their child is at the 50th percentile and think the child is failing, because 50% correct would be a failing grade. They need to be assured that a score at the 50th percentile is, in fact, a fine score and indicates that their child is solidly in the middle, having performed better than 50 percent of those taking the test. In addition, they may not understand how wide the range of "normal" percentiles is and this too must be explained to them.

Standard Scores

Standard scores are raw scores with the same mean (average) and standard deviation (measure of variability or average distance from the mean) as the scores of test takers in the norm group. Standard scores can be used to compare performance across different tests, so they are valuable in classifying and placement decisions. In the standardization of a test, about 68% of the scores will fall above or below 1 standard deviation of the mean of 100. About 96% of the scores will fall within the range of 2 standard deviations above or below the mean. The most common are T scores, Z scores, stanines, and scaled scores. Standard scores are useful because they allow for direct comparison of raw scores from different individuals and different tests.

In interpreting scores, it is important to note what type of standard score is being used. It is also important to understand that all standard scores are based on the presumption of a normal distribution of scores, or a "bell" curve. Variables or scores that do NOT fall on such a normal curve cannot be compared in this way.

Interpretation

It is important for the teacher to correctly interpret the results of any formal assessments used. Most standardized tests will explain how to interpret results so the teacher does not make errors while assessing the test results..

Special care must be taken in interpreting some tests. Intelligence test scores, for example, should be interpreted in terms of performance and not the person's potential. The teacher must read the test manuals and become familiar with the following items:

- Areas measured: Verbal, quantitative, memory, cognitive skills, or the multiple intelligences on some assessments.
- Population: Target age groups, lack of cultural bias, and adaptations or norms for children with physical handicaps such as blindness.
- Standardization information: Mean and standard deviation, scaled scores and what they mean.
- Means of comparing performance among subtests, such as the Verbal and Performance IQ scores of the WISC-IV
- Uses of the results: The test manual will contain information about how the results can be used (e.g., using the K-ABC-II to identify gifted children), or how they are not to be used (e.g., assuming that a 3rd grade student who gets a score like a 5th grader on a 3rd grade test is ready to do 5th grade work, an assumption that would not be correct).

- Information on use with special populations, such as Spanish-speaking students, students with visual impairments, physical impairments, or learning disabilities.
- Information concerning reliability and validity.

Criterion Referenced Tests and Curriculum-based Assessments

These assessments are interpreted on the basis of the individual's performance on the objectives being measured. Such assessments may be commercially prepared or teacher made, and can be designed for a particular curriculum or a scope and sequence. These assessments are made by selecting objectives, task analyzing those objectives, and selecting measures to test the skills necessary to meet those tasks. Results are calculated for each objective, such as Cindy was able to divide 2-digit numbers by 1-digit numbers 85% of the time and was able to divide 2-digit numbers by 2-digit numbers 45% of the time. These tests are used primarily to determine the degree to which a student has mastered certain specific objectives, but they can also be useful for gaining insight into the types of error patterns the student makes. Because the student's performance is not compared to others in a group, results are useful for writing IEPs, as well as for deciding what to teach.

Interpreting Results for Families and Others

Parents and family members will have many questions about their child's testing and diagnosis, but they may not have the specialized educational and psychological background to understand the implications of testing and diagnoses without help. Just as each child is an individual, different from all others in significant ways, each child's family is also different from other families. The teacher must tailor communication strategies to the needs of each individual family, just as she must tailor instruction to each individual child. It is important to define terms and explain procedures that might be confusing to parents without talking down to them or appearing condescending or patronizing.

Interpreting tests and diagnostic results to parents can present special challenges. Parents often see numbers and percentages without understanding their significance. They hear diagnostic terms and labels without understanding what they mean. In addition to the interpretation cautions mentioned above, when reporting test results, it is important to briefly define each test or subtest in terms the parent will understand. Telling parents that their child did well or poorly on the WRAML would not be helpful unless the teacher explains the relevant subtests briefly and outlines the implications for instruction. It is best to be as specific as possible and to give concrete examples of how test results predict learning problems.

For instance, if the test shows a child has poor auditory working memory, the teacher can point out that this may hamper the child's ability to remember lectured facts long enough to relate facts *together* to draw conclusions. This has implications for both instruction (maybe use graphic organizers to outline relationships visually) and for testing accommodations (e.g., allow the use of graphic organizers during a test).

Finally, parents often want to know when their child will be "fixed," or "cured," or "at grade level." This is a very difficult question and most testing and diagnostic assessment simply will not answer it. The teacher needs to help the parents focus on what the results mean for instruction and accommodation. Of course, there will be implications for future planning, but it is unwise to try and turn testing results into predictors of how long the child will need support.

Interpreting results for general education teachers should center on specifics of the student's disability and implications for instructional objectives and methods, as well as accommodations necessary for the student to be successful when in the general education classroom. The special education teacher and general education teacher should consult on the development of lesson plans for any student who spends time in the general education class. This might mean helping the general education teacher modify or differentiate her lesson plans so the student can access the lesson in spite of the disability. It would also mean familiarizing the general education teacher with the accommodations listed in the student's IEP. The teacher is legally bound to provide these instructional and testing accommodations in the general education setting.

Skill 2.5   Identify alternate assessment strategies and procedures (e.g., observations, performance-based assessments, interviews, and portfolios) and their appropriate use

Modifications for Assessment

Test taking is not a pleasant experience for many students with behavioral and/or learning problems. They may lack study skills, may experience anxiety before or during a test, or may have problems understanding and differentiating the task requirements for different tests. The skills necessary to be successful vary with the type of test. Certain students have difficulty with writing answers, but they may be able to express their knowledge of subject matter verbally. Therefore, modifications of content area material may be extended to methods and modifications for evaluation and assessment of student progress.

Teachers of students with special needs will frequently find it necessary to modify their assessment techniques and procedures in order to accurately assess the students' knowledge and skills. Because certain disabilities can interfere with performance on an assessment, it is often necessary for the teacher to break down the task or skill and test each part separately. Many of the common accommodations and modifications in testing are designed to separate the specific skill or knowledge being tested from some other ability or skill impacted by a disability. For example, when testing a student with dyslexia on retention of a concept in science, it would be inappropriate to use solely reading/writing assessments. The student's response to a written test would be confounded by the inability to read the test or to compose readable written responses. In such cases, an oral exam, lab experiment, or project/product-based assessment might more accurately assess the student's science knowledge.

Some of the ways that teachers can modify assessment for individual needs include:

- Help students to get used to timed tests.
- Provide study guides before tests.
- Make tests easier to read by leaving ample space between questions.
- Modify multiple choice tests by reducing the number of choices, reforming questions to yes-no, or using matching items.
- Modify short-answer tests with cloze (fill-in) statements, or provide a list of facts or choices that the student can choose from.
- Essay tests can be modified by using partial outlines for the student to complete, allowing additional time, or including test items that do not require extensive writing.
- Students with visual/spatial issues may need assessments with questions or problems presented one at a time either singly on a piece of paper or enclosed in large boxes with plenty of white space around them.

In general, accommodations or modifications in assessment usually fall into the following categories:

Setting: Changes in the location of the testing, such as separate seating or room, special lighting of noise buffers, adaptive furniture, small group or one to one testing.

Timing and Scheduling: Changes in the duration or time of the test such as allowing extra time or an absence of time limits, frequent breaks, or scheduling the test at a time of day when a student functions best—(or has had specific dosage of medication, etc.)

Presentation of Test: Changes in how the test is given to a student, such as oral testing, large print or Braille, sign language, colored overlays or special paper, etc. This would also include allowing the teacher to clarify directions or read the test to the student.

Student Responses: Changes in how the student is allowed to respond to the test, such as allowing oral responses, multiple choice rather than essay, dictating open responses, use of assistive devices such as computer keyboards, spell checkers, writing software, etc.

Alternative Assessments

Venn (2004) defines *alternative assessments* as a group of informal assessment techniques that emphasize open-ended, criterion referenced evaluation that occurs as an integral part of instruction rather than a separate testing activity. Alternative assessments can be very useful, both in instructional planning and in accurately assessing progress toward specific goals for students with disabilities, particularly where more formal measures would be invalid given the student's disability. There are a number of common forms of alternative assessment currently in use in the special education field.

Authentic Assessments are designed to be as close to real life as possible so they are relevant and meaningful to the student's life. Such an assessment might, for example, involve the student's choosing purchases in a store sale to maximize his available budget. This assessment would be a real world application of both math and reading skills, but would not be made in a typical pencil and paper format.

Anecdotal Records are notes recorded by the teacher concerning an area of interest or concern with a particular student. They should focus on observable behaviors and should be descriptive in nature. They should not include assumptions or speculations regarding affective areas such as motivation or interest. These records are usually compiled over a period of several days to several weeks.

Portfolio Assessments come in many forms and have become quite common. The purpose, nature, and policies of portfolio assessment vary greatly from one setting to another. In general, though, a student's portfolio contains samples of work collected over an extended period. The nature of the subject, age of the student, and scope of the portfolio all contribute to the specific mechanics of analyzing, synthesizing, and otherwise evaluating the portfolio contents. Such portfolios usually are aligned with curriculum goals or standards for a particular child.

In most cases, the student and teacher make joint decisions as to which work samples go into the student's portfolio. A collection of work compiled over an extended time allows teacher, student, and parents to view the student's progress from a unique perspective. Qualitative changes over time can be readily apparent from work samples. Such changes are difficult to establish with strictly quantitative records typical of the scores recorded in the teacher's grade book.

Interviews and Questioning can be an invaluable assessment tools when properly used. It is one of the most frequently occurring forms of assessment in the classroom. As the teacher questions the students, she collects a great deal of information about the degree of student learning and potential sources of confusion for the students. While questioning is often viewed as a component of instructional methodology, it is also a powerful assessment tool. Formal or informal interviews are often conducted by persons who have a close relationship to the student and who can offer valuable information about the student's academic and social progress.

Performance-Based Assessment is a form of testing that requires students to perform a task rather than select an answer from a ready-made list. The teacher then judges the quality of the student's work based on a predetermined set of criteria. Such assessment often uses **student-created formats.** Students create an answer or a response to a question or task. In traditional, inflexible assessments, students choose a prepared response from among a selection of responses, such as matching, multiple-choice, and true or false. When implemented effectively, an alternative assessment approach such as these can exhibit the following characteristics, among others:

- Requires higher-order thinking and problem-solving
- Provides opportunities for student self-reflection and self-assessment
- Uses real world applications to connect students to the subject
- Provides opportunities for students to learn and examine subjects on their own and collaborate with their peers.
- Encourages students to continue learning beyond the requirements of the assignment
- Clearly defines objective and performance goals
- Allows students to demonstrate their knowledge using their individual strengths rather than through a "one size fits all" method.

Teachers are learning the value of giving assessments that meet the individual abilities and needs of students. After the teacher has provided instruction, discussion, questioning, and practice, rather than assigning one task to all students, he or she asks students to generate tasks that will show their knowledge of the information presented. Students are given choices and, thereby, have the opportunity to demonstrate more effectively the skills, concepts, or topics that they as individuals have learned.

For example, following a unit on the life of a famous historical figure, students might choose from among "tests", such as a traditional written report, a poster illustrating important events and contributions of the individual, a timeline of events, a cause and effect web or diagram analyzing the individual's contributions, a skit or oral presentation, a comic book style summary, etc. It has been established that student choice increases student originality, intrinsic motivation, and higher mental processes. In addition, such an approach allows students with varying disabilities demonstrate and to identify a student's strengths and weaknesses in order to plan an individual education program.

Observational Checklists: Please refer to Skill 4.2 for detailed information about observations.

Ecological Assessment is when a child is observed and assessed in different environments to see how he or she will function in different environments. For example, a child may be well-behaved in music class but may misbehave in the library, or a similarly quiet environment.

Skill 2.6 **Identify the factors (e.g., curriculum alignment, cultural bias) that influence disproportionate representation of students from diverse cultural, linguistic, and socioeconomic backgrounds in programs for students with disabilities and recognize the implications for assessment**

Limitations of Tests and Measurements Relating to Multicultural and Linguistic Issues

The term multicultural equality incorporates the idea that all student regardless of their gender and social class or their ethnic, racial, or cultural characteristics should have equal opportunities (Banks & Banks, 1993). This is as true in the evaluation of students as it is in learning in school and in assuring fairness at the work site.

The issue of fair assessment for individuals from minority groups has a long history in the law, philosophy, and education. Salvia and Ysseldyke, 1995 point out three aspects of this issue that are particularly relevant to the assessment of students.

Representation

Individuals from diverse backgrounds need to be represented in assessment materials. It is essential that persons from different cultures be represented fairly. Of equal importance is the presentation of individuals from differing genders in non-stereotypical roles and situations.

Acculturation

It is important that individuals from different backgrounds receive opportunities to acquire the tested skills, information, and values. When students are tested with standardized instruments, they are compared to a set of norms in order to gain an index of their relative standing and to make comparisons. We assume that the students we test are similar to those on whom the test was standardized. That is, we assume that their acculturation is comparable.

Acculturation is a matter of educational, socioeconomic, and experiential background rather than of gender, skin color, race, or ethnic background. Children in American culture will have experience with certain nursery rhymes, historical figures, even television shows and fictional characters. Students from other cultures may not share these experiences and may be confused by offhand references to them by teachers and in literature.

For example, one child from a background that did not contain the Santa Claus figure was very confused by a holiday story that involved hanging stockings by the fire and finding them filled with candy the next morning. The only reason this child could imagine for hanging a stocking by the fire was to dry it out because it had gotten wet. The child, therefore, felt that the Santa figure was mean to put candy in a dirty, wet sock where it would get all mushy. Naturally enough, this child "failed" to identify the "main idea" in the story.

When it is said that a child's acculturation differs from that of the group used as a norm, what is really meant is that the experiential background differed, not simply that the child is of a different ethnic origin (Salvia & Ysseldyke, 1991). Differences in experiential background should therefore be accounted for when administering tests. This is important, in order to avoid bias. Strictly speaking, norm-referenced tests can only be used to assess students from the same cultural group as those upon whom the test was normed. Such tests are NOT valid for assessing students from diverse backgrounds. The inherent cultural bias on many screening and placement assessments accounts for much of the disproportionate representation of students from diverse backgrounds in special education.

Language

The language and concepts that comprise test items should be unbiased. Students should be familiar with terminology and references to which the language is being made when they are administered tests, especially when the results of the tests are going to be used for decision-making purposes. Many tests given in regular grades relate to decisions about promotion and grouping of students for instructional purposes. Tests and other assessment instruments that relate to special education are generally concerned with two types of decisions: (1) eligibility, and (2) program planning for individualized education.

Curriculum Alignment

Educators working in schools often view curriculum alignment as an official structure of information, including purposes, goals, and outcomes, which is provided to students each year. Schools need to examine their curriculum every few years to be sure that the content provided to students is relevant and utilizes recent educational research and norms.

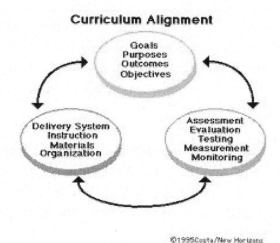

Source: Arthur Costa, California State University

Skill 2.7   **Identify and analyze reliable and valid progress-monitoring methods for assessing individual student progress (e.g., curriculum based assessments, fluency checks, rubrics, storytelling, informal reading inventories, portfolios)**

It is not only necessary to accurately assess a student's needs, once interventions and specialized instruction are in place, it is also necessary to monitor the student's progress toward the goals set by the IEP team. Some of the assessment techniques already discussed (e.g., curriculum based assessments and portfolios) are useful in tracking student progress. Other methods of tracking progress are listed here.

Fluency Checks

Fluency is the ability to read a text quickly, accurately, and with appropriate expression. In silent reading, fluent readers can recognize words automatically, and they fully comprehend what they read. If comprehension is not immediate, these readers can use context clues to grasp the meaning of the sentence or paragraph. When reading aloud, fluent readers display confidence, and they read effortlessly and with expression (prosody). This is in contrast to readers that are not fluent, who read slowly, often one word at a time, so that meaning is lost in an effort to decode words with accuracy.

Fluency is an important skill when learning to read because it helps readers to progress from the word recognition stage to one where they can understand what they read. When readers don't have to spend time focusing on reading individual words, they can group words together to form ideas, which leads to comprehension. Not only can they grasp the main idea of the text, but they can also make connections between the text and their prior knowledge and events in their own lives.

Fluency is a skill that readers have to develop over time and with repeated practice and exposure to literature and opportunities to read for various purposes. Early readers read words rather than phrases and sentences, and the act of reading often appears to be laborious rather than enjoyable. In order to become fluent, readers have to decode the letters and words automatically.

Automaticity is not the same as fluency. This is the fast and effortless recognition of words that only comes through repeated practice. Automaticity refers to accurate reading of words. It does not refer to reading with expression or reading with comprehension. It deals with word recognition only. It is necessary for fluency, but it is not the only factor that determines whether or not a student can read fluently. Eventually, automaticity should lead to comprehension of ideas.

Even when readers do have a repertoire of words that they recognize easily, they may not be fluent readers. This is because the expression is missing from the reading. Reading fluently with expression means that the reader must be able to chunk the text into meaningful segments, i.e., phrases and clauses. Fluency changes over time as readers are exposed to more difficult texts. The most fluent readers at one level may read slowly when they are first introduced to a more difficult text because they need time for comprehension.

Some techniques to use when teaching students to read fluently include:

- Repeated reading of the same text
- Oral reading practice using audio recordings
- Provide models of what fluent reading looks and sounds like
- Read to students
- Choral reading
- Partner reading
- Readers' Theatre

Assessing fluency usually relies on listening to the student read aloud. This can be done informally in group reading and sharing, or more formally through the use of running records. In either case, the teacher is listening for the oral characteristics of automaticity (reading appropriately quickly and with word by word accuracy) and for prosody, or expression, which indicates comprehension. Analysis of a running record or an observational checklist of oral reading can indicate how well the child can decode the words, as well as whether the child understands the text well enough to use appropriate phrasing and expression. A child who reads accurately in a monotone is able to decode the words, but doesn't understand them enough to use the appropriate expression. In addition, a child who comprehends what he/she is reading will chunk word into appropriate phrases based upon the meaning and will not pause at inappropriate times (e.g., when a phrase carries over between two lines). Running records have the advantage of providing clues to the source of any reading problems there may be, as well. A running record can also provide information on a reader's self-monitoring as it notes whether a child retraces his/her steps when a word does not make sense or when the child misinterprets one of the key cues (visual grapho-phonemic, syntactic or semantic).

Running records can also be used to help follow student progress in reading by periodically analyzing errors to see if the student is using the strategies being taught to remedy reading problems. They can also be used to chart advances in the child's independent and instructional levels by increasing the difficulty of the passages on which a running record is taken.

In addition, many of the commercial tests available can be used to track reading progress. There are simple, easy-to-use tests the teacher can give at the beginning and end of a semester or year to help chart progress. The DIBELS testing system, though somewhat controversial, is one simple way to chart progress in word recognition and fluency. The DRA (Developmental Reading Assessment by Pearson) offers leveled reading samples that can be scored for decoding, fluency, and comprehension periodically throughout the year.

Informal Reading Inventories, discussed below, can also provide useful tracking and monitoring formats.

Whether using running records or some more informal strategy for assessing fluency, it is important to take a variety of samples of reading behavior in a several areas, including content areas. A child who can read a simple, chronologically-organized story fluently may not be able to read a more technical science paragraph fluently.

Informal Reading Inventories (IRIs)

These are a series of word lists and samples of texts prearranged in stages of increasing difficulty. By listening to children read through these inventories, the teacher can pinpoint their skill level and the additional concepts they need to work on. Some IRIs also have sentence dictation components that let the teacher assess a student's spelling and phonics level. IRIs usually come with everything a teacher needs for administering and interpreting them, including answer sheets, reproducible materials, and scoring and leveling scales. These assessments can be used to track progress, as well. Examples of commonly used IRIs include: Silvaroli and Wheelock's *Classroom Reading Inventory* (2001), Burns and Roe's (2002) *Informal Reading Inventory,* Qualitative Reading Inventory-V (2010) or Woods and Moe's (2003) *Analytical Reading Inventory.*

Formal Reading Assessments

There are many commercially available tools for assessing various aspects of reading and writing, and for tracking progress in these areas. A few are listed here.

- *The Developmental Reading Assessment (DRA)* is used three times per year in a one on one setting to assess student reading progress. It includes a running record for decoding and miscue analysis, as well as a comprehension piece.

- *The Retelling Profile* (2002) by Mitchell and Irwin uses a checklist to assess text based and inferential comprehension, as well as language fluency. It relies on teacher judgment of five levels of proficiency and can be used to chart progress over time.
- *The Scholastic Reading Inventory* assesses comprehension at all grade levels and provides both a baseline and measures of ongoing progress over the years. It requires access to networked computers.
- *Degrees of Reading Power (DRP)*—this test is designed to assess how well children understand the meaning of written text in real life situations, and measures the process of children's reading, not the products of reading, such as identifying the main idea and author's purpose.
- *CTPIII*—this is a criterion-referenced test that measures verbal and quantitative ability in grades 3-12. It is designed to help differentiate among the most capable students, i.e., those who rank above the 80th percentile on other standardized tests. This is a test that emphasizes higher order thinking skills and process-related reading comprehension questions.
- *Terra Nova/Comprehensive Test Of Basic Skills (CTBS)* by McGraw-Hill is standardized and measures skills in reading and language arts.
- *ISTEP+* assessments measure language arts skills and has a writing component with a 6 point rubric for scoring levels of writing development.

Whether the teacher designs her/his own assessments or chooses commercially available ones, *effective* assessment will have the following characteristics:

1. It should be an ongoing process, with the teacher making some kind of an informal or formal assessment almost every time the child speaks, listens, reads, writes, or views something in the classroom. The assessment should be a natural part of the instruction and not intrusive.
2. The most effective assessment is integrated into ongoing instruction. Throughout the teaching and learning day, the child's written, spoken, and reading contributions to the class or lack thereof, need to and can be continually accessed.
3. Assessment should reflect the actual reading and writing experiences for which that classroom learning has prepared the child. The child should be able to show that he or she can read and explain or react to a similar literary or expository work.
4. Assessment needs to be a collaborative and reflective process. Teachers can learn from what the children reveal about their own individual assessments. Children, even as early as grade two, should be supported by their teacher to continually and routinely ask themselves questions to assess their reading abilities (and other skill progress). They might ask: "How have I done in understanding what the

author wanted to say?" "What can I do to improve my reading?" and "How can I use what I have read to learn more about this topic?" Teachers need to be informed by their own professional observation AND by children's comments as they assess and customize instruction for children.

5. Quality valid assessment is multidimensional and may include, but not be limited to: samples of writings, student retellings, running records, anecdotal teacher observations, self-evaluations, records of independent reading and etc. From this multidimensional data, the teacher can derive a consistent level of performance and design additional instruction that will enhance the level of student performance.

6. Assessment must take into account children's age and ethnic/cultural patterns of learning.

7. Assess to teach children from their strengths, not their weaknesses. Find out what reading behaviors children demonstrate well, and then design instruction to support those behaviors.

8. Assessment should be part of children's learning process; not done ON them, but rather done WITH them.

Selecting and Designing Ongoing Assessments

Several authors have identified principles useful in selecting, designing and interpreting ongoing classroom assessments.

Linn and Gronlund (1995) identify five principles of assessment.

1. Clearly specifying what is to be assessed has priority in the assessment process.
2. An assessment procedure should be selected because of its relevance to the characteristics or performance to be measured.
3. Comprehensive assessment requires a variety of procedures.
4. Proper use of assessment procedures requires an awareness of their limitations.
5. Assessment is a means to an end, not an end in itself.

Stiggins (1997) introduces seven guiding principles for classroom assessment.

1. Assessments require clear thinking and effective communication.
2. Classroom assessment is key.
3. Students are assessment users.
4. Clear and appropriate targets are essential.

5. High-quality assessment is a must.
6. Understanding personal implication is essential.
7. Assessment is a teaching and learning tool.

Drummond lists six critical questions to ask about possible assessments when making a choice among them:

1. What specific assessment judgments and decisions have to be made?
2. What information is needed to make the best decisions?
3. What information is already available?
4. What assessment methods and instruments will provide the needed information?
5. How should appropriate instruments be located?
6. What criteria should be used in selecting and evaluating assessment instruments?

COMPETENCY 3.0   **KNOWLEDGE OF INSTRUCTIONAL PRACTICES IN EXCEPTIONAL STUDENT EDUCATION**

Skill 3.1   **Analyze assessment information to identify a student's educational needs and instructional levels, to select appropriate specialized techniques, strategies, and materials**

Analyze the Purposes, Characteristics, and Uses of Achievement and Diagnostic Tests

The assessment of academic achievement is an essential component of a psycho-educational evaluation. Achievement tests are instruments that directly assess students' skill development in academic content areas. These types of tests measure the extent to which a student has profited from educational and/or life experiences compared to others of like age or grade level. Emphasis needs to be placed upon the kinds of behaviors each test samples, the adequacy of its norms, the test reliability, and its validity.

An achievement test may be classified as a diagnostic test if strengths and weaknesses in skill development can be delineated. Typically, when used as a diagnostic tool, an achievement test measures one basic skill and its related components. For example, a reading test may measure reading recognition, reading comprehension, reading fluency, decoding skills, and sound discrimination. Each skill measured is reported in sub-classifications.

In order to render pertinent information, achievement tests must reflect the content of the curriculum. Some achievement tests assess skill development in many subject areas, while others focus upon single content areas. Within similar content areas, the particular skills assessed and how they are measured differ from test to test. The more prominent areas assessed by achievement tests include math, reading, and spelling.

Achievement test usages include screening, placement, progress evaluation, and curricula effectiveness. As screening tests, these instruments provide a wide index of academic skill development and may be used to pinpoint students for whom educational interventions may be necessary for purposes of remediation or enrichment. They offer a general idea of where to begin additional diagnostic assessment. Skills 2.3 and 2.4 discuss the use of norm-referenced and criterion-referenced assessments in detail.

Placement decisions in special education are typically based on measures of significant academic progress, or lack thereof. It is essential that data from individually administered achievement tests allow the examiner to observe quantitative (i.e. scores) performance as well as to denote specific strengths and weaknesses inherent in qualitative (e.g. attitude, motivation, problem-solving) performance.

Knowing how an individual reacts or produces answers during a testing situation is as relevant as measured skill levels when making placement and instructional decisions. Knowledge of specific skill deficits is needed for developing individualized education plans and designing instruction relevant to a specific child's needs.

Finally, teachers can be provided with measures showing the effectiveness of their instruction. Progress reflected by student scores should be used to review, and often revise, instructional techniques and content. Alternative methods of delivery (i.e. presentations, worksheets, tests) can be devised to enhance the instruction provided to students. Skill 2.5 discusses alternative methods of assessment that might be useful for students with disabilities and that can yield specific data relevant to a student's individual needs.

Applying Test Results to Curriculum and Instruction Decisions

Assessment is the key to providing differentiated and appropriate instruction to all students, and monitoring progress toward objectives. These are the areas in which teachers will most often use assessment. Teachers should use a variety of assessment techniques to determine the existing knowledge, skills, and needs of each student. Depending on the age of the student and the subject matter under consideration, diagnosis of readiness may be accomplished through pre-test, checklists, teacher observation, or student self-report. Diagnosis serves two related purposes—to identify those students who are not ready for the new instruction and to identify for each student what prerequisite knowledge is lacking.

In order to effectively use assessment to drive instruction, a teacher must be able to use assessments to diagnose problems and progress in student ability. Interpretation of test results for purposes of diagnosis goes beyond normative and criterion assessments. It is not enough to know how a student compares with age or grade peers (normative assessments), nor is it enough to know whether a child has mastered a particular set of criteria (criterion referenced assessment). In the field of Special Education, the teacher already knows the student doesn't, for example, read at grade level and hasn't met grade level criteria; that's why the student has been referred for special education help. What the teacher needs to know is *why* the student has these problems, and *what to do about it.* The teacher needs to be able to *interpret* assessment results to determine as closely as possible the exact nature of the student's problem and the best strategy for helping the student to overcome the problem.

Generally, this means the teacher will be using a *combination* of assessment sources, including standardized testing done by the school or outside agencies, classroom quizzes and assessments, informal observations and works samples, even parental input. Some of this information will already be available in the student's IEP or, possibly, 504 document. The teacher will need to be able to interpret and apply this information, as well as her/his own observations.

Standardized intelligence testing can provide clues to the locus of, say, a reading problem. For the teacher, the overall composite intelligence measures are less useful than the subtests. A student might have an overall intelligence rating that is well within normal ranges, or even above normal, but have serious lacks in one or more subtests. It is these specific subtests that the teacher needs for diagnosis and design of instructional methods.

For example, testing may show a student has adequate processing speed, but a very limited working memory. Such a combination may lead to problems that mirror attention difficulties, but have their roots elsewhere. This child is processing information quickly, but can't hold enough pieces of information in working memory long enough to make correct decisions. He/She needs to be taught strategies for expanding working memory, for "chunking" information so more will fit in the limited working memory, and strategies for carrying the pieces along the way to a decision. This might include note-taking and graphic organizers, or other mnemonic devices.

Testing may show another child to have adequate working memory, logic, and long-term memory, and a very slow processing speed. This child needs a very different set of strategies to learn well. Extra time for assignments, avoiding the repetition of verbal instructions (which interrupts his processing), and *written* or *visually-based* instructions may be more efficient learning strategies for this child.

Standardized educational testing done by the school can also provide diagnostic clues to problems and possible treatments in the classroom. Educational testing will often have subtests of individual skills, such as word recognition, fluency, literal or inferential comprehension, writing composition and mechanics, etc. Closely examining these areas can help a teacher diagnose problems and design remedies.

For example, if the educational testing shows a child has adequate sight word recognition skills in isolation, but cannot read connected text fluently, it might be a good idea to go back and look at the student's phoneme and phonic blending skills. Does the student have a basic problem blending at the phoneme level? Combined with the text reading problem this may indicate more than just a phoneme awareness issue, more of an overall problem putting pieces of information together.

Further diagnostic information might be found by looking at the student's ability to handle simple physical puzzles and recognize a whole from parts of a picture. A student with a disability based here will need instruction that helps him/her learn how to put information together. This might start at the most basic physical level with puzzles and progress to the use of word prediction software to help the child generalize this skill to a reading context.

Informal classroom assessments and simply looking at very specific areas of problems can also help the teacher with diagnosis. For example, a student who can answer multiple choice questions correctly, but cannot put that information into writing, may have encoding problems or even a form of Dysgraphia. Examination of what the child *can* do is as important as what he cannot do, because it helps pinpoint the locus of a problem or disability. A child who can correctly compute an entire math worksheet quickly, but cannot do a simple word problem does not have *math* problem; he has a *language or reading* problem. The student needs strategies for relating the vocabulary and language of math to the concrete facts he already knows.

Skill 3.2 Identify characteristics of reliable sources of scientifically based research related to instructional practices

The modern teacher has access to more information than ever before. In addition to what is taught in educational institutions across the country, teachers attend workshops and supplementary courses throughout their professional lives. Countless organizations and groups publish books, articles, slogans, and campaigns about teaching methodologies and theories. Teachers are expected to use the best and most current research available in choosing materials and instructional techniques.

Modern research has made great strides in understanding how the brain learns, what interferes with learning, and what improves learning. Researchers have mapped multiple areas of the brain used in reading and writing, and watched the operation of these areas while the subject carries out these tasks, and then observed which parts falter when students with reading disabilities attempt the same tasks. They have mapped parts of the brain used in complex mathematical calculations and watched male and female brains solve identical problems correctly but *differently*. Researchers have used experimental paradigms to follow specific treatment and instructional methods and analyzed their success or lack of it. It is the teacher's responsibility to be aware of current research that affects the choice of instructional methods, and to use it, where applicable, in the classroom.

Although there will be many opinions, theories, and programs available, only some of them will be based on well-designed current research. In selecting research findings to use in the classroom, the teacher should look at certain factors:

1. Is the study *experimental* in design? That is, does it utilize a scientific approach in which one method or instructional technique is compared to another or to the absence of intervention? Are the results statistically valid?

2. Are the results replicable? Have the same results been found in more than one study? A single instance of effect found amidst multiple studies with the opposite or no effect is suspect.

3. Was the body conducting the research objective and free of special interest contamination? Research conducted by someone who stands to gain financially or in some other way from specific results may not be worthless, but it needs to be corroborated by independent, disinterested parties. Watch for refereed professional journals rather than glossary private brochures. A selection of journals and professional bodies is provided in this section.

4. Are the parameters of the study relevant to your situation? A study conducted on a population very different from your students or in a very different context might be an excellent piece of work, but not useful to you in your situation.

5. Are the procedures and techniques feasible in your situation? It doesn't matter how effective a method is if it is beyond your ability to acquire or to implement.

Fortunately, the teacher is not alone in making decisions about research-based methods. A variety of organizations and publications have professional staff to review research and publications. Various divisional organizations of the Council for Exceptional Children publish professional journals in their area of exceptionality. These journals, their corresponding organizations, and addresses from which journals may be ordered are listed below.

1. Behavioral Disorders
    Council for Children with Behavioral Disorders (CCBD)
    1920 Association Drive
    Reston, VA 22091-1589

2. Career Development for Exceptional Individuals
   Division on Career Development (DCD)
   1920 Association Drive
   Reston, VA 22091-1589

3. Diagnostique
   Council for Educational Diagnostic Services (CEDS)
   1920 Association Drive
   Reston, VA 22091-1589

4. Education and Training of the Mentally Retarded
   Division on Mental Retardation (CEC-MR)
   1920 Association Drive
   Reston, VA 22091-1589

5. Journal of Childhood Communication Disorders
   Division for Children with Communication Disorders (DCCD)
   1920 Association Drive
   Reston, VA 22091-1589

6. Journal of the Division for Early Childhood
   Division for Early Childhood (DEC)
   1920 Association Drive
   Reston, VA 22091-1589

7. Journal for the Education of the Gifted
   The Association for the Gifted (TAG)
   JEG, Wayne State University Press
   5959 Woodward Avenue
   Detroit, MI 48202

8. Journal of Special Education Technology
   Technology and Media Division (TAM)
   JSET, UMC 68
   Utah State University
   Logan, UT 84322

9. Learning Disabilities Focus
   Learning Disabilities Research
   Division for Learning Disabilities
   1920 Association Drive
   Reston, VA 22091-1589

10. Teacher Education and Special Education
    Teacher Education Division (TED)
    Special Press
    P.O. Box 2524, Dept. CEC
    Columbus, OH 43216

11. Exceptional Children
    The Official Journal of the Council for Exceptional Children (CEC)
    1920 Association Drive
    Reston, VA 22091-1589

12. Teaching Exceptional Children
    1920 Association Drive
    Reston, VA 22091-1589

13. Exceptional Child Education Resources
    1920 Association Drive
    Reston, VA 22091-1589

14. Canadian Journal for Exceptional Children
    Publication Services
    4-116 Education North
    The University of Alberta
    Edmonton, Alberta, Canada T6G 2G5

Other journals are published by related fields such as rehabilitation, mental health, and occupational guidance. Some of the sponsoring organizations are included in the Table in Skill 1.8 of this textbook.

Burns, Roe, and Smith (2002) advocate teachers becoming researchers themselves and describe two types of research in which teachers may participate: action research and naturalistic research.

Action research uses experimentally controlled methods and statistical procedures to analyze instructional practices and their usefulness. In effect, the teacher conducts controlled experiments to obtain information.

Naturalistic research involves detailed observations and systematic recordkeeping that allow the teacher to see the effects, or lack of them, of classroom procedures.

Such teacher-based research is described by Burns, et al, as occurring in any of three formats: the individual teacher working alone, a collaborative effort by a group of teachers working with university professionals in a natural setting, or whole school or district-wide efforts. Such teacher-based research can also provide useful information and these efforts have the advantage of being, by definition, relevant to the individual teacher's situation and needs.

Skill 3.3   Identify instructional strategies for acquisition, generalization, and maintenance of skills (e.g., functional and applied academic skills, workplace and career skills, independent living skills) across school, home, work, and community settings

The purpose of practice is to help the student move through the acquisition of learning a skill (initial learning), to maintenance of information (remembering how to do the skill), to generalization of information (applying the skill to new or different situations).

During guided or semi-independent practice, the teacher should provide specific directions and model the procedure on the practice materials while the student follows along. Gradually, the teacher prompts and modeling will fade out as the student becomes more proficient. The teacher should apply positive and corrective feedback at this stage.

During independent practice, the teacher's role is to monitor the students and provide individual attention and modeling as necessary. The student should be encouraged to "think aloud" so the teacher can monitor what strategies and problem-solving skills are being used to answer questions. Again, positive and/or corrective feedback with praise should be used for achievement.

Children who have special learning needs often function at a lower conceptual level than classmates. That is, they have difficulty generating pertinent facts and key concepts inherent in a learning situation. Presenting those key facts and concepts initially is much more effective than asking them to identify the concept alone. Presenting alternative solutions expands their thinking and ensures less learning by chance.

Transfer of Learning

Transfer of learning occurs when experience with one task influences performance on another task. Positive transfer occurs when the required responses are about the same and the stimuli are similar, such as moving from baseball to handball to racquetball, or from field hockey to soccer. Negative transfer occurs when the stimuli remain similar, but the required responses change, such as shifting from soccer to football, tennis to racquetball, and boxing to sports karate. Instructional procedures should stress the similar features between the activities and the dimensions that are transferable. Specific information should emphasize when stimuli in the old and new situations are the same as or similar and when responses used in the old situation apply to the new.

To facilitate learning, instructional objectives should be arranged in order according to their patterns of similarity. Objectives involving similar responses should be closely sequenced; thus, the possibility for positive transfer is stressed. Likewise, learning objectives that involve different responses should be programmed within instructional procedures in the most appropriate way possible. For example, students should have little difficulty transferring handwriting instruction to writing in other areas. However, there might be some negative transfer when moving from manuscript to cursive writing. By using transitional methods and focusing upon the similarities between manuscript and cursive writing, negative transfer can be reduced.

Generalization

Generalization is the occurrence of a learned behavior in the presence of a stimulus other than the one that produced the initial response (e.g., novel stimulus). It is the expansion of a student's performance beyond conditions in which it was initially learned. Students must be able to generalize what is learned to other settings (e.g., reading to math word problems; resource room to regular classroom). It is essential, for example, that students be able to generalize the skills they learn in school to the job and daily life setting they will encounter after they leave school.

Generalization training is a procedure in which a behavior is reinforced in each of a series of situations until it generalizes to other members of the same stimulus class. Stimulus generalization occurs when responses which have been reinforced in the presence of a specific stimulus, the discriminative stimulus (DS), occur in the presence of related stimuli (e.g., bathrooms labeled women, ladies, dames). In fact, the more similar the stimuli, the more likely it is that stimulus generalization will occur. This concept applies to inter-task similarity in that the more one task resembles another, the greater the probability the student will be able to master it. For example, if Johnny has learned the initial consonant sounds of "b" and "d," and he has been taught to read the word "dad," it is likely that when he is shown the word "bad," he will be able to pronounce this formerly unknown word upon presentation.

This is particularly true of functional skills involved in independent living and the workplace. Skills learned in the school setting are far more likely to generalize to home life or the workplace if the school setting resembles the home or work setting. Specific settings and techniques will vary depending upon the individual student's needs, but each student's plan should include specific strategies for helping the student generalize skills learned in school to the workplace and independent living arrangements.

Generalization may be enhanced by the following:

1. Use many examples in teaching to deepen application of learned skills.
2. Use consistency in initial teaching situations, and later, introduce variety in format, procedure, and use of examples.
3. Have the same information presented by different teachers, in different settings, and under varying conditions.
4. Include a continuous reinforcement schedule at first, later changing to delayed and intermittent schedules as instruction progresses.
5. Teach students to record instances of generalization and to reward themselves at that time.
6. Associate naturally occurring stimuli when possible. Arranging for practice in the real life setting can greatly enhance generalization.

Workplace and Career Skills

Skills to assist a special education student in the real world are invaluable. If generalization of skills, as previously mentioned, is permeating many facets of the student's reality, then the transferences of such skills will occur seamlessly when the student is independent and older.

Skills a special education student may need to know include interpersonal skills, job search techniques, basic business math, money management, workplace safety, using a particular computer program, and so forth. A job skills list can be compiled once a targeted job or career is formulated and discussed with a student. He or she can obtain certificates and credentials when necessary, and can integrate workplace skills into the curriculum with the special educator. This may include lessons in budgeting and management money earned from a job. This can also involve 'field trips' to potential jobsites, such as the local grocery store, a restaurant, or an office. Giving the student opportunities to exercise their reality-based skillsets will ease the transition into the world of independence.

Skill 3.4   **Select relevant general education and special skills curricula appropriate for a given student's age, instructional needs, and functional performance across settings**

General Characteristics

When choosing materials, the teacher should first consider the target population and the major goals of the program materials. Cost, compared with similar materials that teach the same skills, as well as durability and timeliness, are factors in material selection. Material that is quickly out of date or does not withstand lots of use, would not be a good choice. Field test data should be available to judge the program's effectiveness.

Teaching Factors

Objectives for the material should be listed, along with a scope and sequence. The skills should proceed from simple to complex and be presented in a logical order. Directions should be clear and concise. The teacher will want to examine the task levels (concrete, semi-concrete, or abstract), as well as the organization of the material (units, chapters or lessons). The teacher should look at the types of stimulus and response modalities used, as well as ways to assess entry level in the curriculum. The teacher should also look for evidence of effective teaching procedures and the pace of the content.

When working with students with disabilities it is important to select curriculum materials that are both accessible to the students and consistent with state guidelines for learning standards. Sometimes this requires searching for materials that address grade level subject matter at a reading level significantly below grade level. A variety of publishing houses specialize in such materials. Rigby, Scholastic and National Geographic Windows on Literacy, for example, all provide nonfiction content area materials for the same standards written at a variety of grade levels.

The materials should provide a means of evaluation and data recording. The material should be judged on the basis of extent of teacher involvement, space and storage requirement, and time requirements. The material should maintain student interest, and there should be reinforcement or suggestions for reinforcement. Students should be able to use the material without disturbing others. The materials should be easy to set up or move and be able to be used within flexible time limits. The teacher should see whether the student would be able to use the materials without constant feedback or intervention from the teacher.

Selecting Teacher-Made and Commercial Materials

The first step in the process would be to make informal assessments of the areas the student is having trouble with, as well as learning styles and preferences. If the materials come with a scope and sequence, or a summary of objectives and skills, the teacher can select those portions that match the student's needs. Since commercial materials are not always written with special needs students in mind, there are things that teachers can do to make these materials easier to use:

1. Review the materials and add advance organizers, cues, prompts, and feedback steps as necessary to make sure that the lesson contains the elements of explicit teaching procedures.
2. Tape record directions, stories, or specific lessons so that the student can listen and play them back as needed.
3. Clarify written directions by underlining key phrases or direction words. If the directions are too lengthy or wordy, simplify or rewrite them.
4. For students who are anxious about seeing what appears to be too much work, tear out individual pages or present portions of the assignment.
5. Students who are distracted by the visual stimulus of a full page can cover the sections that they are not working on at the moment.
6. Change the response directions to underlining, multiple-choice, or marking or sorting if the student has a problem with handwriting. If necessary, give extra space for writing answers.
7. Develop reading guides, outlines of lectures, graphic organizers, and glossaries for content area materials that do not contain them.
8. Develop a method of marking a place in consumable materials, such as the use of post-it notes or arrows.
9. Use tape recorders, computer-assisted instruction, overhead projectors with transparencies, Language Masters, and self-correcting materials.

Skill 3.5 **Identify methods for differentiating, accommodating and modifying assessment, instruction, and materials to meet individual student needs (e.g., related to age, gender, cultural and linguistic background, preferred communication mode)**

In order to make classroom instruction and materials useful for students with disabilities, it will be necessary to make modifications. Although the specific modifications will depend on each individual child's needs, when organizing and sequencing objectives, remember that skills are building blocks. A taxonomy of educational objectives, such as that provided by Bloom (1956), can be helpful in constructing and organizing objectives. Simple, factual knowledge of material is low on this cognitive taxonomy, and should be worked with early in the sequence or with students whose disabilities make more abstract knowledge less accessible. For example, matching or memorizing definitions, or memorizing famous quotes, are lower-level cognitive tasks. Eventually, objectives should be developed to include higher-level thinking such as comprehension (i.e., being able to use a definition); application (i.e., being able to apply the definition to other situations); synthesis (i.e., being able to add other information); and evaluation (i.e., being able to judge the value of something). Such a taxonomy can be used to find entry points for each standard and align a goal not only with the standard, but with the child's current level of performance. This is particularly useful in differentiating instruction to meet the needs of students with disabilities in the classroom.

Differentiated Instruction

In recent years, increasing emphasis has been put on incorporating many principles of *differentiated instruction* into classrooms with students of mixed ability. Tomlinson (2001) states that teachers must first determine where the students *are* with reference to an objective, *then* tailor specific lesson plans and learning activities to help each student learn as much as possible about that objective. The effective teacher seeks to connect all students to the subject matter through multiple techniques with the goal that each student will relate to one or more techniques and excel in the learning process. Differentiated instruction encompasses modifying curriculum in several areas.

- **Content:** What is the teacher going to teach? What does the teacher want the students to learn? Differentiating content means that students have access to aspects of the content that pique their interest, with a complexity that provides an appropriate challenge to their intellectual development, but does not go beyond their frustration level. When students with special needs are included in a classroom, this often means modifying a lesson plan so that it has several levels. One common way to structure such levels is the following.

A *basic* level might address the content of the objective at a cognitively less demanding level (e.g., knowledge, the lowest level on Bloom's taxonomy). Example: The student or student group matches names to planets on a diagram, or they correctly define key vocabulary.

A *moderate* level could address the content at a higher level than basic, but still a fairly low level (e.g., comprehension). Example: After learning that the Earth *orbits* the sun due to the Sun's greater gravity, challenge the student or student group to give other examples of objects orbiting others and explain why in their own words.

A *mastery* level might address the objective at the level most students should reach given state standards (e.g., analysis). Example: The student or student group compares two planets based on a set of variables.

An *advanced* level would address the objective at a higher level aimed at gifted students who can go beyond the required curriculum (e.g., the highest level on Bloom's Taxonomy). Example: The student or student group is given a real or fictional theory of planetary movement and asked to evaluate its accuracy in light of the facts they have learned in the unit, and create a model, video, or drawing demonstrating planetary movement.

- **Process** The classroom management techniques where instructional organization and delivery are maximized for the diverse student group. These techniques should include dynamic, flexible grouping activities, where instruction and learning occur as whole-class, teacher-led activities and in a variety of small group settings, such as teacher-guided small group, peer learning and teaching (while teacher observes and coaches), or independent centers or pairs. Such techniques should also include strategies for anchor activities and smooth transitions from activity to activity.

- **Product**: The expectations and requirements placed on students to demonstrate their knowledge or understanding. The type of product expected from each student should reflect that student's own capabilities. When working with students with special needs, the student's IEP will provide guidelines on the best way to assess the student's progress and any testing accommodations that must be made.

Identifying Basic Instructional Approaches for Content Areas

Instructional alternatives to help students with learning problems may be referred to as compensatory techniques, instructional adaptations, or accommodation techniques. A problem-solving approach to determining what modifications should be made centers around: (a) the requirements of the course, (b) the requirement(s) that the student is not meeting, (c) factors interfering with the student's meeting the requirements, and (d) the identification of possible modifications. Of course, a student's IEP or 504 document may spell out such modifications.

Many of the adaptations and modifications helpful to students with disabilities can be seen in terms of Cummins'(1994) analysis of the cognitive demands of a task or lesson. Such adaptations can be designed to either lighten the cognitive burden of a task or make it easier for the student to carry that burden. Cummins' work with students with limited English proficiency (LEP) led him to analyze tasks in terms of two variables: amount of context, and cognitive demand. Lessons or tasks that have a lot of context for a student will be easier for that student than tasks with little or no context. The more context, the easier the task.

Cognitive demand is a measure of how much information must be processed quickly. A cognitively demanding task requires processing lots of information all at once or in rapid succession, and is more demanding or difficult. Cognitively undemanding tasks or lessons present only single pieces of information or concepts to process, and they separate tasks or lessons into discrete, small steps. When making changes to accommodate students with special needs, it is helpful to focus on changes that will move the task or lesson from a cognitively demanding, low context arena to one of high context and reduced cognitive demand.

Adaptations or changes designed to help the student(s) meet the requirements of a class or standard can take place in a number of areas of curriculum and setting. The following are some of the primary areas in which a special education teacher may need to make changes.

Adapting the Overall Instructional Environment

The teacher can modify the classroom instructional environment in several ways.

I. *Individual Student Variables:* Some students with disabilities benefit from sitting close to the teacher or away from windows. Others (with ADHD, for example) might benefit from wiggle seats or fiddle objects, others from an FM system or cubicles that reduce distractions. Seating that reduces distractions serves also to reduce the cognitive load of lessons, by removing the need for the students to block distractions themselves. 'Preferential Seating' is just one of many accommodations which may appear on a student's IEP.

II. *Classroom Organization*: Many students with learning disabilities benefit from a highly structured environment in which physical areas (e.g., supplies, reading, math, writing) are clearly labeled and a schedule for the day prominently displayed. Individual schedule charts can be useful if some students follow different schedules, such as leaving for a resource room or specialized therapy periodically. Such schedules reduce the cognitive load required to simply get through the day, and provide increased context for the student navigating the daily routine. The teacher can also vary the organization of grouping arrangements (e.g., large group, small group, peer tutoring, paired learning, or learning centers/stations) with student needs in mind.

III. *Classroom Management*: The teacher can vary grading systems, reinforcement systems, and even the rules to accommodate the varying needs of the students. Early teaching and practice of predictable, daily classroom rules and routines can be particularly helpful to students with certain learning disabilities or emotional problems. It may be helpful to pay extra attention to the transitions between tasks, lessons or parts of the day. Some students benefit from having clear stimuli (e.g., a bell, hand signal, or flag) to signal changes and transitions. Attention and time spent on such routines early in the year can pay big dividends in classroom management later in the year. The specific techniques required will depend upon the needs of the students.

Management may also be an area of professional development in which teachers can express interest when it is time to take part in PD days in their district. The school staff, particularly school behaviorists, counselors, and psychologists, have access to a wealth of information and techniques pertaining to behavior.

Presentation of Subject Matter

Subject matter should be presented in a fashion that helps students *organize*, *understand*, and *remember* important information. Advanced organizers and other instructional devices can help students to:

- Connect information to what is already known
- Make abstract ideas more concrete
- Capture students' interest in the material
- Help students to organize the information and visualize the relationships

Organizers can be visual aids, such as diagrams, tables, charts, guides, or verbal cues, that alert students to the nature and content of the lesson. Organizers may be used:

- **Before the lesson** to alert the student to the main point of the lesson, establish a rationale for learning, and activate background information.
- **During the lesson** to help students organize information, keep focused on important points, and aid comprehension.
- **At the close of the lesson** to summarize and remember important points.

Examples of organizers include:

- Question and graphic-oriented study guide
- Concept diagramming: Students brainstorm a concept and organize information into three lists (always present, sometimes present, and never present)
- Semantic feature analysis: Students construct a table with examples of the concept in one column and important features or characteristics in the other column
- Semantic webbing: The concept is placed in the middle of the chart or chalkboard and relevant information is placed around it. Lines show the relationships
- Memory (mnemonic) devices, such as diagrams, charts and tables

Questions can be used to involve all students in class discussions. The higher-level questions should be asked of the high-ability students and less demanding ones of lower-ability students. Questions can be used to have students stretch their thinking and challenge them to extend what they have learned. Opening the lesson with a question can stimulate interest in the upcoming activity and get the students thinking about what will happen in the lesson. Throughout the lesson, teacher questions are usually one of these types:

- Lower level for recall or recognition of basic facts. (Who wrote *White Fang*?)
- Descriptive or comparison questions are used for the acquisition of specific information and organization of information. (Compare the lifestyle of the Native Americans in Mexico before and after the arrival of the Spanish in the 1500s).
- Explanation questions and synthesis/summary questions are used to interpret information and draw conclusions. (How did the novels of Charles Dickens influence social reform in England?)
- Judgmental/open-ended questions require one to apply divergent thinking and evaluate the quality or truth of a relationship or conclusion. (If farmers were not allowed to use some sort of pesticide on their crops, what effect would that have on food prices?)

When students with disabilities are included in the classroom, it is important for the teacher to keep their needs in mind when asking questions. If the teacher knows a particular student will not be able to remember very much about the lesson, she might call on that student *first* so that his/her response is not 'taken' by someone else. Likewise, when calling on a student with disabilities the teacher should carefully consider the cognitive level of the question as described above and be sure to ask a question that is within the ability of the student to answer. Carefully considering a student's cognitive processing time will allow a student to answer questions in a prepared manner, and boost confidence.

Techniques for Modifying Content Areas

Materials, usually textbooks, are frequently modified because of reading level. The goal of modification is to present the material in a manner that the student can more readily understand, while preserving the basic ideas and content. Modifications of course material may take the form of:

Simplifying Texts

a) Using a highlighter to mark key terms, main ideas, and concepts. In some cases, a marker may be used to delete nonessential content.
b) Cut and paste. The main ideas and specific content are cut and pasted on separate sheets of paper. Additional headings or other graphic aids can be inserted to help the student understand and organize material.
c) Supplement with graphic aids or tables.
d) Supplement with study guides, questions, and directed previews.
e) Use self-correcting materials.
f) Allow additional time, or break content material into smaller, more manageable units.

Rewriting Content Material

It may be necessary to simply rewrite the content material to make it accessible to students with reading disabilities. Though the specific modifications will depend upon individual student needs, one of the most common requirements will be finding or revising text for learners who cannot read at grade level or who have difficulty comprehending what they read in content areas such as science and social studies.

The most common specific learning disabilities involve reading difficulties. In order for such students to have equal access to the grade-level curriculum in content areas, it is often necessary to revise printed material so students can access it at their reading comprehension level. Whether selecting published materials, or revising them for the students, these guidelines should be followed in order to increase context, reduce cognitive demand, and provide content material that students with learning disabilities can access.

- Avoid complex sentences with many relative clauses.
- Avoid the passive tense.
- Try to make the topic sentence the first sentence in a paragraph.
- Make sure paragraphs have a concluding sentence that restates the topic sentence in another way.
- Use simple, declarative sentences that have only one main idea or concept at a time.
- Use easy, single syllable, concrete words rather than more complex words (e.g., "an arduous journey" should be "a hard trip").
- Eliminate nonessential information in favor of the main concepts necessary to teach.
- Try to use only one tense in all the sentences.
- Add diagrams and illustrations whenever possible and deliver information through labels rather than complete sentences.
- Whenever possible, include multisensory elements and multimodalities in the presentation.
- Avoid unfamiliar names and terms that will "tie up" the students' cognitive efforts (e.g., while the student is trying to figure out how to read the name " Aloysius" he/she will miss the point of the sentence; change the name to "Al")

Recorded Textbooks

Textbooks can be taped by the teacher or teacher's aide for students to listen to. In some cases, the students may qualify for recordings of textbooks from agencies such as Recordings for the Blind. Modern technology includes most textbooks on CDs that can be highlighted and searched for index items and key words. Furthermore, many electronic devices, such as the iPad or iPod, have recordings which can be purchased or downloaded for listening via headphones. Utilizing modern technology, such as the computer, Kindle, and iPad, can connect students with auditory and visual forms of many textbooks, novels, and other texts.

Parallel Curriculum

Projects such as Parallel Alternative Curriculum (PAC) or Parallel Alternative Strategies for Students (PASS), present the content at a lower grade reading level and come with tests, study guides, vocabulary activities, and tests.

Supplementary Texts

Book publishers, such as Steck-Vaughn, Rigby, Scholastic, and National Geographic Windows on Literacy, publish many series of content-area texts that have been modified for reading level, amount of content presented on pages, highlighted key items, and visual aids. Teachers may always join helpful websites, such as www.scholastic.com, to access short texts, short stories, poems, and worksheets or lesson plans, to supplement curriculum.

Skill 3.6   Identify effective methods of communication, consultation, and collaboration with students, families, parents, guardians, administrators, general education teachers, paraprofessionals, and other professionals including students, families, and team members from culturally and linguistically diverse backgrounds, as equal members of education teams

Teachers of exceptional students are expected to manage many roles and responsibilities, not only those that concern their students, but also with respect to students' caregivers and other involved educational, medical, therapeutic, and administrative professionals. Because the needs of exceptional students are by definition multidisciplinary, a teacher of exceptional children often serves as the hub of a many-pronged wheel, communicating, consulting, and collaborating with the various stakeholders in a child's educational life regularly. Managing these crucial relationships effectively can be a challenge, but is central to successful work in exceptional education.

Students

Useful standards have been developed by the Council for Exceptional Children (2003) that outline best practices in communicating and relating to children and their families. For example, CEC guidelines suggest that effective teachers:

- offer students a safe and supportive learning environment, including clearly expressed and reasonable expectations for behavior;
- create learning environments that encourage self-advocacy and developmentally

appropriate independence; and

- offer learning environments that promote active participation in independent or group activities.

Such an environment is an excellent foundation for building rapport and trust with students, and communicating a teacher's respect for and expectation that they take a measure of responsibility for their educational development. Ideally, mutual trust and respect will afford teachers opportunities to learn and engage students' ideas, preferences, and abilities.

Supporting the healthy learning environments to promote socially acceptable behavior is a priority of general education and special education teachers alike. Positive learning environments may share these principles (Ottowa, 2000):

- A positive learning environment is respectful and caring of all members.
- An inclusive curriculum, recognizing diversity and promoting respect, is needed to help students resolve conflicts peacefully, learn about the law, and acquire social and decision-making skills that contribute to the safety of their schools and communities.
- Fair and consistently implemented class and school policies of behavior contribute to positive environments and reduce racism, bullying, and other forms of harassment.
- Decisions are guided by a problem solving, not punitive, approach as well as by supporting and enabling all members of the community to participate and contribute.

Parents and Families

Families of students know them better than anyone, and are a valuable resource for teachers of exceptional students. Often, an insight or observation from a family member, or his or her reinforcement of school standards or activities, means the difference between success and frustration in a teacher's work with children. A strong line of communication is important for all parties involved. Parents often want to play an active role in planning and aiding a student's IEP goals, and can offer valuable input in meetings.

Suggestions for relationship building and collaboration with parents and families include:

- using laypersons' terms when communicating with families, and make the communication available in the language of the home;

- searching out and engage family members' knowledge and skills in providing services, educational and therapeutic, to the student;
- exploring and discussing the concerns of families and helping them find tactics for addressing those concerns;
- planning collaborative meetings with children and their families and assisting them to become active contributors to their educational team;
- ensuring that communications with and about families is confidential and conducted with respect for their privacy;
- offering parents accurate and professionally presented information about the pedagogical and therapeutic work being done with their child;
- keeping parents abreast of their rights, of the kinds of practices that might violate them, and of available recourse if needed; and
- acknowledging and respecting cultural differences.

See Skill 2.4 for special guidelines on interpreting assessment results for families.

Paraprofessionals and General Education Teachers

Paraprofessionals and general education teachers are also important collaborators with teachers of exceptional students. Although they may have daily exposure to exceptional students, they may not have the theoretical background or experience to assure their effective interaction with such students. They do bring valuable perspective to, and opportunities for breadth and variety in, an exceptional child's education. General education teachers also offer curriculum and subject matter expertise and a high level of professional support, while paraprofessionals may provide insights born of their familiarity with individual students. CEC suggests that teachers can best collaborate with general education teachers and paraprofessionals by:

- offering information about the characteristics and needs of children with exceptional learning needs
- discussing and brainstorming ways to integrate children with exceptionalities into various settings within the school community
- modeling best practices and instructional techniques and accommodations and coaching others in their use
- keeping communication about children with exceptional learning needs and their families confidential
- consulting with these colleagues in the assessment of individuals with exceptional learning needs
- engaging them in group problem-solving and in developing, executing, and assessing collaborative activities

- offering support to paraprofessionals by observing their work with students and offering feedback and suggestions

Related Service Providers and Administrators

Related service providers and administrators offer specialized skills and abilities that are critical to an exceptional education teacher's ability to advocate for his or her student and meet a school's legal obligations to the student and their family. Related service providers — like speech, occupational and language therapists, psychologists, and physicians — offer unparalleled expertise and resources in meeting a child's developmental needs. Administrators are often experts in the resources available at the school and local education agency levels, as well as the culture and politics of a school system, and they can be effective partners in meeting the needs of exceptional education teachers and students.

A teacher's most effective approach to collaborating with these professionals includes:
- confirming mutual understanding of the accepted goals and objectives of the student with exceptional learning needs as documented in his or her IEP
- soliciting input about ways to support related service goals in classroom settings
- understanding the needs and motivations of each and acting in support whenever possible
- facilitating respectful and beneficial relationships between families and professionals
- regularly and accurately communicating observations and data about the child's progress or challenges

Skill 3.7 Identify effective classroom management and flexible grouping strategies for specific instructional activities

One thing teachers can do to help students be successful is to arrange the physical environment and the routine organization and classroom procedures in a way that meets the needs of the students and enhances learning. Although the specific elements of any given classroom organization will vary, some general principles need to be considered when arranging the class. Teachers can review cumulative records, IEPs, and 504 documents for information about student needs, and can also get information about the student preferences through direct interviews or Likert-style checklists in which students rate their preferences.

Physical Settings

A. **Noise**: Students vary in the degree of quiet that they need and the amount of background noise or talking that they can tolerate without getting distracted or frustrated. Students with attention deficit issues may need a quiet, undecorated corner, whereas some students respond well to bright, colorful surroundings.

B. **Temperature and Lighting**: Students also vary in their preference for lighter or darker areas of the room, tolerance for coolness or heat, and ability to see the chalkboard, screen, or other areas of the room. Students with disabilities such as Irlen Syndrome may need shielded light rather than the common florescent light. Allowing the student to wear a cap with a bill can be helpful if alternative lighting is not available.

C. **Physical Factors**: This refers to the student's need for work space and preference for the type of work area, such as a desk, table, or learning center. Some students work better standing up at a counter or even lying down with a clip board. Proximity factors such as closeness to other students, the teacher, or high traffic areas such as doorways or pencil sharpeners, may help the student to feel secure and stay on task, or may serve as distractions, depending on the individual.

In addition to the overall physical organization of the room, classroom groupings can be modified for a variety of needs and purposes. Differentiating instruction is often a high priority in districts, in order to serve a growing, diverse group of students, including those with special needs, gifted tendencies, language barriers, and so forth. Five basic types of grouping arrangements are typically used in the classroom.

A. *Large Group with Teacher*

Examples of appropriate activities include show and tell, discussions, watching plays or movies, brainstorming ideas, and playing games. Science, social studies, and most other subjects, except for reading and math, are taught in large groups.

The advantage of large group instruction is that it is time-efficient and prepares students for higher levels of secondary and post-secondary education settings. However, with large groups, instruction cannot be as easily tailored to high or low levels of students, who may become bored or frustrated. Mercer and Mercer (1985) recommend guidelines for effective large-group instruction, as bulleted.

- Keep instruction short, ranging from 5 to 15 minutes for grades 1 through 7 and 5 to 40 minutes for grades 8 through 12.

- Use questions to involve all students, use lecture-pause routines, and encourage active participation among the lower-performing students.
- Incorporate visual aids to promote understanding, and maintain a lively pace.
- Break up the presentation with different rates of speaking, giving students a "stretch break," varying voice volume, etc.
- Establish rules of conduct for large groups, and praise students who follow the rules.

B. *Small Group Instruction*

Small group instruction usually includes 5 to 7 students and is recommended for teaching basic academic skills such as math facts or reading. This model is especially effective for students with learning problems. Composition of the groups should be flexible to accommodate different rates of progress through instruction. The advantages of teaching in small groups is that the teacher is better able to provide feedback, monitor student progress, and give more instruction and praise. With small groups, the teacher will need to make sure to provide a steady pace for the lesson, provide questions and activities that allow all to participate, and include lots of praise.

C. *One Student with Teacher*

One-to-one tutorial teaching can be used to provide extra assistance to individual students. Such tutoring may be scheduled at set times during the day or provided as the need arises. The tutoring model is typically found more in elementary and resource classrooms than in secondary settings.

D. *Peer Tutoring*

In an effective peer tutoring arrangement, the teacher trains the peer tutors and matches them with students who need extra practice and assistance. In addition to academic skills, the arrangement can help both students work on social skills such as cooperation and self-esteem. Both students may be working on the same material, or the tutee may be working to strengthen areas of weakness. The teacher determines the target goals, selects the material, sets up the guidelines, trains the student tutors in the rules and methods of the sessions, and monitors and evaluates the sessions.

E. *Cooperative Learning*

Cooperative learning differs from peer tutoring in that students are grouped in teams or small groups, and the methods are based on teamwork, individual accountability, and team reward. Individual students are responsible for their own learning and share of the work, as well as the group's success. As with peer tutoring, the goals, target skills, materials, and guidelines are developed by the teacher. In addition, teamwork skills may also need to be taught. By focusing on team goals, all members of the team are encouraged to help each other, as well as improve their individual performance.

Budgeting Time for Activities

Schedule development depends upon the type of class (elementary or secondary) and the setting (regular classroom or resource room). There are, however, general rules of thumb that apply to both types and settings:

1. Allow time for transitions, planning, and setups. Transitions can be particularly difficult for some students with disabilities. It can help to have observable visual or auditory signals to serve as warnings about upcoming changes and transitions, as well as clearly posted schedules and routines.

2. Aim for maximum instructional time by pacing the instruction and allotting time for practice of the new skills.

3. Proceed from short assignments to long ones, breaking up long lessons or complex tasks into short sessions or step-by-step instruction.

4. Follow a less preferred academic subject or activity with a highly preferred academic subject or activity.

5. In settings where students are working on individualized plans, do not schedule all the students at once in activities that require a great deal of teacher assistance. For example, have some students work on math or spelling while the teacher works with the students in reading, which usually requires more teacher involvement. Arrange for anchor activities that allow independent work, as well.

6. Break up a longer segment into several smaller segments with a variety of activities.

Special Considerations for Elementary Classrooms

1. Determine the amount of time that is needed for activities such as P.E., lunch, or recess.

2. Allow about 15 to 20 minutes each for opening and closing exercises. Spend this time for "housekeeping" activities such as collecting lunch money, going over the schedule, cleaning up, reviewing the day's activities, and getting ready to go home.

3. Schedule academics for periods when the students are more alert and motivated, usually in the morning. Take into consideration the effect regular medication for conditions such as ADHD may have on your students.

4. Build in time for slower students to finish their work; others may work at learning centers or other activities of interest. Allowing extra time gives the teacher time to give more attention where it is needed, conduct assessments, or for students to complete or correct work.

Special Considerations for Secondary Classes

Secondary school days are usually divided into five, six, or seven periods of about 50 minutes, with additional time for homeroom and lunch. Students cannot stay behind and finish their work since they have to leave for a different room. Resource room time should be scheduled so that the student does not miss academic instruction in his/her classroom or miss desirable nonacademic activities. In schools where ESE teachers also co-teach or work with students in the regular classroom, the regular teacher will have to coordinate lesson plans with those of the special education teacher. Consultation time will also have to be budgeted into the schedule.

Many students receive extended time as an accommodation on their IEP. Extended time may be used for a student to finish a test, write up a lab, hand in a project, or work on a long-term assignment. The extended time should not conflict with the student's other courses. Perhaps extra/extended time needs can be satisfied during the resource room period, or during a 'free period' in which the student works on homework or study skills.

Homework

Mercer and Mercer (1985) recommend that homework should be planned at the instructional level of the student and incorporated into the learning process of regular class work. However, homework is dependent upon school and district philosophies. Some schools do not give as much homework as other schools, and this may vary even further by teacher preference. Homework is useful when it reinforces previously learned skills, and is not intended to simply be busy work. The number and length of time needed will vary according to the age and grade level. Recommended times are:

- Primary Grades: three 15-minute assignments per week
- Grades 4 to 6: two to four 15 to 45-minute assignments per week
- Grades 7 to 9: up to five 45 to 75-minute assignments per week
- Grades 10 to 12: up to five 75 to 120-minute assignments per week

It should be noted that homework may need to be substantially altered for students with disabilities. For most students with disabilities, homework should be structured at the independent level, rather than the instructional level. In addition, many students with disabilities simply cannot handle the same homework load and will need a reduced or altered homework plan.

Skill 3.8   **Identify effective instructional methods (e.g., explicit and systematic instruction, scaffolding, modeling) for integrating reading, writing, speaking, listening, viewing, researching, and presenting across curricula**

From preschool through third grade, most of a student's education is centered around learning how to read, as well as how to write and express oneself orally. In third grade, the emphasis begins to shift and by fourth grade, students are expected to be reading to learn rather than learning to read. Although students continue to improve and expand their reading and writing abilities, the emphasis is on using their reading ability to learn in the content areas, and using their writing and oral expressive abilities to demonstrate what they know.

Throughout a student's education, therefore, it is important to keep in mind that the goal is for the student to be *using* the reading and writing for purposes that go beyond reading and writing for their own sake. This means that even in the early years, when teachers are helping students learn the various language arts skills, they must be helping students learn strategies that will let them generalize these skills to the content areas. Skill 3.9 provides a more in depth look at various nonfiction text structures. This section presents an overview of how to approach instruction to help students use these skills in other content areas.

The term "comprehension" actually refers to a number of levels and types of comprehension, and teachers must themselves understand those levels, and keep the desired level and type of comprehension in mind when planning lessons. Bloom's (1956) taxonomy of levels of comprehension can be helpful in such planning, and the newer, revised version of Bloom's Taxonomy is also useful (accessible on www.utar.edu.my). Simpler taxonomies of comprehension may outline only three primary levels of comprehension: literal, inferential, and evaluative.

In teaching comprehension of the informational/expository reading common in the content areas, it can be helpful to focus on five key strategies:

1. **Inferencing** is an evaluative process that involves the reader making a reasonable judgment based on the information given, and that engages children in literally constructing their own meaning. In order to develop and enhance this key skill in children, a teacher might have a mini-lesson where the teacher demonstrates this

key skill by reading an expository book aloud (i.e., one on skyscrapers for young children) and then demonstrates or models for them the following reading habits: looking for clues, reflecting on what the reader already knows about the topic (activating prior knowledge), and using the clues in the expository text to figure out what the author means/intends. Throughout the reading, the teacher would "think out loud" and model the strategy.

Note that strategies for inferencing can be taught even in the early grades. Using a common folk tale like *The Three Little* Pigs, students can be taught that different kinds of questions require different strategies to answer.

A. Literal questions can be answered with information that is right there in concrete words. For example, the type of material each pig used to build his house is clearly stated in the text, so if asked about it, the student can find it in a single location in the text (e.g., on page 4 it says the first little pig used straw).

B. Some questions pulling together information that is clearly stated in the text, but in different locations. For example, answering a question about what the wolf did when he could not blow down the house requires looking at information in different parts of the text as it describes the various schemes he used to try to get to the pig. It is all there in the text, but you have to look around for it and put it together.

C. Some questions require the student to put together information in the text with information in their own head, their own background knowledge. If asked, for example, why the third pig left for the apple orchard earlier than suggested by the wolf, the student will not find that information explicitly stated in the text. They have to put together the fact that pigs like to eat apples (in their own head), but don't like to be eaten by wolves, with the fact that the wolf suggested a specific time (in the text). This is a very simple inference.

D. Some questions might require the student to rely primarily on information in his or her own head with very little recourse to the text. For example, asking how the rest of the town might treat the third little pig after the wolf is dead would require the student to combine a whole host of information in his own head to come to a possible conclusion: 1) Other pigs might have felt threatened by the wolf; 2) They would be glad the wolf is gone and might think the third pig was very brave; 3) In the real world, we often give parades for heroes; 4) Maybe they will give a parade for the third pig or hand him the keys to the city, etc. This would be a higher order inference.

All these levels of inferencing can be taught even to early readers, and the skills they learn will be useful to them later when reading in various content areas.

2. **Identifying main ideas** in an expository text can be improved when the children have an explicit strategy for identifying important information. They can be guided to make this strategy part of their everyday reading style by "walking through" the following exercises as a part of a series of guided reading sessions. The child should read the passage so that the topic is readily identifiable to him or her. It will be what most of the information is about. Identifying the main idea is often difficult for students with reading disabilities. They may need additional help in identifying main ideas.

3. The child should be asked to be on the lookout for a **topic sentence** within the expository passage that **summarizes** the key information in the paragraph or in the lengthier excerpt. Then the child should read the rest of the passage or excerpt in light of this information and also note which information in the paragraph is not important. The important information the child has identified in the paragraph can be used by the child reader to formulate the author's **main idea**. The child reader may even want to use some of the author's own language in formulating that idea. It may help to teach them to count sentences that are all about the same thing, or use highlighters or post-it arrows to mark certain sentences. This way they can refer back to the text to see if most of the sentences highlighted are about the same thing—the main idea. Such scaffolding can be gradually reduced as students become more independent with this skill.

4. **Monitoring means self-clarifying**: As a reader reads, the reader often realizes that what he or she is reading is not making sense. The reader then has to have a plan for making sensible meaning out of the excerpt. Cooper and other balanced literacy advocates have a *stop and think* strategy that they use with children. The child reflects, "Does this make sense to me?" When the child concludes that it does not, the child then either: re-reads, reads ahead in the text, looks up unknown words, or asks for help from the teacher.

What is important about monitoring is that some readers ask these questions and try these approaches without ever being explicitly taught them in school by a teacher. However, the key philosophy of many reading theorists is that these strategies need to be explicitly modeled and practiced under the guidance of the teacher for most, if not all, child readers. Students with reading disabilities need such modeling even more, and may also benefit from a monitoring checklist to which they can refer to be sure they are monitoring their comprehension of what they read.

5. **Summarizing** engages the reader in pulling together into a cohesive whole the essential bits of information within a longer passage or excerpt of text. Children can be taught to summarize informational or expository text by following these guidelines. First, they should look at the topic sentence of the paragraph or the text, and delete the trivia. Then they should search for information which has been mentioned more than once and make sure it is included only once in their summary. Next, they should find related ideas or items, and group them under a unifying heading. Then, search for and identify a main idea sentence. Finally, put the summary together using all these guidelines. Graphic organizers can be invaluable tools to help struggling readers keep track of relevant information in a paragraph or longer selection.

Skill 3.9 **Identify instructional strategies that help students comprehend and apply knowledge of informational text structure (e.g., cause and effect, chronological order, compare and contrast) and text features (e.g., index, glossary, subheading)**

Common Text Features

Regardless of the specific subject matter, there are certain common text features children will encounter when reading and understanding the importance of these features significantly enhances comprehension of the text. This is particularly true of nonfiction text, which is often very *dense* in terms of amount of information conveyed.

Understanding the arrangement of nonfiction text with section and chapter titles, heads and subheads, (set in bold type) and other unique organizational devices can provide students with powerful tools to be successful. Students who use such headings as the main points can than fill in additional learning by reading the information below that heading. Also, if looking for a specific piece of information students can utilize Tables of Contents and Indexes, which are generally a part of expository writing. By understanding the structure of the text, students save valuable time and decrease the amount of rereading required.

Generally, there is so much known and valuable information about topics that authors try to share all of that information with the reader. Since there is a large amount of information to be conveyed, authors use specific organizational tools to break the text into smaller, more manageable, chunks. These different structures require the reader to make adjustments to their own personal reading style in order to successfully manage the intake of the new learning.

Most texts provide brief introductions. These introductions can be used by the readers to determine if the information they are seeking is located within the passage to be read. By reading a short passage, the student can quickly ascertain whether he/she needs to do a complete reading or a quick skim will suffice.

When searching for information, students can become much more efficient if they learn to use a glossary and index. Students can find the necessary facts in a more rapid manner and also clarify information that was difficult to understand the first time. Additionally, charts, graphs, maps, diagrams, captions, and photos in text can work in the same way as looking up unknown words in the glossary. They can provide more insight and clarify the concepts and ideas the author is conveying.

Research has shown that students' ability to comprehend nonfiction or expository text-- text that explains facts and concepts--is critical to their success on standardized tests, in their future education, and in adult life. Duke and Bennett-Armistead (2003) describe studies showing that nonfiction periodicals represent the single most common form of adult reading. They further explain that understanding informational text is key to future educational success.

In spite of this, surveys have shown that the vast majority of reading in primary grades is in the fiction genre. Far less attention is paid to nonfiction. This is a critical omission, because nonfiction text structures are more varied and difficult than those of fiction. Most fiction follows a fairly standard structure that is chronological in nature and can be outlined in terms of story grammar markers that list setting, characters, problem or initiating event, a sequence of events, and a resolution. Nonfiction text structures can be found in many different forms and it is important to teach strategies for comprehending them all.

In addition, expository texts are full of information that may or may not be factual and which may reflect the bias of the editor or author. Children need to learn that expository texts are organized around main ideas. They are usually found in newspapers, magazines, content textbooks, and informational reference books (i.e., an atlas, almanac, yearbook, or encyclopedia).

Common Expository Text Structures

The five types of expository texts to which the children should be introduced to through modeled reading and a teacher-facilitated walk through are as follows.

Description process—this usually describes a particular topic or provides the identifying characteristics of a topic. It can be depended upon to be factual. Within this type of text, the child reader has to use all of his or her basic reading strategies because these types of expository texts do not have explicit clue words. Graphic organizers that let the student state the topic or main idea and then briefly list descriptive details are very useful aids.

Causation or Cause-Effect Text—this is one where faulty reasoning may come into play, and the child reader has to use the inferential and self-questioning skills already mentioned to help assess whether the stated cause-effect relationship is a valid and correct one. This text appears in content-area textbooks, newspapers, magazines, advertisements, and on some content-area and general information web sites. Students should be taught to take note of certain clue words, such as: *therefore, the reasons for, as a result of, because, in consequence of,* and *since.* These clues point to a statement of cause and effect relationships. Again, students can differentially highlight cause and effect in the text and use graphic organizers to help with comprehension.

Comparison Text—this is an expository text that is centered on the reader's noting the contrasts and similarities between two or more objects and ideas. Many social studies, art, and science textbooks, as well as non-fiction books include this structure. Sometimes newspaper columnists use it as well in their editorial commentary.

Again, strategies for helping children comprehend the comparison and contrast intended by the author include the use of key clue words and phrases. Among these are: *like, unlike, resemble, different, different from, similar to, in contrast with, in comparison to,* and *in a different vein.* It is important that as children examine texts that are talking about illustrated or photographed entities, they can also review the graphic representations for clues to support or contradict the text. Graphic organizers such as Venn diagrams can be very useful for recording and summarizing details.

Collection Text—this is an expository text that presents ideas in a group. The writer's goal is to present a set of related points or ideas. Another name for this structure of expository writing is a listing or a sequence. The author frequently uses clue words, such *as first, second, third, finally, and next* to alert the reader to the sequence. Based on how well the writer structures the sequence of points or ideas, the reader should be able to make connections.

Simple collection texts that can be literally modeled for young children include recipe making. A class of first graders, beginning readers and writers, were spellbound by the author's presentation of a widely-known copyrighted collection text. The children were thrilled as the author followed the sequences of this collection text and finally took turns stirring the product of the experiment until it was creamy and smooth. After it had cooled, they each had a taste using their plastic spoons. Can you guess what it was? No? What gourmet children's delight would have first graders begging for a taste? Cream Farina from a commercial cereal box that had cooking directions on it (i.e., known as a collection text).

The children had constructed meaning from this five-minute class demonstration and that they would pay close attention to collection texts on other food and product instruction boxes because this text had come to be an authentic part of their lives.

Response structure—this is an expository text that presents a question or problem followed by an answer or a solution. Of course, entire mathematics textbooks, and some science and social studies textbooks, are organized around this type of structure. Again, it is important here to walk the child reader through the excerpt and to sensitize the child to the clue words that signal this type of structure. These words include, but are not limited to: *the problem is, the questions is, you need to solve for, one probable solution would be, an intervention could be, the concerns is, and another way to solve this would be.* It can be helpful for the child to highlight the question or questions in some way and them mark or highlight sentences that provide answers to each question. Graphic organizers to record information can also be useful here.

Newspapers and magazines present excellent opportunities to bring "real" reading into the classroom. A number of news magazines, such as Time For Kids, bring current events into the classroom written at various grade levels. Children see their parents and other adults reading newspapers and magazines all the time. Students who understand the applications of the newspaper, technology, and other real-life situations are able to make the final connection to life-long learning.

What is most intriguing about the use of newspapers as a model and an authentic platform for introducing and teaching children to recognize and use expository text structures, features, and references, is that the children can demonstrate their mastery of these structures by using them to put out their own newspapers detailing their school. They can also create their own timelines for projects or research papers that they have done in class by using newspaper models.

Use of Reading Strategies for Different Texts—as children progress to the older grades (3-6), it is important for the teacher to model for them that in research on a social studies or science exploration, it may not be necessary to read every single word of a given expository information text in order to find the answer to a simple question. For instance, if the child is trying to find out about hieroglyphics, he or she might only read through those sections of a book on Egyptian or Sumerian civilization that dealt with picture writing. The teacher, assisted by a child, should model how to go through the table of contents and the index of the book to identify only those pages that deal with picture writing. In addition, other children should come to the front of the room or to the center of the area where the reading group is meeting. They should then, with the support of the teacher, skim through the book for illustrations or diagrams of picture writing, which is the focus of their need.

Children can practice the skills of skimming texts and scanning for particular topics that connect with their grade social studies, science, and mathematics content area interests.

Skill 3.10   Identify criteria for selecting and evaluating both print and nonprint media (e.g., Internet, software, trade books, textbooks, DVDs, videos) for instructional use to match student needs and interests

Print Media

Evaluating and using print media is significantly different in elementary and middle/high schools. In early elementary school, typically from grades K-3, the child is primarily learning to read. Therefore, all materials must be chosen with the purpose of improving overall reading ability in the child. Somewhere around the end of grade three, and certainly by grade four and later in post elementary grades, children are expected to read to learn. Students are to use their reading skills to learn in the content areas, even to learn more about reading and literature.

Print Media in Elementary Settings

Whatever method is used for selecting literature in an elementary classroom, it must take into consideration the range of reading levels in the room. Although the general categories of reading level may be described in a variety of ways in the educational literature, these four levels are usually included in any discussion:

- **Emergent Readers** understand very basic concepts needed for learning to read: that print conveys a speech message, the directionality of print, and the one to one relationship of printed to oral words. They can recognize some high frequency words, especially those with personal significance. They have the beginnings of the code of letter/sound relationships, but tend to focus only on the beginning sound. They rely heavily on pictures for meaning and may make up interpretations as they go along. They need books with repetitive story and word patterns, simple structure, and backgrounds similar to their own to enhance comprehension.

- **Early Readers** have a much larger sight vocabulary and recognize most high-frequency words. They are able to decode most regularly spelled single syllable words and can use visual, structural, and semantic cues in decoding. They tend to use pictures to *confirm*, rather than convey meaning and can use more problem-solving strategies when they have a problem decoding a word. Repetitive books are still good at this stage, but more complex text structures can be used and longer texts are appropriate.

- **Transitional Readers** have a large sight vocabulary, including many more difficult words. They are able to combine and cross-reference various reading strategies and all three cueing systems to decode words. They can read aloud with more fluency and expression and may enjoy doing so. They may still need help understanding what they read, however, as the decoding task may still take up much of their effort. For this reason, series books are good at this age so the context is familiar and helps comprehension. They can also handle main ideas and simple sets of supportive details.

- **Fluent Readers** read well and for fun. They read with automaticity in terms of decoding, so can self-monitor for meaning and make corrections as necessary. They may enjoy reading series books, but do not need them. They can handle chapter books and textbooks for acquiring additional information and learning.

When selecting literature for a classroom, the literature needs to be selected to cover all these areas in an elementary classroom.

Listed below are a number of strategies for choosing literature to use in the classroom. These would be starting places only; the teacher will need to select books with her students and goals in mind.

- Newberry and Caldecott Award winners are good places to start. These award winners have already been evaluated and are at the top of the "quality" list
- Many teachers like looking to the classics for classroom literature. Some classics, however, are more popular with children and the interest level of the students is important.

- Social significance and relevance to the students' lives are important factors in selecting materials, too. This is particularly true when the classroom has a diverse cultural or ethnic base.
- Letting students make selections on their own is a good practice, as well. Students are more likely to read and enjoy what interests them and the process of selection can help them with evaluation skills.
- Books from all genres (e.g., fiction, nonfiction, traditional literature, biography, informational text, poetry, drama, etc.) need to be selected.
- The state standards for reading and content instruction need to be taken into consideration and the selection of books available must cover these areas.
- Although most fiction material follows a predictable format (chronologically presented information), nonfiction texts have a wide range of formats and present information in a great many ways, including text, illustrations, diagrams, maps, etc. In addition, throughout their school careers students will need to learn about a wide range of content areas. For these reasons, it is wise to have a wide range of nonfiction materials available at a variety of reading levels. See sections 3.8 and 3.9 for more information on nonfiction.
- As adults, periodicals and magazines will be frequent sources of information, so the classroom should have plenty of these at appropriate reading levels.

Print Media at Higher Levels

The same general principle listed above about choosing literature from varied genres, including a variety of nonfiction texts, applies to higher levels as well. However, the social changes of post-World War II significantly affected adolescent fiction literature. The Civil Rights movement, feminism, the protest of the Vietnam Conflict, and issues surrounding homelessness, neglect, teen pregnancy, drugs, and violence have bred a new vein of contemporary fiction that helps adolescents understand and cope with the world they live in.

Popular books for preadolescents deal more with establishing relationships with members of the opposite sex (*Sweet Valley High* series) and learning to cope with their changing bodies, personalities, or life situations, as in Judy Blume's *Are You There, God? It's Me, Margaret*. Adolescents are still interested in the fantasy and science fiction genres, as well as popular juvenile fiction (such as the *Twilight* series, or other vampire or zombie based books). Middle school students still read the *Little House on the Prairie* series and the mysteries of the Hardy boys and Nancy Drew. Teens value the works of Emily and Charlotte Bronte, Willa Cather, Jack London, William Shakespeare and Mark Twain as much as those of Piers Anthony, S.E. Hinton, Madeleine L'Engle, Stephen King, and J.R.R. Tolkein because they're fun to read. Many titles by these authors are still required reading texts in school English curriculums, particularly S.E. Hinton's *Outsiders* and *Rumble Fish*. Newer texts are also emerging in middle grade classrooms, such as *The Curious Incident of the Dog in the Night-Time* and other books by Mark Haddon.

Older adolescents enjoy the writers in these genres.

1. Fantasy—Piers Anthony, Ursula LeGuin, Ann McCaffrey
2. Horror—V.C. Andrews and Stephen King
3. Juvenile fiction—Judy Blume, Robert Cormier, Rosa Guy, Virginia Hamilton, S.E. Hinton, M.E. Kerr, Harry Mazer, Norma Fox Mazer, Richard Newton Peck, Cynthia Voight and Paul Zindel.
4. Science fiction—Isaac Asimov, Ray Bradbury, Arthur C. Clarke, Frank Herbert, Larry Niven and H.G. Wells

These classic and contemporary works combine the characteristics of multiple theories. Functioning at the concrete operations stage (Piaget), being of the "good person" orientation (Kohlberg), still highly dependent on external rewards (Bandura) and exhibiting all five needs from Maslow's hierarchy, eleven- to twelve-year-olds should appreciate the following titles, which are grouped by reading level.

Reading level 6.0 to 6.9

- *Lilies of the Field* by William Barrett
- *Other Bells for Us to Ring* by Robert Cormier
- *Danny, Champion of the World & Charlie and the Chocolate Factory* by Roald Dahl
- *Pippi Longstocking* by Astrid Lindgren
- *Three Lives to Live* by Anne Lindbergh
- *Rabble Starkey* by Lois Lowry
- *The Year of the Gopher & Reluctantly Alice* by Phyllis Naylor
- *Arly* by Robert Newton Peck
- *The Witch of Blackbird Pond* by Elizabeth Speare
- *The Boy Who Reversed Himself* by William Sleator

For Seventh and Eighth Graders

Most seventh- and eighth-grade students, according to learning theory, are still functioning cognitively, psychologically, and morally as sixth graders. As these are not inflexible standards, there are some twelve- and thirteen-year-olds who are much more mature socially, intellectually, and physically than the younger children who share the same school. They are becoming concerned with establishing individual and peer group identities, which presents conflicts with breaking from authority and the rigidity of rules. Some at this age are still tied firmly to the family and its expectations, while others identify more with those their own age or older. Enrichment reading for this group must help them cope with life's rapid changes or provide escape, and thus must be either realistic or fantastic, depending on the child's needs. Adventures and mysteries (the *Hardy Boys* and *Nancy Drew* series) are still popular today. These preteens also become more interested in biographies of contemporary figures rather than legendary figures of the past.

Reading level 7.0 to 7.9

- *Sounder* by William Armstrong
- *National Velvet* by Enid Bagnold
- *Peter Pan* by James Barrie
- *White Fang & Call of the Wild* by Jack London
- *Taking Care of Terrific* by Lois Lowry
- The *Dragonsinger* series by Anne McCaffrey
- *Anne of Green Gables* & sequels by L.M. Montgomery
- *The Pearl* by John Steinbeck
- *The Hobbit* by J.R.R. Tolkein
- *The Pigman* by Paul Zindel

Reading level 8.0 to 8.9

- *I Am the Cheese* by Robert Cormier
- *The Member of the Wedding* by Carson McCullers
- *Rascal* by Sterling North
- *The Adventures of Tom Sawyer* by Mark Twain
- *My Darling, My Hamburger* by Paul Zindel

For Ninth Graders

Depending upon the school environment, a ninth grader may be top dog in a junior high school or underdog in a high school. His peer associations motivate much of his social development, and thus his reading interests. He is technically an adolescent operating at the early stages of formal operations in cognitive development. His perception of his own identity is becoming well defined and he is fully aware of the ethics required by society. He is more receptive to the challenges of classic literature but still enjoys popular teen novels.

Reading level 9.0 to 9.9

- *Bury My Heart at Wounded Knee* by Dee Brown
- *Robinson Crusoe* by Daniel Defoe
- *David Copperfield* by Charles Dickens
- *I Never Promised You a Rose Garden* by Joanne Greenberg
- *Captains Courageous* by Rudyard Kipling
- *Kaffir Boy* by Mark Mathabane
- *Mutiny on the Bounty* by Charles Nordhoff
- *Frankenstein* by Mary Shelley
- *Up From Slavery* by Booker T. Washington

For Tenth-Twelfth Graders

All high school sophomores, juniors and seniors can handle most other literature, except for a few of the very most difficult titles, such as *Moby Dick* or *Vanity Fair*. However, since many high school students do not progress to the eleventh or twelfth grade reading level, they will still have their favorites among authors whose writings they can more easily understand. Many will struggle with assigned novels but still read high interest books for pleasure. A few high interest titles are listed below without reading level designations, though most are 6.0 to 7.9.

- *Squashed* by Joan Bauer
- *When the Legends Die* by Hal Borland
- *Remember Me to Herald Square* by Paula Danzinger
- *Stranger with My Face* by Lois Duncan
- *The Planet of Junior Brown* by Virginia Hamilton
- *The Outsiders* by S.E. Hintion
- *The Great Gilly Hopkins* by Katherine Paterson

Teachers of students at all levels must be familiar with the materials offered by the libraries in their own schools. Only then can they guide their students into appropriate selections for their social age and reading level development.

Off Grade Leveled Materials

Finally, it must be remembered that interest level, emotional level, and reading level are not the same. For older students who do not read well, it is essential to have provide age appropriate high interest materials that are written at a simpler reading level, so poorer readers have access to the same materials their peers do. Many libraries have alternative versions of classics and popular books for those who need simpler text. Publishers such as Rigby and National Geographic Windows on Literacy have nonfiction and genre books of high interest level written in simpler language. Such materials are essential in any diverse classroom.

Nonprint Media

Many of the same principles applied to selecting print media will apply to selecting nonprint media such as videos, DVDs, software, devices, and internet sources. The media must be selected to support state learning standards, meet individual student needs, and be practical and feasible in the classroom. Acquiring attractive (and expensive) video or electronic media materials is only useful if the materials actually support student and curriculum goals.

Mobile learning and nonprint technologies are increasingly important in the classroom environment. Netbooks, Smartboards, iPads, iPods, and e-readers are increasingly becoming educational tools for educators, because educators are preparing twenty-first century learners. Curriculum materials often offer multimedia options for teachers to easily utilize.

Audio-Visual Aides: In addition to texts, appropriately selected video or audio recordings may be useful. For example, a science teacher may wish to show a short clip of a video that demonstrates how to conduct a particular experiment before students do it on their own. Or, a Language Arts teacher may bring in an audio recording of a book to present a uniquely dramatized reading of the book.

Computer Software: Depending upon the resources in a classroom, computer software can enhance learning and make some materials more accessible to students with disabilities. There are a variety of reading programs that allow students to progress at their own rate, read and score their own materials, and make personal reading goals. There are similar math programs, as well. In addition, there are software programs that provide accommodations needed by students with disabilities, such as programs that will scan and read text, that will read back a student's writing to him, or type as the student speaks. Specific software chosen will depend upon very specific student needs. Students with disabilities will often have recommendations in their IEPs concerning such materials.

Internet sources require special care. Students need to be closely supervised and educated about standards for selecting safe and accurate sites for information. As a rule, it is a good idea for the teacher to preselect a set of sites and program links to them so that students do not stray into inappropriate areas. There are many teacher and student friendly sites sponsored by legitimate educational organizations from which to choose.

Application of Comprehension Strategies for Electronic Texts

If electronic materials are being used in the class, additional comprehension strategies and uses can be taught. If the class gets newspapers in the classroom as part of an ongoing Newspapers in Education (NIE) program, it is natural and easy for the teacher to take the time to show children how news is covered online. Many major newspapers have e-news. Children can first do a K-W-L on what they know or think they know about e-news and then actually review their specific daily newspaper's site. There are also sites such as www.newsela.com which are adjusted according to reading level, and the comprehension questions match the passage in connection to the leveled passage.

With the support of the teacher or an older peer, they can examine the resource and perhaps note the following differences in electronic text:

- Use of moving pictures and video to document events.
- Use of sound clips in addition to written text.
- Use of music/sound effects not in printed text.
- Links to other web resources and to other archived articles.

Of course, this can lead to much rich discussion and to further detailed web versus print news resource analysis. For children in grades five and six, this might even include a research investigation of a particular news story or event, including broadcast media coverage.

In addition to current events, a variety of vocational and career related topics can provide authentic situations for reading in the classroom. Everything from employment applications to want ads and grocery store circulars can be used to demonstrate real reading situations.

Skill 3.11   Identify effective instructional methods and supports (e.g., direct instruction, visual supports, manipulatives) for teaching mathematics and integrating mathematics across the curricula

In order to identify and select appropriate instructional and support materials for teaching math, it is first necessary to understand something about the developmental processes that influence the child's acquisition of mathematic concepts. Hatfield, et al (2005) describe the child's developing sense of number and math concepts in terms of Piaget's observations on child development.

Preoperational stage: Although movement through developmental stages is highly individual in terms of exact age, most preschool and first grade children are still in what Piaget calls the *Preoperational Stage*. They are aware that objects have a reality outside that of the child itself, and that objects have properties, which they can describe in a limited way. However, they do not yet understand many of the concepts that are critical to basic, underlying math concepts, and they need a great deal of interaction with objects and manipulatives, as well as guiding questions and time, to develop these concepts.

Concrete Operational Stage: By second grade, many children are beginning to enter the *Concrete operational stage* during which a number of concepts critical to the development of math sense can be learned. Children at this stage can act on operations, can understand an *operation* on an object. They can begin to understand relationships between objects (e.g., size, order) and can carry out operation on objects and *reverse* operations on objects. At this stage, children can learn to sort and classify objects according to a variety of criteria. They can understand that an entire group can be a *part or subset* of another group. They can *reverse actions and operations*. They can successively compare objects and *put them in order*. Most important of all for developing math concepts, they can begin to *conserve numbers* or to understand that the number of objects remains the same even when their arrangement or appearance changes. These concepts are critical to the ability to understand the nature of addition and subtraction, as well as other operations in math.

Formal Operational Stage: By the time children enter middle or high school, many of them will be at the *Formal Operational stage* and they will be capable of learning to conduct operations on other operations independent of any objects or concrete stimuli.

Based on the child's development, Baratta-Lorton described three levels of instruction necessary to help a child move through any mathematics curriculum.

- **Concept Level:** At this level, the child needs *repeated and varied* interaction with manipulatives. The child needs to interact intensively with a variety of objects, to see patterns, combinations, and relationships among the objects before the child can internalize concepts. When introducing new concepts, this is the level at which the child will spend the most time. It is important to remember that the objects are not being used by the teacher to demonstrate concepts, but by the child to *discover* concepts and relationships. The teacher's role is to ask questions that trigger higher order thinking and learning from the child.
- **Connecting Level:** At this level the child learns to assign symbols or representations to the objects and the operations carried out on the objects. However, the objects or manipulatives are still very present and part of the

process. Labeling the objects and operations with symbols in the presence of the objects or manipulatives serves as a connection from the concrete level to the next level. The child can move on from this level more quickly and whenever ready to do so.

- **Symbolic Level:** At this level, the child can use symbols without manipulatives. The child understands the abstract concepts behind the symbols and can operate on and with symbols alone.

The National Council of Teachers of Mathematics (NCTM)'s 2000 outline of principles upon which mathematics instruction should be based outlined a similar process by which math concepts should be taught. This document states that instruction and exploration should go through three stages of *representation* (the procedure for modeling and interpreting organization of objects and mathematical operations). They are:

- Concrete Representations: the extensive exploration and use of objects and manipulatives to discover and then demonstrate operations and relationships.
- Pictorial Representations: The use of concrete pictures of objects and actions often in the presence of the objects as discoveries and demonstrations are made.
- Symbolic Representations: The use of symbols exclusively to conduct operations, explorations and discoveries about math concepts.

A mathematics program based on current research will have certain characteristics.

1. Children will be actively engaged in exploring math concepts and *doing* math. There will be hands-on, concrete exploration, as well talking about, reading about, and writing about math.
2. Students will be encouraged to "stretch" their math sense and "think like mathematicians." High standards will be expected, but the learning setting will be safe enough for children to take risks and make mistakes in order to learn, and enjoy learning.
3. Teachers will be asking questions that stimulate children to make new discoveries and to reveal concepts they already know. Questioning will lead students to make connections between what they know and what they learn.
4. Cooperative learning will take place. Children will learn from talking to one another about math and working together.
5. Math will be part of the "real world" and connections to that real world will be made for all activities and concepts.
6. Content taught will cover a wide range of topics and applications. Children will learn not only computation, but the concepts behind computation and use, and the math language to discuss these connections.

Teaching Strategies Appropriate to the Development of Number Concepts

Numbers appear in many daily situations. Children see numbers on clock faces, on telephone dials or buttons, on mailboxes, on car license plates, on price tags of toys, and on food items. How do children grow in their understanding and use of numbers? Early readiness skills involve classifying, comparing, and ordering numbers, activities that in essence provide some primitive practice in quantification. As mentioned above, early learning requires extensive interaction with manipulatives of all sorts in order to develop a solid grounding in foundation concepts. Stages of concept formation progress as children mature, develop, and experience situations involving numbers.

1. **One-to-One Matching**—children may be asked to match the items in two groups, one-by-one and to describe what they find. One group may be identified as having more or less than another.

2. **Rote Counting**—many young children can count from one to ten or higher using rote memory. They can name the numbers in correct sequence, but may not really understand what the numbers mean. For example, they may be able to sing number songs, but cannot pick up five blocks upon request.

3. **Selection of Correct Number of Objects**—Jean Piaget describes three phases through which children pass in mastering this concept. In the first, a child believes the number changes when the design or number of objects is rearranged. A child in the second phase understands conservation, in the sense that the number is the same no matter how different the set may appear. Children in the final stage can reverse their thinking and understand that the number does not change when objects are returned to their original positions. They can show one-to-one matching of rows of objects. Counting has become meaningful.

4. **Ordinality and Cardinality**—*Ordinality* refers to the relative position or order of an object within a set in relation to the other objects, like first, second and etc. *Cardinality* answers the question of "How many?" in reference to the total number of objects in a group. When counting, children use numbers cardinally as they say "one" for the first object, "two" for the second, and so on. It helps them to move the objects as they are counted. Thus, when the counting is complete, and children can tell that there are four balls in all, they can use the ordinal for any number of the group. The number "4"—a cardinal—is associated with all four objects; the last is the 4th—an ordinal.

5. **Sequencing Numbers to Ten**—Prior work in comparing and ordering quantities is gradually extended. Children learn that five, which is more than three, comes after three in counting sequence.

6. **Zero**—Developmental work with zero occurs within the 1 to 10 sequence rather than first. The meaning of zero as "none at all" is easier for children to

understand when they can use it in relations to known quantities. For example, "There were two cookies on the plate. My dad and I each had one. Now they are all gone."

7. **Symbols**—Children learn to recognize and write numerals in a cognitive manner. The concepts of greater than and less than are also understood. Finally, children learn to name and use numerals of symbols for comparison, even when the objects are no longer present.

8. **Sight Groups**—Children learn to recognize, without counting, the number of objects in groups having four or less items. Eventually, children will learn to sight sub-groups with larger numbers of objects.

9. **Writing Numerals**—After children learn to recognize a numeral and associate it with the correct number of objects, writing begins. However, even when the focus is on writing, continued reference to quantities named should be made.

10. **Sequencing Tasks**—Earlier work, in which children used one-to-one matching to tell whether a group has more, less, or as many objects as another, is extended. Children come to recognize that when a number means more, it comes after another in the process of counting. Conversely, when a number means less, it comes before another in counting.

The stages just described serve as precursors in the development of number concepts. The conceptual understanding of number concepts further extends into mathematical operations, place value, re-groupings, and decimals later.

Communication in Mathematics: Math Vocabulary

Many students with learning disabilities, specifically with math disorders, may have a problem connecting terminology with symbolism in mathematics. For example, multiplication means to multiply or grow larger, and is represented by a multiplication sign, 'x,' when a student is in elementary school. As he or she progresses into higher math courses, the multiplication sign may take on the form of a dot, and eventually fade. Numbers next to one another, such as 5(4) will soon indicate multiplication. It is helpful to explain symbols and their relation to math vocabulary words, not only to explain the underpinnings of problems solving, but also to assist word problem translation. For example, if a word problem asks for the sum of cookies, it is asking the student to add. Vocabulary is a critical component of math, and often needs clarification.

Teaching Students with Disabilities to Succeed in Math

Etiologies of the learning challenges some students face can be diverse, as can their outcomes. Teachers of students with special needs need to be skilled at assessing, observing, implementing, reassessing, and making changes to the educational environment, tools, and approaches they are using with students.

To accomplish this with math instruction, teachers must begin by identifying the nature of math as a curricular area, using that information to task-analyze the concepts, skills, and strategies they want to teach. Then teachers focus on each student's observed and documented strengths and challenges, as well as the relevant information from his/her formal assessments and individualized education plan (IEP). Such analysis may constitute an initial assessment.

In the NCTM journal article, *Planning Strategies for Students with Special Needs* (*Teaching Children Mathematics*, 2004), Brodesky et al. suggest that the next step in deciding on strategies, materials, and resources would be to identify the "barriers" that students' documented and observed challenges will present as they work to meet the goals and objectives of the math curriculum and their IEPs. Data-based assessments are an alternative or adjunct to such observational and record review. This information can help direct teachers' thinking about proactive solutions, including the selection and/or adaptation of the best strategies, materials, and resources.

Once teachers have developed a clear picture of the goals and needs of their math students with learning differences, they can seek resources to ascertain the best practices, including school district-based support, the federal and state departments of education, teacher training programs, and education literature. Ultimately, skilled teachers will layer creativity and keen observation with their professional skills to decide how best to individualize instruction and to facilitate student achievement. Examples include:

- Varying learning modalities (visual, kinesthetic, tactile and aural)
- Integrating technology (calculators, computers and game consoles)
- Providing tools and manipulatives (Cuisinart rods, beans, protractors, real world objects of every sort)
- Developing a range of engaging activities (games, music and storytelling)
- Using real world problem solving (fundraising, school-wide projects, shopping, cooking, baseball cards, etc.)
- Adopting a cross-curricular approach (studying historical events strongly influenced by math and music theory)

- Developing basic skills (guided practice first with manipulatives, then pencil-and-paper computation, journaling and discussing problem-solving strategies)
- Adaptations (extended wait time, recorded lessons, concept videos, ergonomic work areas, and mixed-ability learning groups)

In a paper published by the ERIC Clearinghouse on Disabilities and Gifted Education, Author Cynthia Warger writes, "…for students with disabilities to do better in math, math must be meaningful for them. Both knowing and doing mathematics must be emphasized to enhance the quality of mathematics instruction and learning for students with disabilities." (Warger, 2002)

Real-world applications of mathematics abound and offer highly-motivating opportunities for computational practice and the development of number sense and mathematical reasoning that can give students confidence in their mathematical abilities. Finding the mathematical connections in outdoor games, planning for the purchase of lunch, comparing heights among classmates, calculating the time until recess, and figuring out which sports team is headed for the playoffs are just a few examples.

The Special Connections Project at the University of Kansas suggests a number of strategies in a paper called *Creating Authentic Mathematics Learning Contexts*:

1. Begin where the students are. Their ages, interests, and experiences are excellent clues to the kinds of contexts that will offer the most compelling learning opportunities, whether school-, family- or community-related.
2. Document interests. Comparing and contrasting them can help identify patterns and differences and assist with lesson and activity planning. Documenting and reviewing this information (student name, hobbies, interests, family activities, etc.) could be an activity you share with your students.
3. Model the desired concept, skill, or strategy explicitly and within the real-world context. Observing your problem-solving approach and its outcome helps ground students in the math and begins to strengthen associations between mathematics concepts and real-life situations.
4. Reinforce the associations by demonstrating the relevance of the concept, skill or strategy being taught to the "authentic context."
5. Offer opportunities for guided, supported practice of the concept, skill or strategy; this includes feedback, redirection, remodeling, and if needed, acknowledgement of progress and successes.

Sequence of Mathematics Understanding

The understanding of mathematical concepts proceeds in a developmental context from concrete to semi-concrete to abstract. Children with learning difficulties may still be at the semi-concrete level when their peers are ready to work at the abstract level. This developmental sequence has implication for remedial instruction because the teacher will need to incorporate concrete and/or semi-concrete/representational methodologies into lessons for students who did not master these stages of development in their mathematics background. These levels may be explained as follows:

1   **Concrete:** An example of concrete understanding would be demonstrating 3 + 4 = 7 by using sets of addends (3 and 4) with items, such as buttons, and physically bringing them together to demonstrate the sum (7).

2   **Semi-concrete or representational:** An example of semi-concrete understanding would be using pictures of three buttons and four buttons to illustrate 3 + 4 = 7.

3   **Abstract:** The student solves 3 + 4 = 7 without using manipulatives or pictures.

In summary, the levels of mathematics content involve:

- Concepts such as the understanding of numbers and terms.
- Development of mathematical relationships.
- Development of mathematical skills such as computation and measuring.
- Development of problem-solving ability.

COMPETENCY 4.0   **KNOWLEDGE OF ASSESSING, DESIGNING, AND IMPLEMENTING POSITIVE BEHAVIORAL SUPPORTS**

Skill 4.1   **Analyze the legal and ethical issues pertaining to positive behavior management strategies and disciplinary actions**

Positive behavioral interventions and supports (PBS) are IDEA's preferred strategy for handling challenging behaviors of students with disabilities. IDEA requires PBS to be considered in all cases of students whose behavior impedes their learning or the learning of others.

IDEA requires that "in the case of a child whose behavior impedes his or her learning or that of others," a student's IEP team, while developing an IEP (initial development, review, or revision), is required to "consider, when appropriate, strategies, including positive behavioral interventions, and supports to address that behavior."

PBS involves the use of positive behavioral interventions and systems to attain socially significant behavior change. PBS has four interrelated components. The components are as follows: systems change activities, environmental alterations activities, skill instruction activities, and behavioral consequence activities.

These come together to form a behaviorally-based systems approach, which enhances the ability of schools, families, and communities to create effective environments that improve the link between research-validated practices and the environments in which teaching and learning occur.

According to the Florida Administrative Code, a student can be removed from school for disciplinary reasons for a period of time not exceeding ten consecutive school days. Removals of less than ten consecutive days may be implemented, as long as those removals do not represent an alteration of placement for the student.

The IEP team and additional qualified staff must assess whether the behavior in question is part of the student's disability before a disabled student's placement can be modified as a result of disciplinary action.

If the student's behavior is assessed to be part of the student's disability, then the student's placement cannot be modified as part of a disciplinary tactic. The IEP team may decide that a modification of placement is required in order to provide a free appropriate public education (FAPE) in the least restrictive environment.

The district has to give services to a student with a disability who has been taken from his current placement for more than ten school days in the school year as a result of disciplinary action. School staff can place a student in an interim alternative educational setting (IAES) without the consent of the parent for the same time frame that a student without a disability could be placed, but not more than forty-five calendar days, if the student brings a weapon or firearm to school, or knowingly possesses or used illegal drugs, or sells or solicits the sale of a controlled substance while at school.

The Florida requirements for performing the functional behavior analysis is different from those outlined in the IDEA regulations. The Code of Federal Regulations indicates that a functional behavioral assessment has to be done before a student can be removed from a placement.

In contrast, the Florida Rule states that if a district has not done a functional behavioral assessment for a student, one must be performed before a long-term removal. A long-term removal would consist of the removal of a student with a disability from his or her current placement for longer than 10 school days in a school year. This could or could not mean a change in placement for the student.

After the functional behavioral assessment (FBA) is performed, the IEP team must convene to create the positive behavior intervention plan that addresses the behavior in question and make sure that the plan is put into place. Information from the FBA is utilized to create meaningful interventions and plan for instruction in replacement behaviors. The IEP team must review the positive behavior intervention plan and how it is implemented to decide if changes are needed to make the plan more effective. An example can be found at: http://www.fldoe.org/ese/pdf/tap99-3.pdf

Skill 4.2   Identify data collection strategies to assess student behavior

A behavior measurement plan includes several components. First, it must be decided what behavior will be measured. The dimension or properties of the behavior that can be observed and reliably measured are considered before selecting a measurement scheme. These properties are explained below.

1 **Frequency.** Frequency refers to how often a behavior occurs in a period of time. (Joe completed 20 multiplication problems during math period).
2 **Rate.** When frequency data is expressed in a ratio with time, a measure or rate is expressed. This can be achieved by dividing the numerical count by the time observed. (Joe did 5 of the math problems per minute).

3 **Duration.** How long a behavioral episode lasts describes its duration. (Jerry's temper tantrum lasted for 20 minutes).

4 **Intensity.** Measurements of frequency and duration convey the intensity of the behavior. (Jerry had three temper tantrums during the school day that lasted for a total of 90 minutes).

5 **Latency.** Latency refers to the length of time it takes before a student starts performing a behavior. (Joe stared into space for 6 minutes before beginning his math work).

6 **Topography.** Topography refers to the physical appearance of the behavior or what it looks like. (Joe writes the numeral 4 backwards on his math paper; Jerry kicks, screams, and pulls his hair when he throws a tantrum).

7 **Magnitude or Force.** How strongly or loudly a behavior is performed gives a measure of magnitude or force. (Joe writes so heavily that he makes holes in his paper).

8 **Locus.** Mention of where a behavior occurs describes the locus, or location, of the behavior. (Jerry had his longest temper tantrum on the playground).

Systems of Data Collection

The decision to use a particular system of data collection will be determined partly on the basis of what dimension of behavior is of concern, as well as on the basis of practicality and convenience. Systems of data collection can be classified into three general categories:

1. **Permanent Product Recording.** This system is used when observing tangible products and is sometimes referred to as outcome recording. Numerical counts, rate or percent, or trials to criterion may be obtained by this system. For example, the number of pegs placed in a container or math facts answered correctly are recorded using this system.

2. **Observational Recording System.** This method is used to record a behavior sample as it occurs. The basic observational recording systems are:

    a. *Event recording* is used by teachers interested in recording the number of times a discrete behavior (one that has a beginning and an end, is brief, and can be observed in its entirety) occurs (its frequency or rate of occurrence).

    b. *Interval recording or time sampling* is used to find out during what portion of a specified time period the observed behavior occurs. In interval recording, a behavior is recorded if some part of the behavior is observed to occur within one of a series of continuous time intervals of equal length.

The data consists of some notation indicating whether or not the behavior occurred. In time sampling, a behavior is recorded if some part of the behavior is observed to occur within one of a series of discontinuous time intervals of equal length. Though similar to interval recording, the time intervals in time sampling are typically longer, less frequent, and may be variable.

c. *Duration recording* enables the teacher to determine the length of time that a student spends performing some specific behavior.

d. *Latency recording* measures the length of time that it takes a student to begin performing a behavior.

3. **Anecdotal Recording.** In this method, the teacher writes a short narrative description of the behavior as it occurs. This system has the advantage of permitting the inclusion of such factors as precipitating circumstances, effect of the behavior on witnesses, and outcome. Only factual, objective information should be recorded, with no attempt at subjective interpretations.

Skill 4.3 Analyze individual and group data to select and evaluate proactive interventions that foster appropriate behavior

While educational literature and studies may suggest best practices in fostering appropriate classroom behavior, teachers must rely on their assessment skills, including observation and data collection, to help them identify the most effective and constructive interventions for their students. Using data they collect through permanent products, observational and anecdotal recording, teachers can document individual and group behaviors and preempt or redirect behavior that might be of concern. Because data collection, by definition, requires tracking information regularly over time, patterns, trends, and anomalies are easier to identify and evaluate than through undocumented impressions of behavior.

Teachers may collect information on an individual student either to establish a baseline or to document areas of interest. For example, it may seem that Susan is constantly kicking the back of her classmate's chair during class, but data collection on Susan's kicking behavior may reveal many more or many fewer such kicks, or that it happens only when Susan has missed breakfast, etc. Data collection that centers on the group may reveal that her classmates don't seem to notice her kicking, or it may show that her kicking, if left unchecked, precipitates disruptive behaviors in others throughout the class period. Teachers can use information revealed through such data analysis to inform their intervention choices.

Before selecting behavioral interventions, teachers should first evaluate the environment and culture in their classrooms. Research conducted by the Northwest Regional Educational Library (Cotton, 1990) agrees that prevention of inappropriate behavior in classrooms is far preferable to remediation, but also further suggests that certain baseline practices should be exercised in effective classrooms from the *first day of school*, including:

- providing a functional and organized learning environment and well- organized instruction;
- presenting clear rules and routines and supporting students in adhering to them;
- making plain consequences for inappropriate behavior;
- ensuring consistent and timely enforcement of those rules; and
- fostering a sense of personal responsibility in students, and engendering a culture of shared responsibility for classroom management.

Once those fundamental supports are in place, teachers can examine data for clues about adjustments and tools that may help foster appropriate behavior. They then can implement those changes one at a time or in well-considered clusters, keeping in mind that the effects of their interventions should be documented through continued data collection.

So based on the data recorded, Susan's teacher might decide to try adjusting the position of Susan's chair to make it less likely that her swinging leg will hit other students' chairs *and* to assure that Susan ate breakfast or had access to a snack during morning recess. Her teacher might help Susan become more aware of respecting the personal space of other students and might even engage the class in a discussion about things that distract them from their schoolwork and ways classmates can help one another concentrate, which might include keeping feet near one's own desk. Whatever he or she chooses, the teacher's proactive adjustments and interventions will likely be best informed by an analysis of the data collected on Susan and her classmates.

Skill 4.4   Identify and interpret the essential elements of a functional behavior assessment and a behavior intervention plan

A Functional Behavior Assessment (FBA) is a method of gathering information. The information that is collected is utilized to assess why problem behaviors occur. The data will also help pinpoint things to do that will help alleviate the behaviors. The data from a functional behavioral assessment is used to create a positive behavioral intervention plan.

The Individuals with Disabilities Education Act (IDEA) specifically calls for a functional behavior assessment when a child with a disability has his or her present placement modified for disciplinary reasons. IDEA does not elaborate on how an FBA should be conducted, as the procedures may vary dependent on the specific child. Even so, there are several specific elements that should be a part of any functional behavior assessment.

The first step is to identify the particular behavior that must be modified. If the child has numerous problem behaviors, then it is important to assess which behaviors are the primary ones that should be addressed. This should be narrowed down to one or two primary behaviors. The primary behaviors are then described so that the components of the relevant behavior are clear to everyone involved in the child's treatment. The most typical order of procedures is as follows:

1. Identify and come to an agreement about the behaviors that need to be modified. Find out where the behaviors are most likely to happen and where they are not likely to happen.
2. Identify what may trigger the behaviors to occur.
3. The team will ask these types of questions: What is unique about the surroundings where behaviors are not an issue? What is different in the locations where the problem conduct occurs? Could they be linked to how the child and teacher get along? Does the presence of other students or the amount of work a child is requested to do trigger the difficulty? Could the time of day or a child's frame of mind affect the behaviors? Was there a bus problem or an argument in the hallway? Are the behaviors likely to happen in a precise set of conditions or a specific location? What events seem to encourage the difficult behaviors?
4. Assemble data on the child's performance from as many resources as feasible. Develop a hypothesis about why difficult behaviors transpire. Ask what function the behaviors serve, what the child *gets* from the behaviors. A hypothesis is an educated deduction, based on data. It helps foretell in which location and for what reason problem behaviors are most or least likely to take place. Single out other behaviors that can be taught that will fulfill the same purpose for the child.
5. Test the hypothesis. The team develops and utilizes positive behavioral interventions that are written into the child's IEP or behavior intervention plan.

Assess the success of the interventions. Modify or fine tune as required.

If children have behaviors that place them or others at risk, they may require a crisis intervention plan. Crisis interventions should be developed before they are required. The team should determine what behaviors are crises and what they (and the child) will do in a crisis. By having a plan that guides actions, teachers can assist children through difficult emotional circumstances.

Essential Elements of a Behavior Intervention Plan

A Behavior Intervention Plan is utilized to reinforce or teach positive behavior skills. It is also known as a behavior support plan or a positive intervention plan. The child's team normally develops the Behavior Intervention Plan. The essential elements of a behavior intervention plan are as follows:

- skills training to increase the likelihood of appropriate behavior
- modifications that will be made in classrooms or other environments to decrease or remove problem behaviors
- strategies to take the place of problem behaviors and institute appropriate behaviors that serve the same function for the child
  support mechanisms to help the child use the most appropriate behaviors

The IEP team determines whether the school discipline procedures need to be modified for a child or whether the penalties need to be different from those written into the policy. This decision should be based on an assessment and a review of the records, including the discipline records or any manifestation determination review(s) that have been concluded by the school. A child's IEP or behavior intervention plan should concentrate on teaching skills. Sometimes school discipline policies are not successful in rectifying problem behaviors. That is, the child does not learn what the school staff intended through the use of punishments such as suspension. The child may learn instead that problem behaviors are useful in meeting a need, such as being noticed by peers. When this is true, it is difficult to defend punishment, by itself, as effective in changing problem behaviors.

One of the most useful questions educators can ask when they have concerns about the discipline recommendations for a child is: "Where is the data to support the recommendations?" Special education decisions are based on data. If school staff want to use a specific discipline procedure, they should check for data that support the use of the procedure.

Skill 4.5   Recognize the various concepts and models of positive behavior management.

There are advantages and disadvantages to using various types of reinforcers in the school setting. The four main types of reinforcers are edible, physical, social, and material (activities, objects, tokens).

Edible reinforcers are things that can be eaten, such as snack food, sweets, etc. The advantage of edible reinforcers is that they can be very powerful. They are frequently utilized when beginning to teach a new activity or when working with a student who is new to the teacher. The disadvantages of edible reinforcers are their cost and a possible loss of effectiveness if they are provided too frequently, as well as health issues that might preclude their use for certain students.

Physical reinforcers consist of appropriate physical contact. This reinforcement includes contact such as a gentle touch or hug, or a "high five" hand clap. The advantages to physical reinforcement is that it is always easily available and has been shown to achieve positive gains in young children. The disadvantage is that physical contact can be misconstrued or appear to be inappropriate. One must be cautious about physical contact with students and remember that appropriate contact depends on age, culture, and gender.

Material reinforcers consist of activities or objects given to a student after effectively carrying out an activity. One major advantage of material reinforcers is that they almost always guarantee quick behavioral change, even when other strategies fail. The disadvantage of material reinforcement is that they are often intrusive, and utilizing them effectively can take up large amounts of teacher time and commitment.

Social reinforcers take place the most naturally. They include smiles, praise, attention, and friendly comments. The advantage of social reinforcers is that a lot of behaviors are maintained by social reinforcers, as they are the most convenient and acceptable reinforcer. In addition, social reinforcers become internalized and students can become capable of internally reinforcing themselves. They make students less dependent on outside objects and sources. Social reinforcers should be provided every time another type of reinforcer is utilized. They are also the least invasive, as they mimic the natural consequences of positive behavior. Because they are convenient, practical, and highly effective, they are the most common reinforcers.

The disadvantage of social reinforcement is that effective praise generally is delivered privately. Public uses of praise, such as, "I like the way John is sitting so quietly," have numerous disadvantages. Such statements are normally used to manipulate children into following another child's example. In the example, the message was, "John is doing a better job of sitting than are the rest of you." Over a period of time, young children may start to resent this type of management and resent a child who is the constant recipient of such praise. In addition, in order to be effective, praise must be very individualized and specific (e.g., "You did a good job of spacing your letters neatly on the page," rather than simply," Good work!").

Motivation may be achieved through extrinsic reinforcers or intrinsic reinforcers. This is accomplished by allowing the student a degree of choice in what is being taught or how it will be taught. The teacher will, if possible, obtain a commitment either through a verbal or written contract between the student and the teacher. Adolescents also respond to regular feedback, especially when that feedback shows that they are making progress.

Dr. Glasser originally coined the term "Choice Theory" in 1998. It is an effective theory to use when teaching students and wanting them to achieve intrinsic motivation when learning. This concept can be further researched on the following website: http://www.wglasser.com/

Rewards for adolescents often include free time for listening to music, recreation, or games. They may like extra time for a break or exemption from a homework assignment. They may receive rewards at home for satisfactory performance at school. Other rewards include self-charting progress, and tangible reinforcers. Motivational activities may be used for goal-setting, self-recording of academic progress, self-evaluation, and self-reinforcement.

COMPETENCY 5.0   **KNOWLEDGE OF LANGUAGE DEVELOPMENT AND COMMUNICATION SKILLS**

Skill 5.1   **Identify the sequence of expressive and receptive language development and the components of language structure. Recognize the Normal Sequence of Language Development**

Language is the means whereby people communicate their thoughts, make requests, and respond to others. Communication competence is an interaction of cognitive competence, social knowledge, and language competence. Communication problems may result from any or all of these areas which directly impact the student's ability to interact with others. Language consists of several components, each of which follows a sequence of development.

Brown and colleagues were the first to describe language as a function of developmental stages rather than age (Reid, 1988 p 44). He developed a formula to group the mean length of utterances (sentences) into stages. Counting the number of morphemes per 100 utterances, one can calculate a mean length of utterance, MLU. Total number of morphemes / 100 = MLU e.g., 180/100 = 1.8.

A summary of Brown's findings about MLU and language development:

Stage	MLU	Developmental Features
I	1.0-2.0	• 12-26 months • 14 basic morphemes (e.g. in, on, articles, possessives)
II	2.0-2.5	• 27-30 months • Beginning of pronoun use, auxiliary verbs
III	2.5-3.0	• 31-34 months • Using questions and negative statements
IV	3.0-3.75	• 35-40 months • Use of complex (embedded) sentences
V	3.75-4.5	• 41-46 months • Use of compound

		sentences
V+	4.6+	• 47+ months • Strong command of language

Components of Language

Language learning is composed of five components. Children progress through developmental stages through each component. The five components are: phonology, morphology, syntax, semantics, and pragmatics.

Phonology

Phonology is the system of rules about sounds and sound combinations for a language. A phoneme is the smallest unit of sound that combines with other sounds to make words. A phoneme, by itself, does not have a meaning; it must be combined with other phonemes. Problems in phonology may be manifested as developmental delays in acquiring consonants or reception problems, such as misinterpreting words because a different consonant was substituted.

Morphology

Morphemes are the smallest units of language that convey meaning. Morphemes are root words, or free morphemes that can stand alone (e.g. walk), and affixes (e.g., -ed, -s, -ing). Morphology refers to the system of rules for combining morphemes into words. Content words carry the meaning in a sentence, and functional words join phrases and sentences. Generally, students with problems in this area may not use inflectional endings in their words, may not be consistent in their use of certain morphemes, or may be delayed in learning morphemes such as irregular past tenses.

Syntax

Syntax rules, commonly known as grammar, govern how morphemes and words are correctly combined. Wood (1976) describes six stages of syntax acquisition (Mercer, p 347).

- **Stages 1 and 2** - Birth to about 2 years: Child is learning the semantic system.
- **Stage 3** – Ages 2 – 3 years: Simple sentences contain subject and predicate.
- **Stage 4** - Ages 2 ½ to 4 years: Elements such as question words are added to basic sentences (e.g., where), word order is changed to ask questions. The child

begins to use "and" to combine simple sentences, and the child begins to embed words within the basic sentence.

- **Stage 5** - About 3 1/2 to 7 years: The child uses complete sentences that include word classes of adult language. The child is becoming aware of appropriate semantic functions of words and differences within the same grammatical class.
- **Stage 6** - About 5 to 20 years: The child begins to learn complex sentences and sentences that imply commands, requests, and promises.

Syntactic deficits are manifested by the child using sentences that lack length or complexity for a child that age. The child may have problems understanding or creating complex sentences and embedded sentences.

Semantics

Semantics is language content: objects, actions, and relations between objects. As with syntax, Wood (1976) outlines stages of semantic development:

- **Stage 1** - Birth to about 2 years: The child is discovering meaning while learning his first words. Sentences are one word, but the meaning varies according to the context. Therefore, "doggie" may mean, "This is my dog," or, "There is a dog," or "The dog is barking."
- **Stage 2** - About 2 to 8 years: The child progresses to two-word sentences about concrete actions. As more words are learned, the child forms longer sentences. Until about age 7, things are defined in terms of visible actions. The child begins to respond to prompts (e.g., pretty/flower), and at about age 8, the child can respond to a prompt with an opposite (e.g., pretty/ugly).
- **Stage 3** - Begins at about age 8: The child's word meanings relate directly to experiences, operations, and processes. Vocabulary is defined by the child's experiences, not the adult's. At about age 12, the child begins to give "dictionary" definitions, and the semantic level approaches that of adults.

Semantic problems take the form of:

- Limited vocabulary
- Inability to understand figurative language or idioms; interprets literally
- Failure to perceive multiple meanings of words or changes in word meaning from changes in context, resulting in an incomplete understanding of what is read
- Difficulty understanding linguistic concepts (e.g., before/after), verbal analogies, and logical relationships such as possessives, spatial, and temporal
- Misuse of transitional words such as "although" or "regardless"

Pragmatics

Commonly known as the speaker's intent, pragmatics are used to influence or control actions or attitudes of others. **Communicative competence** depends on how well one understands the rules of language, as well as the social rules of communication, such as taking turns and using the correct tone of voice.

Pragmatic deficits are manifested by failures to respond properly to indirect requests after age 8 (e.g., "Can't you turn down the TV?" elicits a response of "No" instead of "Yes" as the child turning down the volume). Children with these deficits have trouble reading cues that indicate the listener does not understand them. Whereas a person would usually notice this and adjust one's speech to the listener's needs, the child with pragmatic problems does not do this. Pragmatic deficits are also characterized by inappropriate social behaviors, such as interruptions or monopolizing conversations. Children may use immature speech and have trouble sticking to a topic. These problems can persist into adulthood, affecting academic, vocational, and social interactions.

Problems in language development often require long-term interventions and can persist into adulthood. Certain problems are associated with different grade levels:

Preschool and Kindergarten: The child's speech may sound immature, the child may not be able to follow simple directions and often cannot name things such as the days of the week and colors. The child may not be able to discriminate between sounds and the letters associated with the sounds. They might substitute sounds and have trouble responding accurately to certain types of questions. The child may play less with his peers or participate in non-play or parallel play.

Elementary School: Problems with sound discrimination persist, and the child may have problems with temporal and spatial concepts (e.g., before/after). As the child progresses through school, he may have problems making the transition from narrative to expository writing. Word retrieval problems may not be very evident because the child begins to devise strategies such as talking around the word he cannot remember or using fillers and descriptors. The child might speak more slowly, have problems sounding out words, and get confused with multiple-meaning words. Pragmatic problems show up in social situations, such as failure to correctly interpret social cues and adjust to appropriate language, inability to predict consequences, and inability to formulate requests to obtain new information.

Secondary School: At this level, difficulties become more subtle. The child lacks the ability to use and understand higher-level syntax, semantics, and pragmatics. If the child has problems with auditory language, he may also have problems with short-term memory. Receptive and/or expressive language delays impair the child's ability to learn effectively. The child often lacks the ability to organize the information received in school. Problems associated with pragmatic deficiencies persist, but because the child is aware of them, he becomes inattentive, withdrawn, or frustrated.

Skill 5.2   Identify communication deficits and select appropriate interventions

Syntactic deficits are manifested by the child using sentences that lack length or complexity for a child that age. The child may have problems understanding or creating complex sentences and embedded sentences.

Identify Students with Speech/Language Impairments

As a group, youngsters with speech and language impairments score below normal children on measures of intelligence, achievement, and adaptive social skills. However, this is in part attributable to the fact that a large percentage of children with mental, physical, behavioral, and learning disabilities exhibit speech and language disorders secondary to their major disability. Children with markedly deviant or delayed speech and language generally have concurrent difficulties with severe intellectual disabilities, chronic emotional/behavioral disturbances, or acute hearing problems, and function at a delayed developmental level.

Children with speech impairments who have no observable organic defects perform slightly lower than average on tests of motor proficiency. Problems are most likely to occur in the areas of coordination, application of strength, and rhythm. Children with communication disorders tend to demonstrate less interaction with peers.

In addition to these general characteristics, children with cleft palates tend to be underachieving and to show more personality problems (e.g., shyness, inhibition, and social withdrawal) than normal children. Children who with bad stutters exhibit anxiety and have low self-esteem.

Speech Disorders

Children with speech disorders are characterized by one or more of the following:

1. Unintelligible speech, or speech that is difficult to understand, and articulation disorders (distortions, omissions, substitutions).

2. Speech-flow disorders (sequence, duration, rate, rhythm, fluency).

3. Unusual voice quality (nasality, breathiness, hoarseness, pitch, intensity, quality disorders.

4. Peculiar physical mannerisms when speaking.

5. Obvious emotional discomfort when trying to communicate (particularly stutterers and clutterers).

6. Damage to nerves or brain centers which control muscles used in speech (dysarthria).

Language Disorders

Language disorders are often considered just one category of speech disorders, but the problem is really a separate one with different origins and causes. Language-disordered children exhibit one or more of the following characteristics.

1. Difficulty in comprehending questions, commands, or statements (receptive language problems).

2. Inability to adequately express their own thoughts (expressive language problems).

3. Language that is below the level expected for the child's chronological age (delayed language).

4. Interrupted language development (dysphasia).

5. Qualitatively different language.

6. Total absence of language (aphasia).

Understand What Constitutes Effective Communication Skills

Communication occurs when one person sends a message and gets a response from another person. In fact, whenever two people can see or hear each other, they are communicating. The sender is the person who communicates the message; the receiver is the person who ultimately responds to the message. Once the response is given, the receiver changes roles and becomes the sender. The communication process may break down if the receiver's interpretation differs from that of the sender.

Effective teaching depends on communication. By using good sending skills, the teacher has more assurance that she is getting her message across to her students. By being a model of a good listener, a teacher can help her students learn to listen and respond appropriately to others.

Attending Skills

Attending skills are used to receive a message. Some task-related attending skills that have been identified include: (1) looking at the teacher when information or instructions are being presented, (2) listening to assignment directions, (3) listening for answers to questions, (4) looking at the chalkboard, and (5) listening to others speak, when appropriate.

For some students, special techniques must be employed to gain and hold attention. For example, the teacher might first call the student by name when asking a question to assure attending by that individual, or she may ask the question before calling the name of a student to create greater interest. Selecting students at random to answer questions helps to keep them alert and listening. Being enthusiastic and keeping lessons short and interactive assists in maintaining the attention of those students who have shorter attention spans. Some students may be better able to focus their attention when environmental distractions are eliminated, or at least reduced, and non-verbal signals can be used to draw students' attention to the task. Finally, arranging the classroom so that all students can see the teacher helps direct attention to the appropriate location.

Clarity of Expression

Unclear communication between the teacher and special needs students sometimes contributes to problems in academic and behavioral situations. In the learning environment, unclear communication can add to the student's confusion about certain processes or skills he is attempting to master.

There are many ways in which the teacher can improve the clarity of her communication. Giving clear, precise directions is one. Verbal directions can be simplified by using shorter sentences, familiar words, and relevant explanations. Asking a student to repeat directions or to demonstrate understanding of them by carrying out the instructions is an effective way of monitoring the clarity of expression. In addition, clarification can be achieved by the use of concrete objects, multidimensional teaching aids, and by modeling or demonstrating what should be done in a practice situation.

Finally, a teacher can clarify her communication by using a variety of vocal inflections. The use of intonation juncture can help make the message clearer, as can pauses at significant points in the communication. For example, verbal praise should be spoken with inflection that communicates sincerity. Pausing before starting key words, or stressing those that convey meanings, helps students learn concepts being taught.

Paraphrasing

Paraphrasing, that is, restating what the student says using one's own words, can improve communication between the teacher and that student. First, in restating what the student has communicated, the teacher is not judging the content, she is simply relating what she understands the message to be. If the message has been interpreted differently from the way intended, the student is asked to clarify. Clarification should continue until both parties are satisfied that the message has been understood.

The act of paraphrasing sends the message that the teacher is trying to better understand the student. Restating the student's message as fairly and accurately as possible assists the teacher in seeing things from the student's perspective.

Paraphrasing is often a simple restatement of what has been said. Lead-ins such as, "Your position is…" or "It seems to you that…" are helpful in paraphrasing a student's messages. A student's statement of, "I am not going to do my math today," might be paraphrased by the teacher as, "Did I understand you to say that you are not going to do your math today?" By mirroring what the student has just said, the teacher has telegraphed a caring attitude for that student and a desire to respond accurately to his message.

To paraphrase effectively a student's message, the teacher should: (1) restate the student's message in her own words; (2) preface her paraphrasing with such remarks as, "You feel…" or "I hear you say that…"; and (3) avoid indicating any approval or disapproval of the student's statements. Johnson (1978) states the following as a rule to remember when paraphrasing: "Before you can reply to a statement, restate what the sender says, feels, and means correctly and to the sender's satisfaction." (p.139)

Descriptive feedback is a factual, objective (i.e., unemotional) recounting of a behavioral situation or message sent by a student. Descriptive feedback has the same effect as paraphrasing in that: (1) when responding to a student's statement, the teacher restates (i.e., paraphrases) what the student has said, or factually describes what she has seen, and (2) it allows the teacher to check her perceptions of the student and his message. A student may do or say something, but because of the teacher's feelings or state of mind, the student's message or behavior might be totally misunderstood. The teacher's descriptive feedback, which Johnson (1972) refers to as "understanding," indicates that the teacher's intent is to respond only to ask the student whether his statement has been understood, how he feels about the problem, and how he perceives the problem. The intent of the teacher is to more clearly "understand" what the student is saying, feeling, or perceiving in relation to a stated message or a behavioral event.

Evaluative feedback is verbalized perception by the teacher that judges, evaluates, approves, or disapproves of the statements made by the student. Evaluative feedback occurs when the student makes a statement and the teacher responds openly with, "I think you're wrong," "That was a dumb thing to do," or "I agree with you entirely." The tendency to give evaluative responses is heightened in situations where feelings and emotions are deeply involved. The stronger the feelings, the more likely it is that two persons will each evaluate the other's statements solely from his or her own point of view.

Since evaluative feedback intones a judgmental approval or disapproval of the student's remark or behavior; in most instances, it can be a major barrier to mutual understanding and effective communication. It is a necessary mechanism for providing feedback of a quantitative (and sometimes qualitative) instructional nature (e.g., test scores, homework results, classroom performance). In order to be effective, evaluative feedback must be offered in a factual, constructive manner. Descriptive feedback tends to reduce defensiveness and feelings of being threatened because it will most likely communicate that the teacher is interested in the student as a person, has an accurate understanding of the student and what he is saying, and encourages the student to elaborate and further discuss his problems.

To summarize, in the learning environment, as in all situations, effective communication depends upon good sending and receiving skills. Teaching and managing students involves good communication. By using clear, non-threatening feedback, the teacher can provide students with information that helps them to understand themselves better, while at the same time providing a clearer understanding of each student on the teacher's part.

Skill 5.3   Select strategies for integrating communication instruction into educational settings

Identify Activities for Strengthening Integrative Skills

The auditory, visual, and tactile modalities are the ones frequently used in the learning process. The strength of these modalities depends upon intact functioning of channels of communication through which stimuli are received (e.g., speech, writing, movement). A major difficulty in learning has been identified within the integrative (or association) process. Some information that is received requires storage, which involves the memory process. Other information necessitates the neurological process of conversion from one modality to another. That is, information received through one perceptual system must be transferred to or integrated with another sensory channel.

Problems in cross-model perception (or inter-sensory integration) are often discovered in the reading process, where visual symbols must correspond to phoneme sounds. The student who is unable to make this conversion can identify the letters but cannot associate them with their sound equivalents. Conversely, the student who has difficulty converting from the auditory to the visual modality is able to learn the sounds of letters but has problems associating sounds with corresponding graphemes (letter symbols). Another example of a deficit in cross-modal perception is that of planning and executing motor movements.

For instance, to speak, a student must convert auditory memory of words to a motor system in order to say the words. Associative tasks are completed thanks the brain, specifically the hippocampus (Suzuki, 2005), and the neural activity which occurs when students form memories. Techniques for strengthening associative tasks include the following activities from Lerner (1989). The suggested activities are categorized by integrative skills:

Visual Memory

1. *Identifying missing objects.* A collection of objects is shown. The collection is then covered while one object is removed. Again, the collection is shown, and the student is asked to identify the missing object. An alternative is to use an overhead projector, have students view designs or objects, remove one without students looking, and have them recall what is missing.
2. *Drawing from memory.* Following exposure of a simple design, have the student reproduce the design on paper. A variation would be to make a pattern of objects (i.e., beads, blocks). After viewing, have students reproduce the pattern from memory.
3. *Stories from pictures.* Pictures of activities that tell a story are placed on a flannel board. Remove the pictures and have the students recall the story based on their visual memory of the pictures.
4. *Enumerating see objects.* Students are asked to recall objects previously viewed (i.e., looking out window, taking a field trip).

Auditory Memory

1. *Do this.* Place several objects in front of the students and ask them to follow a series of directions. Gradually increase the number of objects.
2. *Number series.* Given a series of numbers, ask students to answer questions. For example, "Write the number closest to your age" (or first one, last one, fourth, largest, or smallest).

3. *Nursery rhymes.* The memorizing of rhymes, poems, and finger plays may be helpful.
4. *Films, videos.* Have students recall certain things, like countries shown or types of transportation.
5. *Going to the moon.* The teacher begins by saying, "I went on a trip to the moon and took my space suit." The first student repeats the statement and adds one item. Trips may be made to other destinations as a variation.
6. *Repetition of Sequences.* Read short sentences and have students repeat them. Advance from short, simple sentences to more complex clauses.

Cross-Modal Perception

1. *Visual to auditory.* Ask the student to look at a pattern of dots and dashes and translate them into rhythmical form.
2. *Auditory to visual.* Have the student listen to a rhythmical beat and select the matching visual pattern of dots and dashes, given several alternatives.
3. *Auditory to visual-motor.* Ask the student to listen to a rhythmical beat and transfer it to a visual form by writing corresponding dots and dashes.
4. *Auditory-verbal to motor.* Play a game like "Simon Says". Have the student listen to commands and transfer the commands to movements of body parts.
5. *Tactile to visual-motor.* Student is directed to feel shapes in a concealed container and draw the shapes on a piece of paper.
6. *Visual to auditory-verbal.* Have the child look at several pictures. Ask, "Which one begins with G? Which rhymes with toy?"
7. *Auditory-verbal to visual.* Describe a picture and have students select the picture from several alternatives presented.

Verbal and Nonverbal Communication

Not all communication is delivered in a verbal manner. Indeed, words spoken are not always true indicators of what a person means and feels. Non-verbal communication, such as body language, facial expression, tone of voice, and speaking patterns, are all clues to the underlying message the student is attempting to deliver. The teacher demonstrates her willingness to listen by sitting close, leaning forward, making eye contact, and showing understanding and acknowledgement by nodding or smiling. By so doing, she is sending the message that she cares, is concerned about the student's feelings, and will take the time necessary to understand what is really being communicated.

To facilitate further communication, the teacher must become an active listener. This involves much more than just restating what the person has said. Her responses must reflect the student's feelings rather than the spoken language. It is essential that the teacher say back what she understands the student's message to mean, as well as the feelings she perceives, and asks for correctness of interpretation. Often, teachers enter into active listening, with body language conveying a willingness to listen, but respond in such a way that judgment or disapproval of the underlying message is conveyed. Evaluative responses from the listener will decrease attempts to communicate. Encouragement toward communicative efforts is enhanced by use of statements rather than questions, when spoken in the present tense and with use of personal pronouns, when reflective of current feelings about the situation, and when offering self-disclosure of similar experiences or feelings if the teacher feels inclined to do so.

Response to the child's feelings is particularly important since his message may not convey what he really feels. For example, a student who has failed a test may feel inadequate and have the need to blame someone else, such as his teacher, for his failure. The student might say to his teacher, "You didn't tell me that you were including all the words from the last six weeks on the spelling test." The teacher, if she were to respond solely to the spoken message, might say, "I know I told you that you would be tested over the entire unit. You just weren't listening!" The intuitive, sensitive teacher would look beyond the spoken words by saying, "You're telling me that it feels bad to fail a test." By responding to the child's feelings, the teacher lets him know her understanding of his personal crisis, and the student is encouraged to communicate further.

Skill 5.4   Select appropriate assistive technology and alternative communication systems to facilitate communication

Augmentative communication devices help individuals produce and understand speech. The technology can range from a board with pictures representing a student's daily needs to sophisticated electronic speech synthesizers. Speech output devices may be simply devices for storing and playing back prerecorded speech or may be true speech synthesizers that use segments of words to produce words. Computers can be equipped with speech synthesizers, and there are portable electronic devices that can produce speech as well.

After the initial assessment, one of the primary tasks is to select the most appropriate Augmentative Alternative Communication (AAC) devices that can be utilized by an individual student.

The first step is to eliminate systems that are not appropriate. Then, it is recommended that the student experiment with one or more AAC systems that appear suitable. The device should be tested by the student for several weeks to evaluate how well the student can use it, how it fits into the settings and activities that make up an average day, and whether or not the child and his family like the communication system.

Unexpected problems or issues may arise when a system is actually being learned and used by the child in regular environments. It is important to keep in mind that students often do not know how, or will even resist using AAC, because it is unfamiliar and may feel invasive. Based on this, if a student does not successfully master the equipment during the trial, this does not mean that the system is not the appropriate one or that the child will never use it.

Communication requirements are different dependent upon the situations, so it is important to have multiple communication models available. It is also crucial to focus on the student's communication goals and the teaching methods that will be used for implementing the communication system.

Everyone in the IEP team should be involved in selecting the appropriate communication mode, with the child and the parents' desires receiving the highest weight in the decision-making process.

The primary categories of Augmentative Alternative Communication modes are as follows:

Graphical communication boards are the use of pictures, drawings, abstract symbols, and text as symbols. Some examples include communication books or wallets or vests that are utilized by pointing, switches, eye gaze, touching, scanning, or indicating to an adult. The symbols on a graphical system may be represented visually, auditorily, and tactually. Graphical communication boards systems tend to be inexpensive and can be made by hand.

Eye gaze techniques are one method of accessing a low- or no-technology AAC system. They can be utilized to indicate real objects directly or symbols on a communication board. Children with severe motor disabilities frequently utilize them. The primary advantage of eye gaze techniques over other methodologies is speed and efficiency of communication. One of the primary disadvantages is that they require considerable effort from the partner to decipher precisely what the child is looking at.

Voice Output Communication Aids (VOCAs) are also graphical systems, but, unlike communication boards, are high technology devices that output speech. VOCA refers to a dedicated electronic speech apparatus. Computers can also fall under this category, as they can also be utilized as speech output devices. In some cases, cassette tape recorders can achieve the same goals as a voice output communication aid. VOCAs vary considerably in their flexibility. They can range from a single message model to a sophisticated model with a large amount of memory and the ability to store an unlimited amount of messages. Vocabulary has to be programmed into the unit, which can be done partially by the manufacturer or entirely by the owner of the unit.

Sign language entails the use of consistent finger and/or hand movements and may consist of conventional (e.g., American Sign Language) and idiosyncratic sign languages (e.g., signs that the child has made up which are understood by family members).

Gestures are physical movements that are cruder than signs, using entire arm or body movements. In many cases, a child's gesturing is created by themselves; however, there are conventional gesturing systems which can be taught in a formal setting.

Speech consists of spoken words that are understandable to at least one other person.

Vocalizations are sounds created by the throat and mouth that are not words or approximations of words, but are able to be utilized for communication reliably.

Concrete objects are tangible objects that are used as symbols for other objects or activities. They may be whole, miniature, or partial objects and are indicated by being pointed to, reached for, touched, or held.

In addition, computer software now available can significantly assist students with certain language disabilities in both reading and writing.

- Talking Word Processing Program with Spell Check: These programs are helpful for students who cannot visually identify the correct word on a traditional spell check program. The talking feature allows the student to "listen" for the correct spelling of the word.

- Talking Word Processor Software: These programs provide feedback by reading aloud what the student has typed in, allowing the student to hear what he has written. This type of multisensory feedback assists the student in identifying and correcting errors.

- Word Prediction Software: This type of software is beneficial for students who have difficulty with spelling and grammar, or with memory and word finding skills. As the first letter or letters of a word are typed in, the computer predicts the word the student is typing. This type of technology is of benefit to students who type slowly as it reduces the number of keystrokes needed to complete a word.

- Voice Recognition Software: This type of software has gained in popularity in recent years due to its wide commercial applications. Voice recognition allows the student to "speak" into the computer and the spoken word is translated into written text on the computer screen.

Skill 5.5   Identify the sequence of typical reading development (e.g., prereading level, learning to read, reading to learn) and the critical components of reading development (e.g., phonological awareness, phonics, fluency, vocabulary, comprehension)

Stages of Reading

Many students follow a typical pattern of initial reading behaviors as they learn to understand turning the pages of a book and pretend reading. As early as toddlerhood, children can identify letters and sounds, and will eventually read by ages four to seven. There are distinct stages for when reading truly unfolds, and the five are delineated below (Dorn & Soffos, 2001).

- Awareness and Exploration of Reading Stage (typically pre-K)
- Emergent Reading Stage (typically pre-K to early Kindergarten)
- Early Reading Stage (typically Kindergarten to early Grade 1)
- Transitional Reading Stage (typically late Grade 1 to Grade 2)
- Fluent Reading Stage (typically Grade 3 and higher)

Strategies that exist to help students who struggle in any of the five stages vary widely. Some investigators hypothesize that strategies for dealing with the letters in words may be relevant (Chall, 1983; Ehri, 1979; Walsh, Price, & Gillingham, 1988). Others hypothesize more general deficits, such as coordination, or some combination of factors (Bauer, 1987; Nicolson & Fawcett, 1990; Shankweiler & Crain, 1986; Tallal & Stark, 1982). It is evident that early intervention, early exposure to text, and read-alouds are critical to the foundation of a student's reading abilities.

As stated on the Florida Center for Reading Research website (www.fcrr.org), research has repeatedly demonstrated the importance of initial instruction that includes the five critical components of reading: Phonological Awareness, Phonics, Fluency, Vocabulary, and Comprehension. To be most effective, the five critical components need to be taught explicitly within classrooms that are strongly positive and engaging, use writing activities to support literacy, and provide students with many opportunities to read interesting text and complete authentic reading and writing assignments. Teachers typically follow a core reading curriculum to guide instruction in whole and small group settings.

Small group instruction should be individualized to reflect the instructional needs of the students. Individual student needs are determined by formal screening and progress monitoring assessments, classroom assessments, and teacher observations. The goal is to use information from multiple sources to group students in a way that makes instruction in critical reading skills most efficient.

Differentiated and guided modes of instruction are imperative when teaching reading and reading strategies. Differentiation must occur on the classroom, small group, and individualized level. Guided reading methods are equally as important, and lesson plans should tailor both types of instruction in order to reach students effectively. Please refer to the Guidance Document for Florida Reading First Schools, "Differentiated Reading Instruction: Small Group Alternative Lesson Structures for All Students: http://www.fcrr.org/assessment/pdf/smallgroupalternativelessonstructures.pdf

Five Essential Components of Reading

Under Reading First (Title I, Part B, Subpart 1), district and school reading programs for K-3 students must include instruction, curriculum, and assessment on:

1. **Phonemic Awareness**—the knowledge and manipulation of sounds in spoken words.
2. **Phonics**—the relationship between written and spoken letters and sounds.
3. **Reading Fluency, including oral reading skills**—the ability to read with accuracy, and with appropriate rate, expression, and phrasing.
4. **Vocabulary development**—the knowledge of words, their definitions, and context.
5. **Reading Comprehension Strategies**—the understanding of meaning in text.

Source: http://lrs.ed.uiuc.edu/students/jblanton/read/5essential.htm

All reading programs used in schools must be based on scientific research. Reading assessments are to be implemented, including screening, instructional, and diagnostic reading assessments. Teachers should also participate in professional development pertaining to reading. Building student motivation and integrating technology whenever possible is also highly encouraged.

Please refer to Skill 5.1 for further information.

Skill 5.6   **Identify the terminology and concepts of literacy development (e.g., oral language, phonological awareness, concepts about print, alphabet knowledge, decoding, vocabulary, text structures, written language, motivation)**

Although some of these terms and concepts are discussed in more detail in other sections, a brief definition and overview of each is presented here.

Alphabetic Principle: This is the concept that spoken words are represented by specific written symbols (letters), and conversely, that letters stand for specific (if often variable) sounds. The National Children's Reading Foundation points out that the *ability to acquire reading skills* is hard wired into the brain, but *actually acquiring them* requires both early exposure to print and explicit instruction. Learning **phonics**, or the specific letter-sound code for English, is critical to learning to read. Numerous summaries of reading research, including those of the International Reading Association (1997), The National Institute of Child Health and Human Development (2000), the National Reading Panel Report on Teaching Children to Read (2002), and the National Institute for Early Education Research (2006), have documented the importance of phonics as a significant part of any reading program.

Decoding: This is both a skill and a process by which the reader translates written symbols (letters of the alphabet) into the words which make up our language. It includes translating letters and combinations of letters into the sounds of our language, as well as using other semantic and syntactic knowledge to translate letters into words and words into sentences. This process and skill is critical to the ability to read. Before meaning can be constructed from printed letters, the letters must be translated (decoded) into words.

Motivation: Burns, Roe, and Smith (2002) define motivation as an incentive to act, the willingness to perform. With regard to reading, motivation refers to the student's incentive or willingness to work to learn the skills necessary to learn to read. A student's motivation can be intrinsically or extrinsically based. Intrinsic motivation is an internal drive by the student who aspires to do his/her best in school, or who has a personal desire to learn to read. This tends to be based in prior learning and conditioning.

For example, children whose parents have frequently read to them, for whom the reading process was an interesting and positive experience, children who see adults and older children enjoy reading, who see how reading can be useful to them in concrete ways, will be more highly motivated to learn to read than children who have not had these experiences. However, even when children have not had these home experiences, skillful teachers can increase motivation by establishing bonds with students and demonstrating confidence and reasonably high expectations in students.

Extrinsic motivation may be as simple as a student wanting to do well in order to carry home a good report card or get privileges that accompany success. In elementary school it is often helpful to provide additional extrinsic rewards, such as sticker charts or tiny rewards. Students with a history of learning difficulties, who have seldom experienced success in school may need such extrinsic rewards in order to become successful.

Oral Language: Spoken language. The development of language and oral language were discussed in detail in section 5.5.

Phonological Awareness: Flippo (2002) states that phonological awareness "refers to an awareness of *many* aspects of spoken language, including words within sentences, syllables within words, and phonemes within syllables and words..." **Phoneme awareness** is one part of phonological awareness, and is the understanding that spoken words are composed of tiny, individual sound units, called phonemes. Children need a strong background in phonemic awareness in order for phonics instruction (sound-spelling relationships in print) to be effective.

The National Reading Panel (2000) specified six phoneme awareness skills crucial to learning to read:

- Phoneme isolation: recognizing individual sounds (/g/ and /O/ in "go")
- Phoneme identification: Recognizing common sounds in different words (/b/ in boy, bike, and bell)
- Phoneme categorization: recognizing sounds in sequence (bus, bun, rug)
- Phoneme blending: hearing a series of individual phonemes, then blending them into a word (hearing /g/ /O/ and saying "go")
- Phoneme segmentation: separating and counting out the sounds in a word (given "go" saying /g/ and /O/)
- Phoneme deletion: recognizing what would be left if one phoneme is removed (hear "flat" and remove the /f/ sound and state that "lat" would be left)

Print Concepts: In *On Solid Ground*, Taberski (2000) 10 basic concepts about print that children need to understand before they can learn to read:

- Print conveys meaning
- the message remains constant through repeated readings
- print moves from left to right
- print moves from top to bottom
- what a letter is
- what a word is
- there are first letters and last letters in words
- you can choose upper or lower case for letters
- there are spaces between words
- different punctuation marks have meaning

Children who have experienced a lot of family reading and read alouds will often pick up many of these concepts before arriving at school. Others will need to be explicitly taught these concepts.

Text Structures: Like oral language, text language has a form and structure, common organization features and convention that can help with comprehension if the reader recognizes and understands them. Text structures include very basic features such as periods and capitals marking the endpoints of sentences, basic punctuation signals, and paragraph concepts such as main ideas being expressed in topic sentences. More advanced text structures include such things as the hierarchical nature of chapter and section headings, captions for illustrations and diagrams, the ordinal nature of the table of contents and the alphabetic organization of the index, glossaries, and reference sections. It also includes the various types and styles of overall organization of ideas, such as cause and effect, chronological, and collection texts. These concepts and methods of teaching them are covered in more detail in section 3.9.

Vocabulary: This term refers to the precise meaning of words, particularly meaning in various contexts. Burns, et al (2002) point out that children acquire vocabulary at a very rapid rate during elementary school years. Early vocabulary development begins with differentiating antonyms, then generalizing (and overgeneralizing) key words without using more accurate synonyms or related words (calling any machine that moves a car, for example). Later vocabulary development includes understanding multiple meaning words, homonyms, synonyms, and more abstract definitions. Still later, children learn the specialized, often technical vocabulary of various content areas (understanding that the word, "line" has a much different meaning in math than in daily use, for example). Since word meaning is variable and fluid, often depending upon context, vocabulary skills are a key part of any reading instruction.

Written Language: Just as the act of reading involves both decoding the print and comprehending its meaning, the act of writing involves both the *composition and organization* of ideas, and the *encoding* of those ideas into print in order to communicate with the reader. These are two very different skills, and many children with learning disabilities will be quite capable of one and severely disabled with the other. Reading and writing are two sides of the same coin, and each can be used to help learn the other. The writing process usually includes prewriting, drafting, revising, editing and publishing or illustrating. Since writing is a more formal skill than oral language, the conventions are slightly different. Many times students write the same way they speak, which is usually unacceptable for written language. The editing process is probably the most effective method for helping students achieve improved use of grammar, spelling, syntax, and semantics. Peer editing and teacher editing provide excellent tools for students

Skill 5.7   **Identify the characteristics and purposes of various reading programs (e.g., core reading program, supplemental reading program, intensive intervention program)**

RTI Model

Response to Intervention (RTI) is a model of instruction described by the Florida Center for Reading Research (FCCR-2006) as a three tier "model for organizing and delivering early reading instruction in elementary schools." Its purpose is to "organize school resources so students that struggle the most can receive timely and intensive intervention before being identified for special education services." Below is a visual example of the RTI Model retrieved from www.scholastic.com :

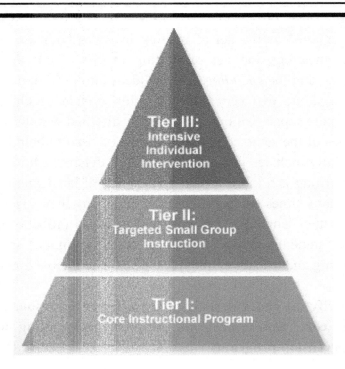

Core Reading Program

A Core Reading Program (often referred to as a Basal Reading Program) is the basic foundation for reading instruction in general education classes. It is usually a commercially published program chosen by the school system. Such a program is designed to meet the reading needs of *most of the students.* This program is provided during the first "tier" of instruction, in which all students participate. According to the Florida Center for Reading Research, an effective core program should include:

- Research-based instructional strategies that explicitly teach strategies and skills;
- Systematic and sequential instruction that moves children from simple to more complex skills and strategies;
- Ample practice opportunities that allow children to practice skills and strategies in reading and writing text;
- A minimum 90 minute or more uninterrupted block of time for reading instruction per day;
- Assessment tools for diagnosing children's needs and monitoring progress; and

Provide professional development that will ensure teachers have the skills necessary to implement the program effectively and meet the needs of their children

Supplemental Reading Program

Even the most effective core program will not reach all students. Some students will need additional help, and supplemental intervention programs are designed to provide that help in one of the five critical areas of reading instruction: phonemic awareness, phonics, fluency, vocabulary, or comprehension. The intent is that these programs can be used to differentiate reading instruction in a general education setting, either through small group or individual work with the teacher or through additional staff assistance. This assistance is provided in a second "tier" through which extra reading assistance is provided daily. The FCCR has a helpful pamphlet with includes parameters and names of such reading programs on the following PDF link: http://www.fcrr.org/science/pdf/arndt/AA_Summer_Institute_July_2007.pdf

Intensive Intervention Programs

Intensive Intervention Programs are designed for students with more severe reading difficulties in a broad range of reading skills. This is usually a much smaller group of students who have been diagnosed as two years or more behind grade level in reading. These programs provide intensive instruction in all five critical areas of reading instruction and typically involve an additional half hour of instruction for children in "tier 3." These programs are designed to be "more intensive, more explicit, more systematic, and more motivating," according to the FCCR (2006).

Skill 5.8   Identify characteristics of reading difficulties

Most reading difficulties fall into one of four broad categories. Some students may, of course, exhibit more than one kind of reading difficulty. The specific instructional techniques and modifications each student needs will depend upon the specific problem.

- Reading/Decoding problems affect the child's ability to identify or remember words and are usually based in difficulties with the sound-letter code. These are problems with the mechanics of reading words and sentences. They impact all aspects of reading, including comprehension if the child is required to decode on his/her own. Children with serious decoding issues expend so much effort decoding, they have nothing left for understanding what is being read. On the other hand, a child with decoding problems may have no difficulty comprehending material read to him/her.
- Reading comprehension problems limit the child's ability to understand and recall what she/he has read. Such a child may be able to decode or read the words correctly, but does not understand them. This child does not understand when

material is read to her/him, either. These problems are based in meaning and abstract inferences.

- Writing/Encoding problems limit the child's ability to correctly spell and write the words he/she wants to use. Often such children cannot spell phonetically and cannot read their own writing after they are finished with it. They may, however, be quite good at composing ideas and organizing the concepts; they just can't write them down. Their problem is with the mechanics of writing.

- Writing/Composing problems involve limitations in the ability to construct sentences, frame or organize ideas, find the right words to use, or communicate verbally or in writing what the child wants to say. These children may be able to carry out the physical act of writing well, have good handwriting, and be able to spell and capitalize well. Their problem is with the content of the message, rather than the mechanics.

Dyslexia

Many students with reading disabilities will have been diagnosed with some form of Dyslexia. Dyslexia is a language learning disorder that is often based on difficulties with phonological awareness and processing. Common symptoms included difficulty decoding words, poor fluency, poor writing and spelling, and sometimes comprehension difficulties as well. These difficulties are present in spite of normal intelligence and instructional methods. The national Association of Special Education Teachers (NASET) Learning Disabilities Report #3 (2008) describes a variety of types of Dyslexia cited by the American Academy of Special Education Professionals' Educator's Diagnostic Manual of Disabilities and Disorders (2007):

- **Direct Dyslexia:** Characterized by the ability of the individual to read words aloud correctly, without comprehension.

- **Dyseidesia Dyslexia:** Characterized by poor sight-word vocabularies, a reliance on time consuming word attack skills (a phonetic approach) for decoding, resulting in labored and inaccurate decoding and poor, though often phonetic, spelling.

- **Dyseidetic Dyslexia:** Characterized by the ability to sound out individual letters phonetically without understanding patterns of letters in groups, as well as deficits in vision and memory of letters and word shapes, making it difficult for them to develop a sight vocabulary.

- **Dyslexia with Dysgraphia** (*Deep Dyslexia*): Characterized by the physical act of writing, as well as understanding word-meanings, phonics, and pronunciation.

- **Dyslexia without Dysgraphia** (*Pure Dyslexia*): Characterized by reading problems without accompanying writing difficulties, and often nearly normal oral language and even oral spelling abilities. It is sometimes accompanied by difficulties with written, though not oral, arithmetic.

- **Dysnemkinesia Dyslexia:** Characterized by minimal dysfunction in the part of the motor cortex responsible for letter formation, and showing the characteristic letter reversals, such as d for b, as in doy for boy.

- **Dysnomia:** Characterized by difficulties in naming and naming speed.

- **Dysphonetic Dyslexia:** Characterized by difficulty relating letters to sounds, and chaotic spelling, though they may have good sight-word recognition and be able to read at near grade level.

- **Literal Dyslexia** (*Letter Blindness*): Characterized by difficulty recognizing letters, particularly in different forms, such as upper case letters with lowercase, as well as naming letters or matching sounds with the corresponding letters.

- **Mixed Reading Disability Dyslexia** (*Alexic Reading Disability*): Includes both the dyseidetic and dysphonic types of reading disorder, and may involve difficulty in both sight vocabulary and phonetic skills. People with this form of dyslexia are usually unable to read or spell.

- **Neglect Dyslexia:** A condition caused by neglect, especially noticeable when reading long words, where the beginning or the end is typically omitted.

- **Phonological Dyslexia:** Characterized by difficulty decoding the sounds of letters in unfamiliar words, as well as decoding nonsense words such as dord.

- **Primary Dyslexia:** Characterized by a dysfunction of, rather than damage to, the left side of the brain (cerebral cortex) that does not change with maturity resulting in an inability to read above a fourth-grade level; often hereditary in nature and found more often in boys than girls.

- **Semantic Dyslexia:** Characterized by distortions of word meaning, such reading a word as its antonym or synonym, or substitution of a related word, particularly with function words such as *of*, *an*, *not*, and *and*.

- **Spelling Dyslexia:** Characterized by difficulty reading all types of words, as well as identifying individual letters, and reading that is choppy and slow even on simple words.

- **Surface Dyslexia:** Characterized by the ability to read words phonetically but poor sight word recognition.

- **Trauma Dyslexia:** Often caused by brain damage and usually classified as Traumatic Brain Injury (TBI) rather than LD.

- **Visual Dyslexia:** Characterized by the inability to learn words as a whole, and visual discrimination, memory synthesis, and sequencing difficulties, as well as word and letter reversals.

History of Dyslexia

Though there is truly a long, arduous past for those with visible special needs and mental challenges, the history of dyslexia is a bit more scientifically driven from the very beginnings of the disorder's naming. Dyslexics were not cast away, but were not readily identified until the nineteenth century. This is perhaps due to the high illiteracy rate among much of humankind throughout the world up until the point of the industrial revolution, when suddenly, reading became a marketable skill for those who wanted to become lawyers, doctors, businessmen, and the like.

Prior to this, writing or scribing, as well as reading, were highly specific skills. Priests and trained scholars were readers and writers - not the majority of the population by any means. It was not commonplace for the average working man, and especially the woman, to ever need the skill of reading, or even writing. Early school houses served rudimentary curriculums for students who were not required to show up to class regularly for any set amount of years or skill levels. Many professionals were self-reliant, and reading was not necessary to be a farmer, or a homesteader, or an indentured servant. For centuries upon centuries, education was for the elite, the upper-class, and nobility..

Dyslexia's identification dates back to 1869 when Sir Francis Galton, a psychologist, started to look into the individual differences in children's learning abilities. At that time, educators and psychologists were not investigating the causes of childhood learning difficulties. In fact, public schools were just barely beginning to form in the United States, as America slowly shifted from the one-room, multi-aged school house model. Medical professionals were the people who treated learning difficulties, if at all, because learning problems were considered a medical condition.

By 1878. Adolph Kussmaul, a German neurologist, began the first recorded study of people with reading difficulties. He felt there was an underlying neurological impairment. He noted his patients wrote and read words 'in the wrong order' and he used the term 'word blindness' to label the problem.

In 1891, Dr. Dejerne wrote an article in the Lancet journal and reported a story of one his patients, who suffered brain injury after being struck in the head by a crowbar. Dr. Dejerne claimed his patient could no longer read, and the patient lost other language functions as well. It was now believed that people with difficulty reading had some form of brain damage or brain injury.

In the 1930s, dyslexia appeared often in professional literature and by 1967, the Orton Dyslexia Society began. The main goal of the Society was to raise public awareness and describe the remedial needs of dyslexics.

The US Department of Education recognized dyslexia as a disorder or disability in 1994. Professionals still used the term 'dyslexia' and 'specific learning difficulties', although dyslexia was now specifically acknowledged. In 1997 the Orton Dyslexia Society changed its name to the International Dyslexia Association because they dealt with dyslexia across the globe and not just in the US.

Skill 5.9   Identify and select prevention and intervention methods for addressing reading difficulties

Teachers are at something of a disadvantage in *preventing* reading difficulties, since so much of the foundation for reading development is typically laid *before* the child gets to school. The National Institute for Early Education Research (NIEER) included described the following factors in its Preschool Policy Brief (2006):

- **Experiences with print (through reading and writing) help preschool children develop an understanding of the conventions, purpose and functions of print.** Children learn about print from a variety of sources, and in the process, come to realize that print carries the story. They also learn how text is structured visually (i.e., text begins at the top of the page, moves from left to right and carries over to the next page when it is turned). While knowledge about the conventions of print enables children to understand the physical structure of language, the conceptual knowledge that printed words convey a message also help children bridge the gap between oral and written language. Many of these concepts are developed at home when parents read to children.

- **Knowledge of the alphabet and the ability to discriminate among the alphabetic symbols** contribute to initial reading acquisition by helping children develop efficient word recognition strategies.

- **Opportunities to write and draw** both for self-expression and in response to questions prepare children for communicating through the written word. The child who has had many such opportunities at home has a significant advantage in learning to read and write in school.

- **Storybook reading and extensive early literacy experiences** prepare children for learning basic reading strategies. This factor is one of the most influential and well-documented factors affecting acquisition of reading skills.

Since, children arrive in class with differing levels of experience with storybook reading and different degrees of experience with print, literacy, writing, and drawing, the teacher is often required to "level the field" by providing remedial literacy experiences for those whose background does not contain them.

This means that the teacher will need to provide a "print-rich" environment and many daily opportunities for reading, drawing, and writing experiences both individually and as a group. Reading aloud to students, Big Books and guided reading and writing are important stepping stones.

In order to provide each child with what they need to develop their reading ability, however, it is first necessary to know what each child's level of reading readiness and ability are. Skills 2 and 3.1 discuss assessment in great detail. Accurate assessment of what the child does and does not know is crucial to both preventing and intervening in reading difficulties.

Skill 5.7 discusses a school wide method of addressing reading difficulties through an RTI model. Skills below, including 5.11 through 5.16 discuss approaches for specific types of reading problems.

Regardless of the overall approach taken, the individual teacher should keep in mind that, as mentioned in Skill 5.8, reading difficulties typically fall into one of four broad areas: 1) Reading/decoding problems often based in phonological awareness difficulties, 2) Reading Comprehension problems, 3) Writing/Encoding problems with spelling and writing mechanics, and 4) Writing composition difficulties generating ideas, organizing them and recalling words for expressing them.

One of the best overall strategies for developing instructional interventions for students with severe disabilities in these areas is to *separate* these areas in your plans. Design instruction that *targets only one of them at a time* and assessments that assess only one at a time. Of course, eventually, the goal is to get the two levels back together. However, some children have such severe learning disabilities related to literacy that they will always struggle with some aspect of reading. The goal, then, is to be sure that the disability in one area does not limit the child's demonstration of ability in another.

For example, separate the decoding piece from comprehension for the student who cannot decode by teaching decoding at one level and comprehension at another. Conduct decoding lessons using materials appropriate to the child's decoding level, but target higher level comprehension abilities through books on CD, iPad, Kindle, computer, or other electronic media. The teacher can integrate the two areas by designing special decoding pieces that relate the current decoding lesson to words taken from the CD, sound file, video, or other electronic media. Another method is to select reading materials that deliver higher level comprehension strategies through selections written at a more easily decoded level, one that follows appropriate decoding sequences. Software discussed in Skill 5.4 can also be helpful.

For a student who can decode but struggles with comprehension modifications, the strategies discussed in Skill 5.15 can help. If the child has difficulty encoding (spelling) or with the physical act of writing, but can compose ideas and sentences well, it is usually best to separate composition from encoding by letting the child use some form of dictation for the composition and organization part of writing, then dictating back to the child to provide encoding practice. This allows the child to demonstrate his/her ability to compose and communicate independently of the ability to associate sounds and letters. For the child who can encode well, who spells well but cannot find the right words or organize thoughts, graphic organizers and software for organizing writing, such word prediction software, can be very useful.

In 2000, the National Reading Panel released its now well-known report on teaching children to read. This report side-stepped the debate between phonics and whole-language approaches and argued, essentially, that both letter-sound recognition and comprehension of the text are important in successful reading. It identified five critical areas of reading instruction, as explained earlier: phonemic awareness, phonics, fluency, vocabulary, and comprehension.

Methods used to teach these skills are often featured in a "balanced literacy" curriculum that focuses on the use of skills in various instructional contexts. For example, with independent reading, students independently choose books that are at their reading levels; with guided reading, teachers work with small groups of students to help them with their particular reading problems; with whole group reading, the entire class will read the same text and the teacher will incorporate activities to help students learn phonics, comprehension, fluency, and vocabulary. In addition to these components of balanced literacy, teachers incorporate writing so that students can learn the structures of communicating through text.

Skill 5.10   **Identify the early phases of word recognition within the decoding process (e.g., pre-alphabetic, partial-alphabetic, full-alphabetic, consolidated-alphabetic)**

Ehri and others at the Graduate Center, City University of New York, have outlined 5 stages of learning to decode words in reading. These stages are not considered universal, nor are they "hard-wired" into the brain, but the model can be useful in conceptualizing a child's progress in decoding and in helping students at various stages of decoding development. Ehri and McCormick (1998) and Ehri (1999) provide a table of these stages with detailed descriptions of the characteristics of each, and McLoughlin and Lewis (2001) enhance this information be providing lists of published assessments that can be used at each stage.

A brief overview of Ehri's stages is provided below:

It should be noted that prior to these phases, Ehri sees the child as engaged in acquiring phonemic awareness, as discussed in similarly in Skill 5.6. Without this awareness, the child will not be able to move smoothly through these stages of decoding ability.

1. **Pre-alphabetic phase** (also called the logographic phase): Children respond to words as visual gestalts in context by memorizing their visual features. They do not yet understand phoneme/letter correspondence. They might recognize the word "stop" inside the usual hexagon shaped sign, but not recognize it in connected text.

2. **Partial-alphabetic phase** (also called the rudimentary alphabetic stage): Children can recognize and name some letters of the alphabet and apply sounds to many of the consonants. They can use this knowledge along with the visual and context cues from stage one to remember more words and identify them in different

contexts. They can do some invented spelling using the sounds of the words, but don't recognize common spelling patterns.

3. **Full-alphabetic phase** (also called the spelling-sound phase): Children have a good understanding of the graphophonemic system and fully grasp the connection between graphemes and phonemes. They can decode letter by letter and spell phonetically (i.e., their spelling is reasonable and their words, even when misspelled, are recognizable). They can decode unfamiliar words and store sight words in memory.

4. **Consolidated-alphabetic phase** (also called orthographic phase): Children tend to see words as whole units and use all their decoding skills in unison to decode unfamiliar words. This grouping of units allows them to decode multi-syllable words and decode words by analogy (if i can read 'bang' I can read 'hang'). At this stage they can also use such things as prefixes and suffixes as clues to decoding new words.

5. **Automatic phase:** At this phase, the child's decoding has reached a state of automaticity where word-level reading predominates, and reading is fluent and comprehension rivals that of listening comprehension. That is, so little effort is needed to decode that the reader can understand the material as easily as if someone is reading it to them.

In order to successfully help students move from one phase to another, it is necessary for the teacher to understand where each child 's abilities lie on this continuum of skills in decoding, then to provide the instruction and literacy experiences appropriate to that level. Much of differentiated instruction will center on these phases in early elementary school.

Skill 5.11   Identify explicit and systematic instructional methods for promoting the development of phonological and phonemic awareness

Phonological Awareness "refers to an awareness of *many* aspects of spoken language, including words within sentences, syllables within words, and phonemes within syllables and words…" (Flippo, 2002). Phoneme awareness is one part of phonological awareness, and is the understanding that spoken words are composed of tiny, individual sound units, called phonemes.

The key in phonemic awareness is that it can be taught with the students' eyes closed. In other words, it's all about sounds, not about ascribing written letters to sounds. To be phonemically aware means that the reader and listener can recognize and manipulate specific sounds in **spoken** words. Phonemic awareness deals with sounds in words that are spoken. The majority of phonemic awareness tasks, activities, and exercises are, therefore, oral.

Since the ability to distinguish between individual phonemes within words is a prerequisite to association of sounds with letters and manipulating sounds to blend words—a fancy way of saying "reading"—the teaching of phonemic awareness is crucial to emergent literacy (early childhood K-2 reading instruction). Children need a strong background in phonemic awareness in order for phonics instruction (sound-spelling relationships in print) to be effective.

The Role of Phonemic Awareness in Reading Development

Children who have problems with phonics, learning the letter-sound code of English, often have deficits in these phonemic awareness skills. Often, they have not acquired or been exposed to phonemic awareness activities usually fostered at home and in preschool to second grade, such as extensive songs, rhymes and read–alouds. In other cases, the child may have a disability that affects phoneme awareness, and needs more explicit instruction and/or more practice with these skills.

Blevins (1997) describes the earlier work of theorist Marilyn Jager Adams in designing five types of phoneme awareness tasks that can be used in the classroom. These align well with the International Reading Associations' Reading Panel Report, *Teaching Children to Read* (2002) and its analysis of phoneme awareness skills.

Task 1—the ability to hear rhymes and alliteration—for example, the children listen to a poem, rhyming picture book or song and identify the rhyming words heard.

Task 2—the ability to do oddity tasks (recognize the member of a set that is different [odd] among the group)—for example, the children look at the pictures of a door, a dog, and a cat. The teacher asks which starts with a different sound.

Task 3—the ability to orally blend words and split syllables—for example, the children can say the first sound of a word (e.g., /b/) and then the rest of the word (/at/) and then put it together as a single word (bat), as in onsets and rimes.

Task 4—the ability to orally segment words—for example, the ability to count sounds. The children would be asked as a group to count the sounds in "sat" (/s/, /a/, /t/--3 sounds).

Task 5—the ability to do phonics manipulation tasks—for example, replace the "r" sound in rose with a "n" sound and say "nose."

Other instructional methods that may be effective for teaching phonemic awareness include:

- Clapping the SOUNDS (not syllables) in words. (e.g., "bat" has three sounds, /b/, /a/, /t/)

- Games where students must identify the beginning, middle, or end sound (not letter) of a word (e.g., "Find something that begins with the /t/ sound").

- Games with common nursery rhymes where the students change one sound in several words (e.g., "Jack and Jill went up the hill..." Now change Jack and Jill to begin like 'Mary")

- Using visual cues and movements to help children understand when the speaker goes from one sound to another. This can also be done with colored blocks, a different color for each sound, and children can move their blocks around as the teacher moves the sound around (e.g. starting with three different colored blocks for "cat" and changing the "word" to "tac.")

- Singing familiar songs (e.g., Happy Birthday, Knick Knack Paddy Wack) and replacing key words with words with a different ending or middle sound (oral segmentation).

- Dealing children a deck of picture cards and having them sound out the words for the pictures on their cards or calling for a picture by asking for its first and second sound.

- Onset and rhyme games where children are given a beginning sound and told to blend it with a specific series of endings (e.g., "OK, start with /ch/ and add "eep' then "eet" etc.)

- Games like "I'm going on vacation and I'm taking a (something that begins or ends with a particular phoneme)

Multisensory Considerations

Make sure the student is counting the sounds rather than the letters in a word. Visual or tactile learners may need to visually represent words, syllables, or phonemes with a manipulative (e.g., tokens, blocks, etc.). A kinesthetic learner may benefit from tapping, jumping, moving hands together (for blending) and moving them apart for (segmenting). Start lessons with the level(s) a student has demonstrated mastery in. This allows for reteach or review, and builds student confidence. Then a new concept can be introduced. The student should move at their own pace and model teacher examples. The lesson may end with a new or novel phonological task such as a board or card game, experimentation with nonsense words, or a computer game. A few minutes with phonemic software, which may come with the district program, may serve as a closing activity or reward (or both). A student may also close the lesson with a separate computer game that is not connected to district-purchased software, such as *Reader Rabbit*, SIPPS, or a website game hub, such as *Starfall* or *ABCMouse*.

Knowledge of Phonemes

In order to assess and teach phoneme awareness and, subsequently, phonics, a teacher must be familiar with the phonemes of the English language. A **phoneme** is the smallest unit of sound that can distinguish one word from another. The phoneme is said to have mental, physiological, and physical substance: our brains process the sounds; the human speech organs produce the sounds; and the sounds are physical entities that can be recorded and measured. Consider the English words "pat" and "sat," which appear to differ only in their initial consonants. This difference, known as *contrastiveness* or *opposition*, is sufficient to distinguish these words, and therefore the "p" and "s" sounds are said to be different phonemes in English. They sound different, our mouths and tongues move differently to produce them, and we can process the difference mentally. A pair of words, identical except for such a sound, is known as a *minimal pair*, and the two sounds that distinguish each from the other are separate phonemes.

Where no minimal pair can exist to demonstrate that two sounds are distinct, it may be that they are *allophones*. An allophone is a slight variation in a phoneme's sound, a variation not recognized as distinct by a speaker, and not meaningfully different in the language, so these "allophones" are perceived as being the same. An example of this would be the heavy sounding "l" when landed on at the end of a word like "wool," as opposed to the lighter sounding "l" when starting a word like "leaf." This demonstrates allophones of a single phoneme. While it may exist and be measurable, such a difference is unrecognizable and meaningless to the average English speaker. The real value is as a technique for teaching reading and pronunciation. Identifying phonemes for students and applying their use is a step in the process of developing language fluency. American English has 44 phonemes, and they are usually listed like this:

Phoneme	Sound and sample spellings (graphemes)
/A/	a (table), a_e (bake), ai (train), ay (say)
/a/	a (flat)
/b/	b (ball)
/k/	c (cake), k (Key), ck (back)
/d/	d (door)
/E/	e (me), ee (feet), ea (leap), y (baby)
/e/	e (pet), ea (head)
/f/	f (fix), ph (phone)
/g/	g (gas)

PHONEME	SOUND AND SAMPLE SPELLINGS
/h/	h (hot)
/I/	i (I), i_e (bite), igh (light), y (sky)
/i/	i (sit)
/j/	j (jet), dge (edge), g (gem)
/l/	l (lamp)
/m/	m (map)
/n/	n (no), kn (knock)
/O/	o (okay), o_e (bone), oa (soap), ow (low)
/o/	o (hot)
/p/	p (pie)
/kw/	qu (quick)
/r/	r (road), wr (wrong), er (her), ir (sir), ur (fur)
/s/	s (say), c (cent)
/t/	t (time)
/U/	u (future), u_e (use), ew (few)
/u/	u thumb, a (about)
/v/	v (voice)
/w/	w (wash)
/gz/	x (exam)
/ks/	x (box)
/y/	y (yes)
/z/	z (zoo), s (nose)
/OO/	oo (boot), u (truth), u_e (rude), ew (chew)
/oo/	oo (book), u (put)
/oi/	oi (soil), oy (toy)
/ou/	ou (out), ow (cow)
/aw/	aw (saw), au (caught), al (tall)
/ar/	ar (car)
/sh/	sh (ship), ti (nation), ci (special)
/hw/	wh (white)
/ch/	ch (chest), tch (catch)
/th/	th (thick)
/*th*/	th (this)
/ng/	ng (sing)
/zh/	s (measure)

The oral production of these phonemes provides kinesthetic feedback that children have unconsciously learned as they learn to speak their language at home. The teacher can use this to help children discriminate among these sounds by calling attention to the different ways we produce the sounds, the differing positions of lips, tongue, and teeth. Children will differ in the amount of help they will need to develop their phoneme awareness. Once children have a good grounding in phoneme awareness, they are ready to study phonics.

Skill 5.12   Identify the processes and skills (e.g., graphophonemic, morphemic, syntactic, semantic) that effective readers use for word recognition

Effective word recognition involves use of multiple cueing systems and readers must learn to use them all in unison, relying on one set more heavily in some situations, and on other cues in other situations. The teacher must not only teach these skills, but help the student learn strategies for determining which skill or combination of skills will be most useful in different situations.

Phonics (graphophonemic cues)

Phonics is the letter-sound correspondence in written language. It is also known as the *code* for which letter or letter combinations represent which phonemes in the language. It is the connection between the sounds we say and the letters on the page, and it is absolutely crucial to learning to read. Students must be taught how to produce a correct sound for a letter or letter combination and blend the sounds for several letters together into a recognizable word. Word recognition is taught through grapheme (letter symbol)-phoneme associations (use of graphophonemic cues), with the goal of teaching the student to independently apply these skills to new words. Unlike phoneme awareness activities, phonics requires students to LOOK at what they are doing. It requires coordination of visual and auditory senses. See section 5.16 for more details on methods for teaching phonics.

Morphemic (Word Structure) Cues

Morphology is the system of rules for making words, including such things as making plurals, possessives, inflections, etc. Morphemes are the smallest units of language that convey meaning. Free morphemes are morphemes that can stand alone as base or root words, such as 'dog' or 'walk.' Bound morphemes are morphological units that cannot stand alone. They convey or alter meaning when attached to other morphemes, and include such things as affixes, endings and inflections (e.g. pre-, -ed, -s, -ing).

175

Structural analysis is a process of examining the words in the text for meaningful word units, or morphemes, such as affixes, base words, and inflected endings. There are six word types that are formed and therefore can be analyzed using structural analysis strategies. They include:

1. Common prefixes or suffixes added to a known word ending with a consonant
2. Adding the suffix –*ed* to words that end with consonants
3. Compound words
4. Adding endings to words that end with the letter *e*
5. Adding endings to words that end with the letter *y*
6. Adding affixes to multisyllabic words

When teaching and using structural analysis procedures, teachers should remember to make sound decisions on which to introduce and teach. Keeping in mind the number of primary words in which each affix appears and how similar they are will help the teacher make the instructional process smoother and more valuable to the students.

Adding affixes to words can be started when students are able to read a list of one-syllable words by sight at a rate of approximately 20 words correct per minute. At the primary level, there is a recommended sequence for introducing affixes. The steps in this process are:

- Start by introducing the affix in the letter-sound correspondence format
- Practice the affix in isolation for a few days.
- Provide words for practice which contain the affix (word lists/flash card).
- Move from word lists to passage reading, which includes words with the affix (and some from the word lists/flash cards).

Some teachers choose to directly teach structural analysis, in particular, those who teach by following the phonics-centered approach for reading. Other teachers, who follow the balanced literacy approach, introduce the structural components as part of mini lessons that are focused on the students' reading and writing.

Structural analysis of words as defined by J. David Cooper (2004) involves the study of significant word parts. This analysis can help the child with pronunciation and constructing meaning.

Key Structural Analysis Components (Morphemic elements) Defined

Base Words. These are stand-alone linguistic units (free morphemes) which cannot be deconstructed or broken down into smaller meaningful units. They stand alone as words, and often form the base of other words when affixes or inflections (bound morphemes) are added to them. For example, in the word *retell*, the base word is "tell."

Root Word. This term is often used interchangeably with 'base word' for a free morpheme. However, it can also refer to the word (often from another language) from which another word is developed. The second word can be said to have its "root" in the first, such as *vis* in visor or vision.

Regardless of the term you use to describe them, base words and roots can be illustrated by a tree with roots to display the meaning for children. Children may also want to literally construct root words using cardboard trees to create word family models.

ELL students can construct these models for their native language root-word families, as well for the English language words they are learning. ELL students in the 5th and 6th grade may even appreciate analyzing the different root structures for contrasts and similarities between their native language and English. Learners with special needs can focus in small groups or individually with a paraprofessional on building root-word models.

Contractions. These are shortened forms of two words in which a letter or letters have been deleted. These deleted letters have been replaced by an apostrophe.

Prefixes. These are beginning units of meaning which can be added (the vocabulary word for this type of structural adding is "affixed") to a base word or root word. They cannot stand alone. They are also sometimes known as "bound morphemes" because they cannot stand alone as a base word. Examples are *re-, un-,* and *mis-.*

Suffixes. These are ending units of meaning which can be "affixed" or added on to the ends of root or base words. Suffixes transform the original meanings of base and root words. Like prefixes, they are also known as "bound morphemes," because they cannot stand alone as words. Examples are *-less, -ful,* and *-tion.*

Compound Words. These occur when two or more base words are connected to form a new word. The meaning of the new word is in some way connected with that of the base word. Examples are *firefighter, newspaper,* and *pigtail.*

Inflectional Endings. These are types of suffixes that impart a new meaning to the base or root word. These endings in particular change the gender, number, tense, or form of the base or root words. Just like other suffixes, these are also termed "bound morphemes." Examples are *–s* or *-ed.*

Activities for improving structural analysis

Word Study Group: This is a strategy generally used with children in grades 3-6. It involves the teacher taking time to meet with children in a small group of no more than six children for a word study session. Taberski (2000) suggests that this meeting take place next to the word wall. The children selected for this group are those who need to focus more on the relationship between spelling patterns and consonant sounds.

It is important that this not be a formalized traditional reading group that meets at a set time each week. Rather the group should be spontaneously formed by the teacher based on the teacher's quick inventory of the selected children's needs at the start of the week. Taberski has templates in her book of *Guided Reading Planning Sheets.* These sheets are essentially targeted word- and other skills sheets with her written and dated observations of children who are in need of support to develop a given skill.

The teacher should try to meet with this group for at least two consecutive 20- minute periods daily. Over those two meetings, the teacher can model a *Making Words Activity.* Once the teacher has modeled making words the first day, the children would then make their own words. On the second day, the children would "sort" their words.

Other topics for a word study group within the framework of the *Balanced Literacy Approach* that Taberski advocates are: inflectional endings, prefixes and suffixes, and/or common spelling patterns. These are covered later in this chapter.

Discussion Circles: This is an activity that fits nicely into the balanced literacy lesson format. After the children conclude a particular text, they respond to the book in discussion circles. Among the prompts, the teacher-coach might suggest that the children focus on words of interest they encountered in the text. These can also be words that they heard if the text was read aloud. Children can be asked to look for words that show various structural elements or changes. Through this focus on children's response to words as the center of the discussion circle, peers become more interested in word study.

Banking, Booking, and Filing It:. Children can realize the goal of making words their own and exploring word structures through creating concrete objects or displays that demonstrate the words they own. They can maintain their own files of words they have learned and sets of affixes or inflections that can be added to them to change the meaning of each word. Games in which children "play" with the structural elements of words can help them understand and manipulate these elements in their reading and writing.

Write Out Your Words, Write with Your Words. Ownership of words can be demonstrated by having the children use the words in their writings. The children can author a procedural narrative (a step-by-step description) of how they went about their word searches to compile the words they found for any of the activities. If the children are in grades K–1, or if the children are struggling readers and writers, their procedural narratives can be dictated. Then they can be posted by the teacher. Children can also keep "word wallets" of base words with lists of affixes that can alter the meaning.

Children with special needs may model a word box or wallet on a specific holiday theme, genre, or science/social studies topic with the teacher. Initially, this can be done as a whole class. As the children become more confident, they can work with peers or with a paraprofessional to create their own individual or small team/pair word boxes.

Special needs children can create a storyboard with the support of a paraprofessional, their teacher, or a resource specialist. They can also narrate their story of how they all found the words, using a digital recorder.

Knowledge of Greek and Latin Roots That Form English Words. Knowledge of Greek and Latin roots which comprise English words can measurably enhance children's reading skills and can also enrich their writing.

Word Webs. Taberski (2000) does not advocate teaching Greek and Latin derivatives in the abstract to young children. However, when she comes across (as is common and natural) specific Greek and Latin roots while reading to children, she uses that opportunity to introduce children to these useful resources. For example, during readings on rodents (a favorite of first and second graders), Taberski draws her class's attention to the fact that beavers gnaw at things with their teeth. She then connects the root *dent* with other words with which the children are familiar. The children then volunteer *dentist, dental, denture.* Taberski begins to place these in a graphic organizer, or word web.

When she has tapped the extent of the children's prior knowledge of *dent* words, she shares with them the fact that *dens/dentis* is the Latin word for teeth. Then she introduces the word *indent,* which she has already previewed with them as part of their conventions of print study. She helps them to see that the *indenting* of the first line of a paragraph can even be related to the *teeth* Latin root in that it looks like a "print" bite was taken out of the paragraph.

Taberski displays the word web in the Word Wall Chart section of her room. The class is encouraged throughout, say, a week's time to look for other words to add to the web. Taberski stresses that for her, as an elementary teacher of reading and writing, the key element of the Greek and Latin word root web activity is the children's coming to understand that if they know what a Greek or Latin word root means, they can use that knowledge to figure out what other words mean.

She feels the key concept is to model and demonstrate for children how fun and fascinating Greek and Latin root study can be.

Syntactic cues

Syntax is the set of rules, commonly known as grammar, that governs how morphemes and words are correctly combined to make sentences. As children learn oral language, they adopt the syntactic and grammatical patterns of the adults around them. They learn that certain words or classes of word *sound right* and others *sound wrong* in various parts of a sentence. However, children with reading disabilities may struggle to learn these rules without very explicit instruction.

Many of the syntactic rules that provide contextual clues to help identify words are based on *word classes* such as parts of speech (e.g., nouns, verbs, adjectives). However, words do not fall into such conceptual categories in fixed, constant ways. A particular word's syntactic class can vary depending upon how it is used in the sentence. The word *fish*, for example, can be a noun in one sentence (e.g., "I like to eat fish."), and a verb in another (e.g., "I like to fish on the lake."). Other syntactic cues depend upon placement in the sentence, or upon related words in a sentence, and this, too, is an abstract concept that means a word can mean one thing in one place and another in a different place, or that different forms of a word should be used in different places. It also means that words that *look* very different can be essentially different forms of the same word (e.g., be, is, are).

Children whose oral language development has been different from that of mainstream English, or who have language disabilities, will need extra help to learn how to use syntactic cues. Section 5.14 presents more details on developing lessons to help teach these concepts.

Semantic cues

Semantic cues are based upon word meanings. Children can deduce the meaning of an unknown word based upon the meaning of the passage as a whole, and the sentences immediately around the unknown word, as well. Illustrations and diagrams can also provide cues to meaning. When the probable meaning of a word is clear, the student can compare the idea or meaning with the letters and figure out the word. Once again, children with language disabilities may struggle to use this cueing system because it requires pulling information together from different parts of a sentence or paragraph, holding it in working memory, and putting it together to form a conclusion. Section 5.14 presents some ideas for lessons to help teach use of this cueing system.

Skill 5.13   **Identify explicit and systematic instructional methods for developing reading fluency (e.g., practice with high frequency words, timed readings, repeated readings, read alouds, choral reading, recorded books**

Reading fluency, most frequently defined as the rate of accurate reading (correct words per minute), is more than a status symbol for children; it is an important indicator of reading ability (Hunt & Marshall, 2005). Students with fluency problems may read aloud in a word-by-word manner without appropriate inflection or rhythm, unable to relate the patterns of spoken language to the printed word. Students with weakness in this area often dread being asked to read in class (Friend, 2005). According to Salvia and Ysseldyke (1998), common oral fluency problems include the following:

- **Omissions.** The student skips individual words or groups of words.
- **Insertions.** The student inserts one or more words into the sentence being orally read.
- **Substitutions.** The student replaces one or more words in the passage by one or more meaningful words.
- **Gross mispronunciation of a word.** The student's pronunciation of a word bears little resemblance to the proper pronunciation.
- **Hesitation.** The student hesitates for two or more seconds before pronouncing a word.
- **Inversions.** The student changes the order of words appearing in a sentence.
- **Transpositions.** Reading words in the wrong order ("She away ran" instead of "she ran away").
- **Unknown words.** Being unable to pronounce certain words in a reasonable amount of time.
- **Slow choppy reading.** Not recognizing words quickly enough (20 to 30 words per minute).
- **Disregard of punctuation.** The student fails to observe punctuation; for example, may not pause for a comma, stop for a period, or indicate a vocal inflection, a question mark, or an exclamation point.

Reading fluency has been shown to have strong correlations to comprehension skills, which are the goal of any reading activity. Therefore, it is very important for students to have well developed fluency skills. For students who do not naturally develop their fluency skills, the teacher must provide strategies or activities that help develop them. A few instructional techniques for improving fluency are presented below.

Choral Reading. Choral reading is an effective reading strategy used to increase fluency. Students can read with a group or the teacher to build their fluency. In this strategy, reading should be done at an appropriate pace and with good prosody. For children with language disabilities, this can be very helpful. The choral reading provides a lot of context and modeling that helps improve fluency over time.

Reader's Theater. This strategy helps to bring drama back into the classroom by creating scripts with different parts for different characters. The students practice the script in small groups for a few days, and then they complete a reading with good fluency for their peers. There is no preparation of costumes or set design, but it allows the students to have the practice of reading different parts. It also means that the child will be reading and rereading the same text, which is also helpful.

Frequent Independent Reading. The more opportunity students have to practice reading, the more fluent they will become. The key is that the reading is on their independent level and the text is enjoyable for the reader. Students need to have some independent reading time daily.

Paired Reading. Students are sometimes the best teachers. Paired reading is an opportunity for them to provide effective instruction to their peers. For the struggling readers, this is an excellent strategy to increase reading fluency. Sometimes, students can graph the results of their *words correct per minute* (wcpm) with their student helpers to have a visual representation of their progress. There are different things to consider when pairing students, including: reading level, ability to work together and stay on task, and appropriate materials for both partners to read.

In any given pair, one child may be a more accomplished reader than the other, but this should not be a problem. The struggling reader would be reading at their *independent level,* which means that they should be able to read it reasonably well. When the more accomplished reader reads his or her more difficult selection, it also serves as a model for the less accomplished reader.

Repeated Readings. Repeated reading passages are one of the most effective strategies for increasing oral reading fluency. This can be done individually or in pairs. Tying graphing, paired reading, and repeated oral reading into one time frame within the classroom can provide teachers and students with a specific strategy easily incorporated for a few minutes a day into the classroom routine.

Although most teachers would immediately equate fluency with the number of words per minute read correctly, reading fluency is more than reading speed. Students must also demonstrate good prosody. Prosody refers to reading with expression, appropriate phrasing, and good inflection.

Generally considered a part of fluency, prosody is an important element on all rubrics used to evaluate reading fluency. Prosody is what takes otherwise robotic reading and makes it into something enjoyable to hear. The punctuation we use as part of grammar provides the cues for reading with good prosody.

Modeling is one of the most effective strategies a teacher can use with students to enhance their prosody skills. Teachers need to provide examples of good reading, as well as non-examples where the teacher reads "robotically." In this way, students can hear the differences between good oral reading and poor oral reading.

Prosody can only be built by using oral reading, so any of the already mentioned strategies for improving fluency can also be used to increase the prosody of the same students. It is important for students to clearly understand that reading is not a race. It is not all about the number of words read correctly in a minute, but rather about the number of *well-read* words.

Recorded Books. One way to model correct prosody is to allow students to listen to well-read books on tape or CD. As the students listen and scan the text at the same time, they not only hear the words modeled, they also experience rapidly putting the letter image they *see* with the sound they *hear*.

High-Frequency Sight Words. Since fluency is dependent, in part, on rapid recognition of words being read, students benefit from practice learning instant recognition of high frequency words. Automatic recognition contributes to both accuracy and speed.

While the majority of reading will occur silently in the student's head, it is necessary to take the time to practice reading out loud to ensure students develop this more natural flow of language. Such practice makes it more likely the phrasing and expression will transfer into the silent reading, and this will enhance comprehension, as well. If students are unable to do the task orally, the reading in their head may be just as robotic or choppy which can impact comprehension in a negative manner.

Skill 5.14 **Identify explicit and systematic instructional methods and strategies for increasing vocabulary acquisition (e.g., appropriate choice of words for instruction; multiple exposures; teaching word learning strategies, such as word analysis and contextual analysis)**

According to Burns, et al (2002), vocabulary develops in humans as they listen to conversation around them while they develop. Therefore, a language-rich environment stimulates vocabulary development in children and a language impoverished environment can result in deficits in vocabulary development. In addition, some language disabilities also limit vocabulary acquisition. Such deficits have serious implications for ultimate reading comprehension.

Biemiller (2003) cites research results indicating that the listening vocabulary for a 6th grader who tests at the 25th percentile in reading is equivalent to that attained by the 75th percentile 3rd grader. This deficit in vocabulary presents a formidable challenge for the 6th grader to succeed, not only on reading tests, but also in various content subjects in elementary school and beyond. His research also indicates that those children entering 4th grade with significant vocabulary deficits demonstrate increasing reading comprehension problems. Evidence shows that these children do not catch up, but rather continue to fall behind.

The National Reading Panel has put forth the following conclusions about vocabulary instruction as it relates to overall reading comprehension:

- There is a need for direct instruction of vocabulary items required for a specific text.
- Repetition and multiple exposures to vocabulary items are important. Students should be given items that will be likely to appear in many contexts.
- Learning in rich contexts is valuable for vocabulary learning. Vocabulary words should be those that the learner will find useful in many contexts. When vocabulary items are derived from content learning materials, the learner will be better equipped to deal with specific reading matter in content areas.

- Vocabulary tasks should be restructured as necessary. It is important to be certain that students fully understand what is asked of them in the context of reading rather than focusing only on the words to be learned.
- Vocabulary learning is effective when it entails active engagement in learning tasks.
- Computer technology can be used effectively to help teach vocabulary.
- Vocabulary can be acquired through incidental learning. Much of a student's vocabulary will have to be learned in the course of doing things other than explicit vocabulary learning. Repetition, richness of context, and motivation may also add to the efficacy of incidental learning of vocabulary.
- Dependence on a single vocabulary instruction method will not result in optimal learning. Research shows that a variety of methods can be used effectively with emphasis on multimedia aspects of learning, richness of context in which words are to be learned, and the number of exposures to words that learners receive.
- The Panel found that a critical feature of effective classrooms is the instruction of specific words that includes lessons and activities where students apply their vocabulary knowledge and strategies to reading and writing. Included in the activities were discussions where teachers and students talked about words, their features, and strategies for understanding unfamiliar words.

There are many methods for directly and explicitly teaching words. In fact, the Panel found twenty-one methods that have been found effective in research projects. Many emphasize the underlying concept of a word and its connections to other words, such as semantic mapping and diagramming that use graphics. The keyword method uses words and illustrations that highlight salient features of meaning. Visualizing or drawing a picture, either by the student or by the teacher, was found to be effective. Many words cannot be learned in this way, of course, so it should be used as only one method among others. Effective classrooms provide multiple ways for students to learn and interact with words. The Panel also found that computer-assisted activities can have a very positive role in the development of vocabulary. A few such strategies and techniques are mentioned here.

Strategy One: Word Map Strategy. This strategy is useful for children in grades 3–6 and beyond. The target group of children for this strategy includes those who need to improve their independent vocabulary acquisition abilities. The strategy is essentially teacher-directed learning where children are "walked through" the process. The teacher helps the children to identify the type of information that makes a definition. Children are also assisted in using context clues and background understanding to construct meaning.

The *word map graphic organizer* is the tool teachers use to complete this strategy with children. Word map templates are available online from the Houghton Mifflin web site and from *Read Write Think*, the web site of the NCTE (see webliography section). The word map helps children to visually represent the elements of a given concept.

The children's literal articulation of the concept can be prompted by three key questions: What is it? What is it like? What are some examples? For instance, the word "oatmeal" might yield a word map with boxes that have the answers to each of the three key questions. What is it? (A hot cereal) What's it like? (Mushy and Salty) What are some examples? (Plain or Apple-Flavored)

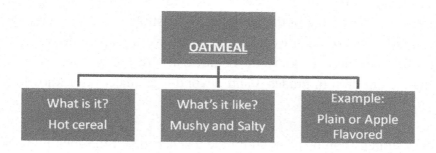

To share this strategy with children, the teacher selects three concepts familiar to the children and shows them the template of a word map with the three questions asked on the map. The teacher then helps the children to fill in at least two word maps with the topic in the top box and the answers in the three question boxes. The children should then independently complete the word map for the third topic. To reinforce the lesson, the teacher has the children select a concept of their own to map either independently or in a small group. As the final task for this first part of the strategy, the children, in teams or individually, write a definition for at least one of the concepts using the key things about it listed on the map. The children share these definitions aloud and talk about how they used the word maps to help them with the definitions.

For the next part of this strategy, the teacher picks an expository text or a textbook the children are already using to study mathematics, science, or social studies. The teacher either locates a short excerpt where a particular concept is defined or uses the content to write original model passages of definition.

After the passages are selected or authored, the teacher duplicates them. Then they are distributed to the children along with blank word map templates. The children will be asked to read each passage and then to complete the word map for the concept in each passage. Finally, the children share the word maps they have developed for each passage, and explain how they used the word in the passage to help them fill out their word map. Lastly, the teacher reminds the children that the three components of the concept—class, description, and example—are just three of the many components for any given concept.

This strategy has assessment potential because the teacher can literally see how the students understand specific concepts by looking at their maps and hearing their explanations. The maps the students develop on their own demonstrate whether they have really understood the concepts in the passages. This strategy serves to ready students for inferring word meanings on their own. By using the word map strategy, children develop concepts of what they need to know to begin to figure out an unknown word on their own. It assists the children in grades 3 and beyond to connect prior knowledge with new knowledge.

This word map strategy can be adapted by the teacher to suit the specific needs and goals of instruction. Illustrations of the concept and the comparisons to other concepts can be included in the word mapping for children grades 5 and beyond. This particular strategy is also one that can be used with a research theme in other content areas.

Strategy Two: *Preview in Context*—This is a direct teaching strategy that allows the teacher to guide the students as they examine words in context prior to reading a passage. Before beginning the strategy, the teacher selects only two or three key concept words. Then the teacher reads carefully to identify passages within the text that evidence strong context clues for the word.

Then the teacher presents the word and the context to the children. As the teacher reads aloud, the children follow along. Once the teacher has finished the read-aloud, the children reread the material silently. After the silent rereading, the children are coached by the teacher on a definition of one of the key words selected for study. This is done through a child-centered discussion. As part of the discussion, the teacher asks questions that can help the children activate their prior knowledge and use the contextual clues to figure out the correct meaning of the selected key words. The teacher makes certain that the definition of the key concept word is finally made by the children.

Next, the teacher helps the children to expand the word's meaning by having them consider the following for the given key concept word: synonyms, antonyms, other contexts, or other kinds of stories/texts where the word might appear. This is the time the children check their responses to the challenge of identifying word synonyms and antonyms by having them go to the thesaurus or the dictionary. In addition, the children are asked to place the synonyms or antonyms they find in their word boxes or word journals. The recording of their findings will guarantee them ownership of the words and deepen their capacity to use contextual clues.

The main point to remember in using this strategy is that it should only be used when the context is strong. It will not work with struggling readers who have less prior knowledge. Through listening to the children's responses as the teacher helps them to define the word and its potential synonyms and antonyms, the teacher can assess students' ability to successfully use context clues. The key to this simple strategy is that it allows the teacher to draw the children out and to learn about their thinking process through their responses. The more talk from the child the better.

The Role of Systematic, Non-contextual Vocabulary Strategies

Hierarchical and Linear Arrays. The very complexity of the vocabulary used in this strategy description may be unnerving for the teacher. Yet this strategy, included in the Cooper (2004) literacy instruction, is very simple once it is outlined directly for children.

The term *"hierarchical and linear" arrays* refers to how some words are grouped based on associative meanings. The words may have a "hierarchical" relationship to one another. For instance, the sixth grader is lower in the school hierarchy than the eighth grader. Within an elementary school, the fifth or sixth grader is at the top of the hierarchy and the pre-K or kindergartener is at the bottom of the hierarchy.

Words can have a linear relationship to one another in that they run a spectrum from bad to good. An example for K–3 children might be *pleased–happy–overjoyed*. These relationships can be displayed in horizontal boxes connected with dashes. The following is another way to display hierarchical relationships.

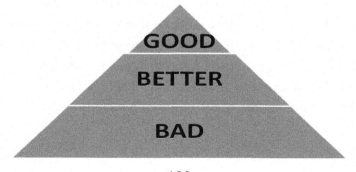

Once you get past the seemingly daunting vocabulary words, the arrays turn out to be another excellent graphic organizer tool which can help children see how words relate to one another.

To use this graphic organizer, the teacher should pre-select a group of words from a read-aloud or from the children's writing. Show the children how the array will look using arrows for the linear array and just straight lines for the hierarchy. In fact, invite some children up to draw the straight hierarchy lines as the array is presented. This lets the children have a role in developing even the first hierarchical model.

Create one hierarchy array and one linear array of the pre-selected word with the children. Talk them through filling in (or helping the teacher to fill in) the array. After the children have had their own successful experience with arrays, they can select the words from their independent texts or familiar, previously read favorites to study. They will also need to decide which type of array, hierarchical or linear, is appropriate.

This strategy is best used *after* reading because it will help children to expand their word banks.

Contextual Vocabulary Strategies

Vocabulary Self-Collection. This strategy is one in which children, even on the emergent level from grade 2 and up, take responsibility for their learning. It is also by definition, a student centered strategy, which demonstrates student ownership of their chosen vocabulary.

To start, ask the children to read a required text or story. Invite them to select one word for the class to study from this text or story. The children can work individually, in teams, or in small groups. The teacher can also do the self-collecting so that this becomes the joint effort of the class community of literate readers. Tell the children that they should select words that interest them or are unique in some way.

After the children have had time to make their selections and to reflect on them, make certain that they have time to share them with their peers as a whole class. When each child shares the word he/she has selected, have them provide a definition for the word. Each word that is given should be listed on a large experiential chart or even in a BIG BOOK format, if that is age and grade appropriate. The teacher should also share the word he/she selected and provide a definition. The teacher's definition and sharing should be somewhere in the middle of the children's recitations.

The dictionary should be used to verify the definitions. When all the definitions have been checked, a final list of child-selected and teacher-selected words should be made.

Once this final list has been compiled, the children can choose to record all or part of the list in their word journals. Some students may record only those words they find interesting. It is up to the teacher at the onset of the vocabulary self-collection activity to decide whether the children have to record all the words on the final list or can eliminate some.

To further enhance this strategy, children, particularly those in grades 3 and beyond, can be encouraged to use their collected words as part of their writings or to record and clip these words as they appear in newspaper stories or online. This type of additional recording demonstrates that the child has truly incorporated the word into his/her reading and writing. It also habituates children to be lifelong readers, writers, and researchers.

Assessment is built into the strategy. As the children select the word for the list, they share how they used contextual clues. Further, as children respond to definitions offered by their peers, their prior knowledge can be assessed.

Knowledge of Common Sayings, Proverbs, and Idioms

Common sayings, idioms, and proverbs may create some misunderstandings among children, and with those who are learning English as a second language. Common sayings such as: "A bird in the hand is worth two in the bush" may leave a child confused.
The lesson below provokes a child to seek understanding from reliable sources on this type of language.

The Fortune Cookie Strategy (Reissman, 1994). Grades 3 and up—Distribute fortune cookies to the children. Have them eat the cookies and then draw their attention to the enclosed fortunes.

First, the teacher will model by reading aloud his/her own fortune. After reading the fortune aloud, the teacher will explain what the fortune means using its vocabulary as a guide. Finally, the teacher may share whether or not they agree with the statement made in the fortune.

Similarly, children can read their fortunes aloud, explain the saying, and tell whether they agree with the proverb or prediction.

Following this activity, children can be asked to go home and interview their parents or community members to get family proverbs and common sayings.

Once the children return with the sayings and proverbs, they can each share them and explain their meaning. The class as a whole can discuss to what extent these sayings are true for everyone. Proverbs and sayings can become part of a word wall or be included in a special literacy center. The teacher can create fill-in, put-together, and writing activities to go with the proverbs. These tie in nicely with cultural study in grades 3–6 including the study of Asian, Latin American, and African nations.

This strategy also highlights, in a positive way, both the uniqueness and commonality of the family proverbs contributed by children from ELL backgrounds. If possible their proverbs can also be posted in their native languages as well as in English.

Extending a Reader's Understanding of Familiar Words

Dictionary and Thesaurus Use. Dictionaries are useful for spelling, writing, and reading. Thesauruses can expand a children's understanding of specific words and help them understand how different words are related. It is very important to expose and habituate students to using these resources.

Model the correct way to use the dictionary for children even as late as the third to sixth grade. Many have never been taught proper dictionary skills. The teacher needs to demonstrate to the children that as an adult reader and writer, he/she routinely and happily uses the dictionary and learns new information that makes him or her better at reading and writing.

It is possible to begin dictionary study and use as early as kindergarten, because of the proliferation of lush picture dictionaries that can be introduced at that grade level. Children can not only look at these picture dictionaries, but also begin to make dictionaries of their own at this grade level filled with pictures and beginning words..

In early grade levels, use of the dictionary can nicely complement the children's mastery of the alphabet. They should be given whole-class and small-group practice in locating words.

As the children progress with their phonetic skills, the dictionary can be used to show them phonetic re-spelling using the pronunciation key.

Older children in grades 3 and beyond need explicit teacher demonstrations and practice in the use of guide words. They also need to begin to learn about the hierarchies of various word meanings. In the upper grades, children should also explore using special content dictionaries and glossaries located in the backs of their books.

Thesauruses can be used in conjunction with the "word wallets" mentioned earlier. Children can construct packets of colorful 3X5 cards, each with a set of word families of synonyms with various connotations for concept words. They can use these to help understand words they find in print, as well as to improve word choice in their own writing.

Vocabulary Instruction for Students with Disabilities

Students with language and reading disabilities may have significant difficulties acquiring, remembering, or using vocabulary correctly. Words are labels for things such as objects, ideas, actions, and relationships among these and other concepts. Word referents range from literal ("dog" stands for a particular animal), to the very abstract ("analogous" stands for a concept concerning the relationship between abstract ideas). In order to properly comprehend and use words correctly, the word must be understood, stored, and retrieved when needed. It may also be necessary to hold a number of words and their referents in working memory while reading a complex passage or composing a sentence with them. A disability in any of these areas of attaching meaning to a word, storing it, or retrieving and working with it can seriously affect vocabulary development. Children with such disabilities may not acquire vocabulary as efficiently as children without disabilities, even if they *are* in a language rich environment. Children with disabilities may need more explicit instruction, practice with strategies, and accommodations to learn the vocabulary necessary to become good readers.

Most children develop vocabulary skills as they read or are read to by parents and teachers. They hear words and attach meanings to them based on the context in which they hear them. However, children with learning disabilities may not be able to use context without explicit training and practice. Some children will "read" or listen to a passage and be able to parrot back the words, but do not understand what they mean in context.

There are a number of strategies for explicitly teaching children how to use context to determine what a word means. One method is to design a sort of "Mystery Word" game in which sentences with blanks or nonsense words are recorded on colorful cards and set up in a box for students. Students take a card or set of cards and try to figure out what word will fit in the blank. Context clues can be of two types:

Syntax clues are clues related to a parts of speech and grammar; a word's job in the sentence (for example, in "The _____ ran up the wall," the word in the blank would have to be a noun of some sort).

Semantic clues are based on meaning in the sentence and the word (for example, in "My dad drove the _____ to work," the blank would have to be some sort of a vehicle, not a butterfly or a feeling).

A set of sentences can be developed that provide increasing context clues to the meaning of the word. An example of a set of cards with increasing semantic clues would be:

a. We have a new _____ at our house. (Not much in the way of semantic clues, though it should be a noun; could be a pet, a piece of furniture, a book, a baby, whatever).

b. We have a new _____ at our house and it is bigger than the one that broke. (OK, so NOT a baby or a pet...).

c. We have a new _____ at our house and it is bigger than the one that broke so we can put TWO gallons of milk in it at a time (Now, we are probably talking about a refrigerator).

Children can guess at each word and discuss their guesses with the teacher. The teacher can guide the student to evaluate their guesses and clues and look at both syntactic and semantic context. The object in such lessons is NOT the actual vocabulary, but rather the *strategy* of using context to determine a word's meaning. Such an activity can be modified to include actual vocabulary words necessary for reading once the student has mastered the use of the strategy.

Since some students with disabilities will have more problems with semantic clues, while others will have problems with syntactic clues, such lessons must be individualized for each problem type.

When handling problems with semantic cues, a teacher can use prompts such as:

1. You said (child's word/incorrect attempt). Does that make sense to you? Can it DO that?
2. If someone said (repeat the child's attempt), would you know what he or she meant?
3. You said (child's incorrect attempt). Would you write that?

When handling syntactic problems, a teacher can use prompts such as:

1. You said (child's incorrect attempt). Does that sound right?
2. You said (child's incorrect attempt). Can we say it like that?
3. Since some children come from backgrounds where incorrect grammar contributes to the problem, say: Would your *teacher* say it that way? Or: Would you say it that way in class?

Another strategy for helping students with disabilities to acquire necessary vocabulary is to make the vocabulary as concrete as possible and present it in a multimedia manner. Wherever possible illustrate the word with a picture or an accompanying action. If working memory is a problem, maintaining a visual bank of words or pictures from which to choose, will help the student manipulate vocabulary correctly.

Skill 5.15   Identify explicit and systematic instructional methods for facilitating students' reading comprehension and critical-thinking skills (e.g., use of graphic and semantic organizers; use of multiple strategy instruction; teaching summarizing, monitoring, question answering, question generating, and recognizing story structure as comprehension strategies)

An overview of several levels of comprehension, as well as strategies for recognizing common text features was presented in Skill 3.8. In addition to the strategies in that section, there are a number of other methods a teacher can use to help students improve comprehension.

Questions as Guideposts

Generating questions can also motivate and enhance children's comprehension of reading in that they are actively involved in generating their own questions and then answering these questions based on their reading. The following guidelines will help children generate meaningful questions that will trigger constructive reading of expository texts.

First, children should preview the text by reading the titles and subheads. Then they should also look at the illustrations and the pictures. Finally, they should read the first paragraph. These first previews should yield an impressive batch of specific questions.

Next, children should get into their Dr. Seuss mode, and ask themselves a "THINK" question. For younger children, having a "THINK" silly hat in the classroom might be effective, as well, so that the children could actually go over and put it on. Make certain that the children write down the question. Then, have them read to find important information to answer their "Think" questions. Ask that they write down the answer they found and copy the sentence or sentences where they found the answer. For students with writing difficulties, they can put a numbered post-it on the part of the text that holds the answer or clue. Also, have them consider whether, in light of their further reading through the text, their original questions were good ones or not.

Finally, ask them to be prepared to explain why their original questions were good ones or not. Once the children have answered their original "think" questions, have them generate additional ones, and then find their answers and judge whether these questions were "good" ones in light of the text.

Use of Comprehension Skills Before, During, and After Reading

Cooper (2004) advocates that the child ask himself or herself what a text is about before he or she reads it, and even as he or she is in the process of reading the text, and that he or she notes what he or she thinks the text is going to be about. While the child is reading the text, the child can be continually questioning himself or herself as to whether the text confirmed the child's predictions. Of course, after completing the text, the child can then review the predictions and verify whether they were correct.

Pre-reading strategies such as looking over the expository text subheads, illustrations, captions, and indices to get an idea about the book can also be helpful.

During the reading, the child is asking, "Am I finding the answer to my question?"

After the reading, the child notes: "I have found the answer to my question. This book or electronic text is an excellent source of information for me about my question." (Or perhaps, "No, I have not found the answer to my question. This book or electronic text is not a good source of information for me about my question. I will have to look for other resources.").

Think Alouds. Thinking aloud is one of the most effective strategies both for teaching comprehension and for working through complex concepts presented in some texts. When using the think-aloud approach, the teacher is simply speaking out loud every thought that would normally be going on silently in her head. As the teacher demonstrates and explains the connections he/she is making while reading, the students begin to understand how the teacher arrived at these connections. Integrating new information with the old information is a valuable skill for students to master. Students can practice their own think alouds by reviewing the questions they have chosen to set a purpose for reading.

Visualization is the process of creating a mental picture corresponding to the words on the page. Generally, good readers have a mental image of what they are reading. The phrasing and author's voice provide clear details that allow multiple readers to have the same basic vision. When working with visualization it can sometimes be helpful for students to take the additional step of drawing out the picture as they see it in their mind. Working with the teacher, the students can advance their comprehension even if key concepts are missing.

Strategic reading occurs when students are reading to gain information. The purpose for reading is simply to learn. Typically, strategic reading occurs with nonfiction or expository texts. The students are generally given some guidance on what information they are to find.

In strategic reading however, it is not a simple recall of facts. This is not literal comprehension. The students are required to read a great deal of information about a topic. Then they need to take all of that information and build their own foundation of knowledge. Constructing knowledge is what makes strategic reading different from simple literal recall. It is through this process that information is connected to prior knowledge.

These connections are key factors in the success of comprehension. Strategic reading requires the reader to be able to tie new and old learning together to compound it into useful information. This process of thinking about reading and manipulating all *that is* learned is known as metacognition. Metacognition is a complex set of variables for the reader. The reader needs to be aware of the reading process and be able to recognize when information does not make sense. At this point, the reader needs to adjust the things they are doing in order to clarify and make the necessary connections.

Throughout this process, the reader must continue to integrate the new and old. Strategic readers call into play their meta-cognitive capacities as they analyze texts so they are aware of the skills needed to construct meaning from the text structure.

When reading strategically, students need to keep in mind several factors:

Self-Monitoring. When students self-monitor, they are able to keep track of all the factors involved in the process. In this way, they are able to process the information in the manner that is best for them.

Setting the Purpose for Reading. In strategic reading, the child has a specific reason for reading the text—to gain information. This reason should be clear to the student. If it is unclear, the student will not be successful.

Rereading. Rereading is one of the most used methods for taking in an overwhelming amount of information. By revisiting the text more than once, the student is able to note and take in smaller pieces of information that he/she might have missed during the first read.

Adjusting Reading Rates and Strategies. Similar to self-monitoring, students must be able to understand that sometimes it will be necessary to read more slowly than at other times. Sometimes they will need to make adjustments to the way they are reading in order to be successful at gaining the information they want to gain.

Topic and Concluding Sentences. As we teach students to write, we often spend a lot of time focusing on writing paragraphs with topic sentences and concluding sentences. However, we also need to focus on how these same features—topic and concluding sentences—may be used to better understand the text. These parallels can help students better understand what they are reading and develop their writing skills. Understanding that topic sentences tell the main idea of the paragraph, and that concluding sentences restate that idea, can help students' comprehension as well.

Note Taking Learning how to take notes when reading is a tough skill to master and to teach. It requires the reader to understand the main ideas in a passage and immediately be able to summarize those ideas into something meaningful. This process requires a great deal of higher-order thinking and may need to be scaffolded for younger students. A method of providing support is to provide a rough outline with some information missing that the students can find when they are reading. Such an outline/cloze form can be modified as the child becomes more accomplished at note taking, with fewer and fewer pieces provided by the teacher, and more by the student.

Semantic Mapping. Another beneficial tool for students is *semantic mapping*. In semantic mapping, students begin to make the connections between the information they already know about the topic and the new information they are learning. It is typically a more graphic representation of the information, but it is built upon words and ideas. Mapping generally increases knowledge and improves vocabulary development. This is a strategy that can be used to reach all learning styles and therefore is an important one to teach. It is exactly what its name implies—a map of the reading.

Just as a road map helps the driver get from point A to point B, so it is for a reading map. It helps the reader maneuver through the information in a meaningful manner. Maps can use words with key ideas connected to smaller chunks of information. They can also use pictures instead of words to help the more visual learner. Adding color to a map can help certain ideas stand out. This can be particularly helpful for students to begin to understand the process of prioritization in skills. Combining words and pictures is probably the most commonly used type of map. Lines are drawn between connecting concepts to show relationships and because the reader is creating it himself or herself, it is meaningful only to them. Maps are individual creations and revolve around the reader's learning and prior knowledge.

Other types of graphic organizers can also help students acquire information from content area texts. Mind mapping, for example, is a strategy that combines pictures and words to convey the underlying concepts of what was read. There are many different types of graphic organizers from which a teacher can draw to support students. However, students need to be able to apply these skills on their own. In other words, they need to be able to create their own graphic organizer to meet the needs of the task before them. A personally created organizer can become the most efficient and most meaningful strategy of all.

Reading comprehension is the ultimate goal of any reading activity. As students progress through the grades, it becomes increasingly important that they be able to read factual information in the content areas, like science and social studies, with as much efficiency and solid comprehension as possible. So much learning and teaching occurs through the use of texts that students need to be taught specific methods to gain comprehension from these books.

Typically, content-area texts are nonfiction in nature. Therefore, students can use specific strategies to help gain more insight. First, students can begin by analyzing the text itself. Looking at the organization and layout of the text can provide:

- Cues students may use to filter out non-pertinent information.

- Pointers to the specific places in the text where the answers sought may be located.
- Additional ways to connect information to prior knowledge, thus making the content more meaningful.

This analysis of text structure is a critical skill for students to achieve.

Children can practice the skills of skimming texts and scanning for particular topics that connect with their grade social studies, science, and mathematics content-area interests.

Use of Multiple Approaches

The Balanced Reading Approach is taking on new meaning after publication of the well-known report, *Teaching Children to Read* from the National Reading Panel (2000). A comprehensive and well-balanced reading program is becoming more complex and difficult to define.

In general, such a program should include instruction in phonemic awareness, phonics, fluency, comprehension, and vocabulary. There also needs to be time when the teacher reads *to* the children, when the teacher reads *with* the children, and where the children read for themselves. The catch phrase, "To, With, and By," has often been used to remind teachers of the types of reading that must occur within the classroom.

In reading *to* students, teachers generally use a read-aloud approach. The read-aloud helps build vocabulary and listening comprehension. It allows modeling of fluent reading and builds a love of reading.

When reading *with* students, teachers use two different approaches: shared reading and guided reading. Shared reading allows the teacher to share more difficult texts with the students than they might be able to read on their own. The teacher generally focuses on comprehension skills and will often complete think alouds or use other comprehension strategies to increase the development of these skills. Vocabulary development and modeling appropriate fluency are also key factors in shared reading. In guided reading, the students are reading texts on their instructional levels. In these small groups, skill development occurs regularly. This is where the phonics skills and phonemic awareness skills can be focused on specifically for a small group of students.

Finally, independent reading (*by* students) provides each child the opportunity to practice all of the parts of reading. Children are able to get multiple repetitions of the same skills taught otherwise to build the automatic nature with which they read.

No one part of the reading program as described above would be sufficient to help the students develop and become proficient readers. It is the inter-relationship of all these parts that makes the program work. If one part is removed, not only are skills missed, but also the practice opportunities and modeling opportunities are lost.

While all of the components of good reading instruction can be taught or practiced in each section individually, it is when they are combined that the most economical use of the time occurs.

Teachers should have a toolkit of instructional strategies, materials, and technologies to encourage and teach students how to solve problems and think critically about subject content. With each curriculum chosen by a district for school implementation comes an expectation that students must master benchmarks and standards of learning skills. There is an established level of academic performance and proficiency in public schools that students are required to master in today's classrooms. Research of national and state standards indicate that there are additional benchmarks and learning objectives in the subject areas of science, foreign language, English language arts, history, art, health, civics, economics, geography, physical education, mathematics, and social studies that students are required to master in state assessments (Marzano and Kendall, 1996).

Higher Order and Critical Thinking Skills

Students use basic skills to understand things that are read such as a reading passage, a math-word problem, or directions for a project. However, students apply additional thinking skills to fully comprehend how what was read could be applied to their own life or how to make comparisons or choices based on the factual information given. These higher-order thinking skills are called *critical thinking skills* as students think about thinking and teachers are instrumental in helping students use these skills in everyday activities.

- Comparing shopping ads or catalogue deals
- Finding the main idea from readings
- Applying what's been learned to new situations
- Gathering information/data from a diversity of sources to plan a project
- Following a sequence of directions
- Looking for cause and effect relationships
- Comparing and contrasting information and synthesizing information

Teachers who couple diversity in instructional practices with engaging and challenging curriculum and the latest advances in technology can create the ultimate learning environment for creative thinking and continuous learning for students. Teachers who are innovative and creative in instructional practices are able to model and foster creative thinking in their students. Encouraging students to maintain journals and portfolios of their valued work from projects and assignments will allow students to make conscious choices on including a diverse range of their creative endeavors in a filing format that can be treasured throughout the educational journey.

Helping students become effective note-takers and stimulating a diversity of perspectives for spatial techniques that can be applied to learning is a proactive teacher strategy for creating a visual learning environment where art and visualization become natural parts of learning. In today's computer-laden environment, students must understand that computers cannot replace the creative thinking and skill application that comes from the greatest computer on record, the human mind.

Strategies for identifying point of view, distinguishing facts from opinions and detecting faulty reasoning in informational/expository texts:

Newspapers provide wonderful features that can be used by the teacher as read-alouds to introduce children in grades 3-6 to point-of-view distinctions; specifically, editorials, editorial cartoons, and key sports editorial cartoons. Children can also come to understand the distinction between fact and fiction when they examine a newspaper advertisement or a supermarket circular for a product they commonly use, eat, drink, or wear which that includes exaggerated claims about what the product can actually do for the individual in question.

Differentiating fact from opinion can be extremely difficult for some children with language or reading disabilities. Children need to be taught the difference between statements that are factual in nature and those that state an opinion. In the early grades it helps to define facts as statements that can be proven to be correct, and opinions as statements that cannot be proven, about which people may disagree. To do this, a child must be taught what constitutes "proof," and this may involve some discussion. Some forms of proof are sensory; you can see, hear or touch it (the table is blue, the bell is ringing, etc.) Other statements may require finding a reference or expert to consult (checking the dictionary to see how a word is spelled, an encyclopedia to see where tigers live, or the teacher to see what tonight's homework is). Local events can be used to illustrate this. The statement, "The Chicago Cubs play baseball in Wrigley Field in Chicago," can be verified as fact by looking it up in a book, a magazine, or on a map.

However, the statement "Baseball is a fun game to watch," cannot be proved and it is likely the students will disagree on whether it is true or not.

Children can be taught to look for key words or ideas that signal an opinion. Any value judgment or use of the word "should" will be an opinion, for example. Children often have difficulty understanding that just because they agree with an opinion does not make it a fact (e.g., just because they like baseball does not make the 'baseball is fun' statement a fact). They will also have problems understanding that just because a statement is *wrong* does not make it an opinion (e.g., if someone miscounts and says there are 13 children in the room when there are actually only 12, it is not an opinion, just a mistake.).

Skill 5.16 Identify explicit and systematic instructional methods for developing phonics skills

As noted in earlier sections, most children diagnosed with specific reading disabilities, as well as most of those who are slow to learn to read show deficits in phoneme awareness, phonics, or both. Most forms of Dyslexia include phonics or phoneme awareness deficits, though some may involve other deficits as well. The National Reading Panel's review of research on teaching reading (2000) clearly stated that phoneme awareness and phonics instruction were critical for reading success, particularly in children with reading difficulties. Skill 5.11 provides an overview of methods for facilitating phoneme awareness. This section deals with the other side of the coin: phonics.

Phonics refers to instruction in and learning of the letter/sound code of the language. Once the child can discriminate among the various phonemes of the language and manipulate them in verbally presented words, it is necessary to attach those sounds to certain letters and letter combinations.

Phonics instruction may be synthetic or analytic. In the synthetic method, letter sounds are learned before the student goes on to blend the sounds to form words. This usually means repeated drills on individual letters or letter combinations and sounds. Once the students can reliably produce a correct sound for a letter or combination of letters, the task of blending them into words begins.

The analytic method teaches letter sounds as integral parts of words. Regularly spelled sight words are memorized first, then the sounds in each are mapped out with the teacher's help. This approach is more common in classes using the whole language approach in reading. However, both methods can be used and students with disabilities or limited phoneme awareness backgrounds may need at least some practice with a synthetic approach in order to master the code. Many students with severe deficits in phonemic awareness will need long-term, intensive instruction in phonics.

The sounds are often taught in this sequence: vowels, consonants, consonant blends at the beginning of words (e.g., bl and dr) and consonant blends at the end of words (e.g., ld and mp), consonant and vowel digraphs (e.g., ch and sh), and diphthongs (e.g., ow and oy). However, some methods that emphasize kinesthetic feedback to help identify sounds will teach consonant pairs first, because they are the most easily distinguished and have the most consistent spellings. In addition, consonant sounds are more easily differentiated *kinesthetically* through the positions of the lips, teeth, and tongue. This provides additional feedback to a child struggling with phoneme awareness preceding the phonics piece. Vowels would then be taught as a group since they are both more difficult to distinguish and have more varied spellings.

Some languages have very consistent grapheme-phoneme relationships. English does not, although the relationship is more consistent than many may think. There are, however, significant variations in the English grapheme-phoneme code. One letter or group of letters can make more than one sound in different contexts, and most phonemes can be represented by a number of different letters. Examination of the phoneme-grapheme chart in Section 5.11 shows that most sounds have multiple spellings. This is particularly true for vowel phonemes, which can have many grapheme representations (e.g., 'i', 'i-e', 'igh', or '-y' for long I). In addition, *digraphs* are multiple letter combinations that represent only one phoneme (e.g., 'ph' or 'f' for /f/, or 'ch' or 'tch' for /ch/). There are also vowel *diphthongs*, a single vowel phoneme that slides or glides from one sound to another in a fluid roll such as the 'ow' sound in 'cow,' or the 'oi' sound in 'boy.'

There are many programs and techniques for teaching phonics, and some children will pick it up more easily than others. However, most will require multiple exposures to specific phonics patterns and a step by step approach to the instruction. This can be accomplished through specifically decodable readers, readers with very controlled letter sound patterns that emphasize one or a family of phonics concepts at a time. Such readers usually include certain high frequency irregular words for practice, as well. This approach can be particularly effective with ELL students or students with decoding disabilities such as Dyslexia, because they may need extensive practice to master the code.

Other students can learn through phonics presented through a whole language or basal reader approach where the phonics portion is included in the "real" literature. Lists of children's picture books that emphasize certain phonics principles are available from many publishers and libraries.

Examples of phonics series are *Science Research Associates, Merrill Phonics* and DML's *Cove School Reading Program.*

When teaching phonics, the teacher can assist students to attend to graphophonemic cues (see Skill 5.12) by the use of skillful questioning when the child makes an error. For example:

- Does what you said match the letters?
- If the word you said was _____, what letter would it have to start (or end) with?
- Look carefully at the first letters. Then, look at the middle letters. Then, look at the last letters. What could it be?
- If the word was _____, what letter or letters would it end with?
  If you were writing *(the child's incorrect attempt)* what letter would you write first? What letters would go in the middle? What letters would go last?

It should be noted that most programs that teach phonics also teach phoneme awareness, and teachers need to assess the individual child's level of phoneme awareness before moving to phonics.

Programs That Teach Phoneme Awareness and Phonics

There are a great many programs available to teachers and choosing among them can be difficult. It is important to know the student population for which the intervention is intended and to select based upon individual needs rather than some universal standard. The American Federation of Teachers in *Building From the Best: Learning From What Works* (1999) described five remedial reading programs that research had shown were effective for various populations and problems, and that include phonics instruction:

- Direct Instruction (DI)—This is a very highly structured approach for at-risk students and involves mastery of early reading skills, as well as comprehension and analysis. It has scripted lesson plans, research-based curriculum objectives, including extensive phoneme awareness activities, and involves achievement grouping of students, a rapid pace, and the use of outside coaches and facilitators.
- Early Steps—This is a tutorial-style program for reading and language arts intervention in the first grade. It presents a balanced approach including phoneme awareness and phonics as well as reading experiences based on the Reading Recovery model, word study, and a writing component.
- Exemplary Center for Reading Instruction (ICRI)—This is a research-based program for grades 1-12 and is based on early literacy instruction, word

recognition, vocabulary, critical and inferential comprehension, writing, and study skills.

- Lindamood-Bell—This program for individual use with students grade 1-12 involves a highly structured program for multisensory instruction in phoneme awareness and phonics; followed by word study, vocabulary, and spelling; and culminating in structured use of visualizing and verbalizing techniques to aid comprehension.

- Reading Recovery—This program involves pull-out tutorials for first grade students and is meant as a supplement to regular reading classwork and instruction. It includes literature-based activities that start with familiar material and move to new areas. It includes letter and word study, and writing.

Other commonly used programs include:

- The Wilson Reading program for decoding and encoding, an outgrowth of dyslexia research with the Orton-Gillingham phonics based program. These are intensive, sequential phonics based programs that teach word formation with a multisensory approach.

- Phonografix, a phonics and spelling program that teaches letter sound correspondence through use of "sound pictures" made of letter combinations

- Open Court, a reading program with a heavy emphasis on phonics

Whatever program or programs a teacher chooses, it is important to remember that students with reading disabilities may need many months of daily instruction in phoneme awareness and phonics in order to master the code for reading and move on from "learning to read" to "reading to learn."

COMPETENCY 6.0   KNOWLEDGE OF SKILLS RELATED TO TEACHING INTERPERSONAL INTERACTIONS AND PARTICIPATION

Skill 6.1   **Select appropriate instructional procedures for teaching adaptive life skills based on observations, ecological assessments, family interviews, and other student information**

Adaptive life skills refer to the skills that people need to function independently at home, school, and in the community. Adaptive behavior skills include communication and social skills (intermingling and communicating with other people); independent living skills (shopping, budgeting, and cleaning); personal care skills (eating, dressing, and grooming); employment/work skills (following directions, completing assignments, and being punctual for work); and functional academics (reading, solving math problems, and telling time).

Teaching adaptive behavior skills is part of the special education program for students with disabilities. Parent input is a critical part of the adaptive behavior assessment process since there are many daily living skills that are observed primarily at home and are not prevalent in the educational setting.

The measurement of adaptive behavior should consist of surveys of the child's behavior and skills in a number of diverse settings, including his class, school, home, neighborhood, and community. Since it is not possible for one person to observe a child in all of the primary environments, measurement of adaptive behavior depends on feedback from a number of people. Because parents have many opportunities to observe their child in an assortment of settings, they are normally the best source of information about adaptive behavior. The most prevalent method for collecting information about a child's adaptive behavior skills in the home environment is to have a school social worker, school psychologist, or guidance counselor interview the parents using a formal adaptive behavior assessment rating scale. These individuals may interview the parents at home, or they may hold a meeting at the school to talk with the parents about their child's behavior. Adaptive behavior information is also procured from school personnel who work with the student in order to understand how the child functions in the school environment.

There are a variety of strategies for teaching adaptive life skills, including incorporating choice, which entails allowing students to select the assignment, and allowing students to select the order in which they complete tasks. In addition, priming or pre-practice is an effective classroom intervention for students with disabilities. Priming entails previewing information or activities that a student is likely to have problems with before he or she begins working on that activity.

Partial participation or multi-level instruction is another strategy, and it entails allowing students with disabilities to take part in the same projects as the rest of their class, with specific adaptations to the activity so that it suits a student's specific abilities and requirements. Additional instructional practices include self-management, which entails teaching the student to function independently without relying on a teacher or a one-on-one aid. This strategy allows the student to become more involved in the intervention process, and it improves autonomy.

Cooperative groups are an effective instructional technique for teaching social skills. Working in groups has been known to result in increased frequency, duration, and quality of social interactions. Peer tutoring entails two students working together on an activity, with one student giving assistance, instruction, and feedback to the other.

Reinforcement Schedules: When trying to establish new patterns of behavior, it can be helpful to keep in mind that there are a variety of reinforcement schedules that can be used. Each type of reinforcement schedule affects learned behavior differently.

Continuous Reinforcement is reinforcement given every single time the desired behavior occurs. It is most useful for building and establishing new behavior patterns. For example, if you are trying to teach a student to wait his turn patiently without barging in, then during the initial stage of this process, you would reward him every time he waits patiently.

Partial Reinforcement is reinforcement given only part of the time, not every time the behavior occurs. It is usually used *after* the behavior is occurring regularly in order to wean the student off of continuous reinforcement and make the behavior less resistant to extinction. There are several types of partial reinforcement schedules and the teacher should choose the one that suits the student, the student's stage of learning, and the particular behavior and type of reinforcer.

- **A fixed-ratio schedule** reinforces a behavior after a specific number of correct responses. It can lead to a high, steady rate of responding with a brief pause after reinforcement.
- **A fixed-interval schedule** rewards the behavior the first time it occurs after a specific amount of time has passed. It produces higher rates of responding with the behavior near the end of that time and slower rates right after reinforcement.

- **A variable-ratio schedule** rewards the behavior after a changing and unpredictable number of correct responses and results in a very high and steady rate of responding. This is why gambling and lottery games use this sort of schedule.

- **A variable-interval schedule** rewards the behavior after an unknown and varying interval of time has passed. It produces a slow, steady rate of responding.

In general, ratio schedules result in higher rates of responding or behavior than interval schedules, and they tend to have a brief pause after reinforcement. Variable schedules produce higher rates of response than fixed schedules and are better at making the new behavior resistant to extinction. The variable ratio schedule results in the highest rate of behavior as well as the greatest resistance to extinction. This is particularly relevant when helping a child learn new behaviors as it is important that the behavior continue to occur even when there is no one present to reinforce it on a regular basis.

Skill 6.2   Identify methods for evaluating and documenting student progress in acquiring, generalizing, and maintaining skills related to interpersonal interactions and participation in activities across settings (e.g., at school, at home, and in the community)

After a student has been taught appropriate social and interpersonal skills there are a variety of ways to evaluate and document their progress. Some methods are as follows:
A **communication notebook** is a notebook passed from teacher to parent or other persons involved with the student to discuss the student's behavior. This allows teachers and parents to monitor the generalization of skills from one setting to another. It can also be used to discuss the individual's social and interpersonal skills across settings.

Direct observation is another way of evaluating and documenting interpersonal interactions. See Competency Skill 4.2 for detailed information about observations and Competency 2 for assessment options, such as rating scales and behavioral checklists. **Naturalistic Assessments** (informal/authentic) address the functional skills that enhance a person's independence and social interactions in a variety of settings (i.e., school, home, community, etc.). Functional skills best addressed by this method are vocational skills, such as following directions, socially acceptable behavior, and measurable work ethics. Naturalistic assessment requires planning for instruction to occur in various settings. The advantages of this method include a "real world setting," while allowing for culturally-appropriate materials. The disadvantages of this method are the requirements for long-range planning and reduced efficiency in both teaching and assessing the skill that is to be measured. See Skill 4.2 for more information on data collection on behavior.

See also Competency 7, which deals with teaching and assessing adaptive behaviors in naturalistic settings as part of the transition process.

Skill 6.3   Identify skills necessary for students with disabilities to engage in self-determination and self-advocacy

Self-concept may be defined as the collective attitudes or feelings that one holds about oneself. Children with disabilities perceive, early in life, that they are deficient in skills that seem easier for their peers without disabilities. They also receive expressions of surprise or even disgust from both adults and children in response to their differing appearance and actions, again resulting in damage to the self-concept. For these reasons, the special education teacher want to direct special and continuing effort to bettering each child's own perception of himself.

The poor self-concept of a child with disabilities causes that student at times to exhibit aggression or rage over inappropriate things. The teacher can ignore this behavior unless it is dangerous to others or too distracting to the total group, thereby reducing the amount of negative conditioning in the child's life. Further, the teacher can praise this child, quickly and frequently, for the correct responses he makes, remembering that these responses may require special effort on the student's part to produce. Further, correction, when needed, can be done tactfully and in private.

The child whose poor self-concept manifests itself in withdrawn behavior should be pulled gently into as many social situations as appropriate. This child must be encouraged to share experiences with the class, to serve as a teacher helper for projects, and to be part of small groups for tasks. Again, praise for performing these group and public acts is most effective if done immediately. The teacher must be careful, however, to "load the dice" in favor of the child to help ensure they experience success.

The teacher can plan, in advance, to structure the classroom experiences so that aversive situations will be avoided. Thus, settings that stimulate the aggressive child to act out can be redesigned, and situations that stimulate group participation can be set up in advance for the child who acts in a withdrawn manner.

Frequent, positive, and immediate are the best terms to describe the teacher feedback required by children with disabilities. Praise for very small correct acts should be given immediately when each correct act is repeated. Criticism, when necessary, should be done in private. The teacher should first check the total day's interactions with students to ensure that the number and qualitative content of verbal stimuli is heavily on the positive side. While this trait is desirable in all good teaching, it is fundamental and utterly necessary to build the fragile self-concept of youngsters with disabilities.

The teacher must have a strategy for use with the child who persists in negative behavior outbursts. One system is to intervene immediately and break the situation down into three components. First, the teacher requires the child to identify the worst possible outcome from the situation, the thing that he fears. To do this task, the child must be required to state the situation in the most factual way he can. Second, he is required to state what would really happen if this worst possible outcome happened and to evaluate the likelihood of it happening. Third, he is asked to state an action or attitude that he can take after examining the consequences in a new light. This process has been termed *rational emotive therapy*.

Self-Advocacy is learning how to speak up for yourself, making your own decisions about your own life, learning how to get information so that you can understand things that are of interest to you, finding out who will support you in your journey, knowing your rights and responsibilities, problem solving, listening and learning, reaching out to others when you need help and friendship, and learning about self-determination, according to the Wrightlaw website (2014).

There are LD Self Advocacy manuals and internet resources available on the internet. Once helpful guide for students is by Dr. Scott Crouse, "Uncovering the Mysteries of Your Learning Disability: Discovery Self Awareness and Self Discovery." http://www.ldpride.net/selfadvocacy.htm

Self-determination is quite similar in nature; a student with a disability has the right to express him or herself fully, and can become a successful person. The student has the right to exercise control over his or her choices. He or she can exhibit control and knowledge of services and supports being received. He or she can obtain needed services if deemed necessary. The student is an advocate for him or herself, and can even take part in training others in self-advocacy, and policy-making. Self-determination is powerful for a student with a disability, and allows the student to become who he or she envisions the future self to be.

COMPETENCY 7.0   KNOWLEDGE OF THE TRANSITION PROCESS

Skill 7.1   Identify activities relevant to the four stages of career development (i.e., awareness, exploration, preparation, and placement)

Career development is the complex process of acquiring the knowledge, skill, and attitudes necessary to create a plan of choosing and being successful in a particular field. Career development typically has four different stages. The stages of career development are awareness, exploration, preparation, and placement.

A. Career Awareness

Career Awareness activities focus on introducing students to the broad range of career options. First, students must be provided with current, in-depth information about careers, including job-related skills, necessary education and training, and a description of typical duties, responsibilities, and tasks. Students must be instructed on how to access the variety of available resources, such as the internet, professional magazines, newspapers, and periodicals. Guest speakers and career fairs are provided for students to speak with and interview workers with first-hand experiences.

B. Career Exploration

Career exploration focuses on learning about careers through direct, hands-on activities. This stage is also important to gain insight into the characteristics of these occupations, as well as personal interests and strengths. These activities can be provided through in-school and work-based experiences. In-school activities include contextual learning activities, simulated work experiences, and career fairs. Work-based experiences can be either non-paid or paid. These activities include job shadowing, mentors, company tours, internships, service learning, cooperative education, and independent study.

C. Career Preparation

Career preparation provides students with the specific academic and technical knowledge and skills needed in order to be successful at a particular occupation. This may include Career and Technical Education programs or postsecondary education. They include the core activities of career assessments (formal and informal) and work-readiness skills (soft-skills development, computer competency, and job search skills). Community organizations, employers, and professional organizations are also available to provide training and insight on accommodations that may be provided for students with special needs.

D. Career Placement

Students transitioning from high school need to work collaboratively with involved parents, teachers, and guidance counselors to successfully enter either the workplace or post-secondary education. Placement should depend on the student's aptitude, skills, experiences, and interests.

Skill 7.2   Identify the essential domains of transition planning (e.g., personal/social, general community functioning, employment, leisure/recreational) for students with disabilities

Transition services will be different for each student. Transition services must take into account the student's interests and preferences. Evaluation of career interests, aptitudes, skills, and training may be considered.

The transition activities that have to be addressed, unless the IEP team finds it uncalled for, are: (a) instruction, (b) community experiences, and (c) the development of objectives related to employment and other post-school areas.

a) Instruction – The instruction part of the transition plan deals with school instruction. Students should have a portfolio completed upon graduation. They should research and plan for further education and/or training after high school. Education can be in a college setting, technical school, or vocational center. Goals and objectives created for this transition domain depend upon the nature and severity of the student's disability, the student's interests in further education, plans made for accommodations needed in future education and training, and identification of post-secondary institutions that offer the requested training or education. (See Skill 7.1 for more information).

b) Community experiences – This part of the transition plan investigates how the student utilizes community resources. Resources entail places for recreation, transportation services, agencies, and advocacy services. It is essential for students to deal with the following areas:
   - recreation and leisure - examples: movies, YMCA, religious activities.
   - personal and social skills - examples: calling friends, religious groups, going out to eat.
   - mobility and transportation - examples: passing a driver's license test or utilizing Dial-A-Ride.
   - agency access - examples: utilizing a phone book and making calls.
   - system advocacy- example: have a list of advocacy groups to contact.
   - citizenship and legal issues - example: registering to vote.

c) Employment and post school areas- This segment of the transition plan investigates becoming employed. Students should complete a career interest inventory. They should have chances to investigate different careers. Many work skill activities can take place within the classroom, home, and community. Classroom activities may concentrate on employability skills, community skills, mobility, and vocational training. Home and neighborhood activities may concentrate on personal responsibility and daily chores. Community-based activities may focus on after-school and summer part-time work, cooperative education or work-study programs, individualized vocational training, and volunteer work.

d) Daily living skills – This segment of the transition plan is also important although not essential to the IEP. Living away from home can be an enormous undertaking for people with disabilities. Numerous skills are needed to live and function as an adult. In order to live as independently as possible, a person should have an income, know how to cook, clean, shop, pay bills, get a job, and have a social life. Some living situations may entail independent living, shared living with a roommate, or supported living or group homes. Areas that may need to be looked into include: personal and social skills; living options; income and finances; medical needs; and community resources and transportation.

Skill 7.3   **Demonstrate knowledge of transition planning using student and family (e.g., socioeconomic status, gender, cultural and linguistic background) to develop desired post-school outcomes**

Transition planning is mandated in the Individuals with Disabilities Education Act (IDEA). The transition planning requirements ensure that planning is begun at age 14 and continued through high school. Transition planning and services focus on a coordinated set of student-centered activities designed to facilitate the student's progression from school to post-school activities. Transition planning should be flexible and focus on the developmental and educational requirements of the student at different grades and times.

Transition planning is a student-centered event that necessitates a collaborative endeavor. Responsibilities are shared by the student, parents, secondary personnel, postsecondary personnel, and even community resources, who are all members of the transition team.

It is important that the student play a key role in transition planning. This will entail asking the student to identify preferences and interests and to attend meetings on transition planning. The degree of success experienced by the student in postsecondary educational settings depends on the student's degree of motivation, independence, self-direction, self-advocacy, and academic abilities developed in high school. Student participation in transition activities should be implemented as early as possible and no later than age 16.

In order to contribute to the transition planning process, the student should: understand his learning disability and the impact it has on learning and work; implement achievable goals; present a positive self-image by emphasizing strengths while understanding the impact of the learning disability; know how and when to discuss and ask for needed accommodations; be able to seek instructors and learning environments that are supportive; and establish an ongoing personal file that consists of school and medical records, individualized education program (IEP), resume, and samples of academic work.

The primary function of parents during transition planning is to encourage and assist students in planning and achieving their educational goals. Parents also should encourage students to cultivate independent decision-making and self-advocacy skills.

Transition planning involves input from four groups: the student, parents, secondary education professionals, and postsecondary education professionals. Working together, these groups can help the student analyze his or her individual needs and aptitudes. The result of effective transition from a secondary to a postsecondary education program is a student with a learning disability who is confident, independent, self- motivated, and striving to achieve career goals. This effective transition can be achieved if the team consisting of the student, parents, and professional personnel work as a group to create and implement effective transition plans.

Post-Secondary Considerations

The school is responsible for including the student, parents, and any involved community agencies in writing and developing the transition services. This plan then becomes a long-range goal to ensure the post-secondary outcomes the student hopes to achieve can be achieved. This may involve specific course selection, which would then need to be coordinated through the IEP. Finding the courses and enrolling the student becomes the school's responsibility, as is providing the necessary modifications and adaptations for the student to be successful.

External supports may be needed. Throughout the process, from age sixteen until graduation, or earlier, the level and frequency of these external supports may vary. It is also important that the services available at post-secondary institutions be explored completely. These services might include disability services, job placement services, written language support services, computer access services, or other such services.

When choosing a post-secondary institution, it is necessary to find a balance between curriculum and course offerings and the necessary services. Be sure to research if the university of college has a strong student support center, writing center, and learning specialists on hand, as well as tutors and peer tutors. Understand the degree offerings, or certification offerings, of each school, to deem what is appropriate for the student. Consider the class sizes, number of students on campus, and the living quarters.

Students need to have met the necessary requirements for graduation and any other prerequisites. Some post-secondary agencies have additional requirements, which must be completed for students with identified needs. It is the responsibility of the ARD committee to review and incorporate these into the transition plan.

In addition, functional vocational evaluations, employment goals and objectives, independent living goals and objectives, community experiences, acquisition of daily living skills, and governmental agency involvement should also be considered and discussed as appropriate.

Skill 7.4   Identify resources and strategies to assist students in functioning in a variety of environments to which they will be transitioning

Managing Transitions in General: Children on the Autism Spectrum, and Students with Time Management Problems

Children with Autism, or related disorders, have difficulty managing their time efficiently. Routines and knowing what will come next in the schedule is soothing, and predictable, thus managing potential outbursts or changes in behavior. There are many tools are available to help students and young adults organize their time. Here are helpful skills from The Autism Transition Handbook, accessible on
http://autismhandbook.org/index.php/Time_Management

1. Break each day up into chunks: Assign various tasks for each time period. For example, your child may be in school from 8 a.m.–3 p.m. From 3–4 p.m., he may work on homework; from 4–5 p.m., update his schedule for the next day; from 5–6 p.m., help with dinner, and so on. By chunking the tasks, it will help your child stay organized and not get overwhelmed.

2. Create an individualized activity schedule: You can help your student put together a "To Do" list of items, including homework, chores, and appointments or leisure/recreation activities. Over time, allow your young adult to do this on his own and check his progress (self-monitoring).

3. Use an organizer: − Simple paper organizer: These organizers can be divided by tabs and include sections for "To Do" lists, homework assignments, and a schedule of activities. Again, help your young adult establish a routine to check and update the organizer.

4. Electronic organizer (PDA): If your young adult likes technology, this could be a fun way to learn about organization. Most organizers have calendars and places to create "To Do" lists with pop-up reminders when a task should start. Help your student learn how to use these organizers. Create a routine to update the list and schedule every night.

Vocational Training

Vocational training is an important element in transition programs. One of the first steps in determining the appropriate vocational program entails performing a functional vocational evaluation. This evaluation gives information about a student's aptitudes, interests, and skills in relation to employment. It concentrates on practical skills related to a specific job or goal that a student has. It consists of information that is collected through situational assessments while the student is on the job. It may include surveys, observations, interviews, and other methods. The information obtained during the evaluation is utilized to define the transition activities needed for the students.

It also provides information on the student's strengths and weaknesses in the vocational area. It includes suggestions regarding potential career paths and training programs that are deemed appropriate for the student. This will make the preparation for vocational education more precise and eliminate students entering vocational programs that are ill suited and don't reflect the students likes or strengths.

Vocational educators that have knowledge of vocational training and job requirements can help provide career information to students. They can also help develop realistic assessment activities for students to determine if they have the aptitude or skills necessary to complete a particular program.

The transitional plan in the IEP should reflect appropriate vocational training that appeals to both the student's aptitude, skills, strengths, and likes. It should be based on decisions involving a variety of people, including the student, family, teachers, vocational educators, and other interested parties.

Vocational Training

Vocational education programs prepare students for entry into occupations in the labor force. Through these programs, it is intended that they become self-sufficient, self-supporting citizens. This training has typically incorporated work-study programs at the high school and post-secondary levels. These programs include training while students are in school and on-the-job training after leaving school. Instruction focuses on particular job skills and on integral activities such as job opportunities, skill requirements for specific jobs, personal qualifications in relation to job requirements, work habits, money management, and academic skills needed for particular jobs. Such vocational training programs are based on three main ideas (Blake, 1976):

1. Students need specific training in job skills. They must acquire them prior to exiting school.
2. Students need specific training and supervision in applying skills learned in school to requirements in job situations.
3. Vocational training can provide instruction and field-based experience which will meet these needs and help enable the student to work in specific occupations.

In order to ensure that the various skills learned in school can generalize to a variety of post school setting, it will be necessary for the student to practice them in varied settings, preferably those closest in form to those they will encounter after school. For further information, see Skill 1.2.

SAMPLE TEST

1. **The Individuals with Disabilities Education Act (IDEA) was signed into law in and later reauthorized through a second revision in what years?**
   (Rigorous) (Skill 1.1)

   A. 1975 and 2004

   B. 1980 and 1990

   C. 1990 and 2004

   D. 1995 and 2001

2. **How was the training of special education teachers changed by the No Child Left Behind Act of 2002?**
   (Rigorous) (Skill 1.1)

   A. It required all special education teachers to be certified in reading and math.

   B. It required all special education teachers to take the same coursework as general education teachers.

   C. If a special education teacher is teaching a core subject, he or she must meet the standard of a highly-qualified teacher in that subject.

   D. All of the above

3. **The No Child Left Behind Act (NCLB) affected students with Limited English Proficiency (LEP) by:**
   (Rigorous) (Skill 1.1)

   A. Requiring these students to demonstrate English Language Proficiency before a High School Diploma is granted.

   B. Providing allowances for schools not to require them to take and pass state Reading Exams (RCTs) if the students were enrolled in U.S. schools for less than a year.

   C. Providing allowances for these students to opt out of state math tests if the students were enrolled in a U.S. school for less than one year.

   D. Both B and C

4. **Which of the following is a specific change of language in the IDEA?**
   (Rigorous) (Skill 1.1)

   A. The term "Disorder" changed to "Disability."

   B. The term "Children" changed to "Children and Youth."

   C. The term "Handicapped" changed to "Impairments."

   D. The term "Handicapped" changed to "With Disabilities."

5. **Which component changed with the reauthorization of the Education for all Handicapped Children Act of 1975 (EHA) 1990 EHA Amendment?**
    (Rigorous) (Skill 1.1)

    A. Specific terminology

    B. Due process protections

    C. Non-discriminatory reevaluation procedures

    D. Individual education plans

6. **The definition of assistive technology devices was amended in the IDEA reauthorization of 2004 to exclude what?**
    (Average Rigor) (Skill 1.1)

    A. iPods and other hand-held devices

    B. Computer enhanced technology

    C. Surgically implanted devices

    D. Braille and/or special learning aids

7. **Which is untrue about the Americans with disabilities Act (ADA)?**
    (Rigorous) (Skill 1.1)

    A. It was signed into law by President Bush the same year as IDEA.

    B. It reauthorized the discretionary programs of EHA.

    C. It gives protection to all people on the basis of race, sex, national origin, and religion.

    D. It guarantees equal opportunities to persons with disabilities in employment, public accommodations, transportation, government services, and telecommunications.

8. **Requirements for evaluations were changed in IDEA 2004 to reflect that no 'single' assessment or measurement tool can be used to determine special education qualification, furthering that there was a disproportionate representation of what types of students?**
    (Average Rigor) (Skill 1.1)

    A. Disabled

    B. Foreign

    C. Gifted

    D. Minority and bilingual

9. **What determines whether a person is entitled to protection under Section 504?**
   (Average Rigor) (Skill 1.1)

   A. The individual must meet the definition of a person with a disability.

   B. The person must be able to meet the requirements of a particular program in spite of his or her disability.

   C. The school, business, or other facility must be the recipient of federal funding assistance.

   D. All of the above

10. **Effective transition was included in:**
    (Rigorous) (Skill 1.1)

    A. President Bush's 1990 State of the Union Message

    B. Public Law 101-476

    C. Public Law 95-207

    D. Both A and B

11. **The Free Appropriate Public Education (FAPE) describes Special Education and related services as?**
    (Easy) (Skill 1.2)

    A. Public expenditure and standard to the state educational agency.

    B. Provided in conformity with each student's individualized education program, if the program is developed to meet requirements of the law.

    C. Including preschool, elementary, and/or secondary education in the state involved.

    D. All of the above

12. **Jane is a third grader. Mrs. Smith, her teacher, noted that Jane was having difficulty with math and reading assignments. The results from recent diagnostic tests showed a strong sight vocabulary and strength in computational skills, but a weakness in comprehending what she read. This weakness was apparent in mathematical word problems as well. The multi-disciplinary team recommended placement in a special education resource room for learning disabilities two periods each school day. For the remainder of the school day, her placement will be:**
    (Easy) (Skill 1.2)

    A. In the regular classroom

    B. At a special school

    C. In a self-contained classroom

    D. In a resource room for intellectual disabilities

13. **Which of the following must be provided in a written notice to parents when proposing a child's educational placement?**
(Average Rigor) (Skill 1.2)

    A. A list of parental due process safeguards

    B. A list of current test scores

    C. A list of persons responsible for the child's education

    D. A list of academic subjects the child has passed

14. **Zero Reject requires all children with disabilities be provided with what?**
(Average Rigor) (Skill 1.2)

    A. Total exclusion of functional exclusion

    B. Adherence to the annual local education agency (LEA) reporting

    C. Free, appropriate public education

    D. Both B and C

15. **Students who receive special services in a regular classroom with consultation generally have academic and/or social-interpersonal performance deficits at which level of severity?**
(Easy) (Skill 1.2)

    A. Mild

    B. Moderate

    C. Severe

    D. Profound

16. **IEPs continue to have multiple sections; one section, present levels, now addresses what?**
(Average Rigor) (Skill 1.3)

    A. Academic achievement and functional performance

    B. English as a second language

    C. Functional performance

    D. Academic achievement

17. **What is true about IDEA? In order to be eligible, a student must:**
(Easy) (Skill 1.4)

    A. Have a medical disability

    B. Have a disability that fits into one of the categories listed in the law

    C. Attend a private school

    D. Be a slow learner

18. **Changes in requirements for Current Levels of performance require:**
(Average Rigor) (Skill 1.4)

  A. student voice in each Present Level of Performance.

  B. CSE chair must tell parents when child has unrealistic goals.

  C. Parent/Guardian must attend either by phone conference or in person.

  D. Teachers must write post adult outcomes assigning a student to a specific field.

19. **Developmental Disabilities:**
(Rigorous) (Skill 1.4)

  A. Is the categorical name for intellectual disabilities in IDEA

  B. Includes congenital conditions, such as severe Spina Bifida, deafness, blindness, or profound intellectual disability

  C. Includes children who contract diseases, such as polio or meningitis, and who are left in an incapacitated functional state

  D. Both B and C

20. **Which of the following goals reflects new IDEA requirements?**
(Rigorous) (Skill 1.3)

  A. Janet wants to be a doctor.

  B. Frank plans to attend the Culinary Institute.

  C. Janet will go to college.

  D. Carmel currently lives independently on her own.

21. **The definition for "Other Health Impaired (OHI)" in IDEA:**
(Rigorous) (Skill 1.4)

  A. Is the definition that accepts heart conditions

  B. Includes deafness, blindness, or profound intellectual disability

  C. Includes Autism and PDD

  D. Includes cochlear implants.

22. **Which is an educational characteristic common to students with mild intellectual learning and behavioral disabilities?**
(Easy) (Skill 1.5)

  A. Show interest in schoolwork

  B. Have intact listening skills

  C. Require modification in classroom instruction

  D. Respond better to passive than to active learning tasks

23. **In general, characteristics of students with learning disabilities include:**
(Average Rigor) (Skill 1.5)

   A. A low level of performance in a majority of academic skill areas

   B. Limited cognitive ability

   C. A discrepancy between achievement and potential

   D. A uniform pattern of academic development

24. **Michael's teacher complains that he is constantly out of his seat. She also reports that he has trouble paying attention to what is going on in class for more than a couple of minutes at a time. He appears to be trying, but his writing is often illegible, containing many reversals. Although he seems to want to please, he is very impulsive and stays in trouble with his teacher. He is failing reading, and his math grades, though somewhat better, are still below average. Michael's psychometric evaluation should include assessment for:**
(Average Rigor)(Skill 1.5)

   A. Mild intellectual disability

   B. Specific learning disabilities

   C. Mild behavior disorders

   D. Hearing impairment

25. **Joey is in a mainstreamed preschool program. One of the means his teacher uses in determining growth in adaptive skills is that of observation. Some questions about Joey's behavior that she might ask include:**
(Average Rigor) (Skill 1.5)

   A. Is he able to hold a cup?

   B. Can he call the name of any of his toys?

   C. Can he reach for an object and grasp it?

   D. All of the above

26. **Which of the following statements about children with an emotional/behavioral disorder is true?**
(Average Rigor) (Skill 1.5)

   A. They have very high IQs.

   B. They display poor social skills.

   C. They are poor academic achievers.

   D. Both B and C

27. **Which behavior would be expected at the mild level of emotional/behavioral disorders?**
(Average Rigor) (Skill 1.5)

    A. Attention seeking

    B. Inappropriate affect

    C. Self-Injurious

    D. Poor sense of identity

28. **Autism is a condition characterized by:**
(Easy) (Skill 1.5)

    A. Distorted relationships with others

    B. Perceptual anomalies

    C. Self-stimulation

    D. All of the above

29. **As a separate exceptionality category in IDEA, autism:**
(Average Rigor) (Skill 1.5)

    A. Includes emotional/behavioral disorders as defined in federal regulations

    B. Adversely affects educational performance

    C. Is thought to be a form of mental illness

    D. Is a developmental disability that affects verbal and non-verbal communication

30. **The CST coordinates and participates in due diligence through what process?**
(Average Rigor) (Skill 1.6)

    A. Child study team meets for the first time without parents.

    B. Teachers take child learning concerns to the school counselor.

    C. School counselor contacts parents for permission to perform screening assessments.

    D. All of the above

31. **Which of the following examples would be considered of highest priority when determining the need for the delivery of appropriate special education and related services?**
(Rigorous) (Skill 1.6)

    A. An eight-year-old boy is repeating first grade for the second time and exhibits problems with toileting, gross motor functions, and remembering number and letter symbols. His regular classroom teacher claims the referral forms are too time-consuming and refuses to complete them. He also refuses to make accommodations because he feels every child should be treated alike.

    B. A six-year-old girl who has been diagnosed as autistic is placed in a special education class within the local school.

Her mother wants her to attend residential school next year even though the girl is showing progress.

C. A ten-year-old girl with a profound intellectual disability who is receiving education services in a state institution.

D. A twelve-year-old boy with mild disabilities who was placed in a behavior disorders program but displays obvious perceptual deficits (e.g., reversal of letters and symbols and inability to discriminate sounds). He originally was thought to have a learning disability but did not meet state criteria for this exceptionality category based on results of standard scores. He has always had problems with attending to a task and is now beginning to get into trouble during seatwork time. His teacher feels that he will eventually become a real behavior problem. He receives social skills training in the resource room one period a day.

32. **When a student is identified as being at-risk academically or socially what does Federal law hope for first?**
(Rigorous) (Skill 1.6)

A. Move the child quickly to assessment.

B. Place the child in special education as soon as possible.

C. Observe the child to determine what is wrong.

D. Perform remedial intervention in the classroom.

33. **What do the 9th and 10th Amendments to the U.S. Constitution state about education?**
(Average Rigor) (Skill 1.8)

A. That education belongs to the people

B. That education is an unstated power vested in the states

C. That elected officials mandate education

D. That education is free

34. **The IDEA states that child assessment is?**
(Average Rigor) (Skill 2.1)

    A. At intervals with teacher discretion

    B. Continuous on a regular basis

    C. Left to the counselor

    D. Conducted annually

35. **Safeguards against bias and discrimination in the assessment of children include:**
(Average Rigor) (Skill 2.2)

    A. The testing of a child in Standard English

    B. The requirement for the use of one standardized test

    C. The use of evaluative materials in the child's native language or other mode of communication

    D. All testing performed by a certified, licensed psychologist

36. **Which is characteristic of group tests?**
(Average Rigor) (Skill 2.3)

    A. Directions are always read to students.

    B. The examiner monitors several students at the same time.

    C. The teacher is allowed to probe students who almost have the correct answer.

    D. Both quantitative and qualitative information may be gathered.

37. **For which of the following uses are standardized individual tests MOST appropriate?**
(Rigorous) (Skill 2.3)

    A. Screening students to determine possible need for special education services

    B. Evaluation of special education curricula

    C. Tracking of gifted students

    D. Evaluation of a student for eligibility and placement, or individualized program planning, in special education

38. Which of the following is an advantage of giving informal individual rather than standardized group tests?
(Easy) (Skill 2.3)

    A. Questions can be modified to reveal a specific student's strategies or misconceptions.

    B. The test administrator can clarify or rephrase questions.

    C. They can be inserted into the class quickly on an as needed basis.

    D. All of the above

39. Mrs. Stokes has been teaching her third grade students about mammals during a recent science unit. Which of the following would be true of a criterion-referenced test she might administer at the conclusion of the unit?
(Average Rigor) (Skill 2.3)

    A. It will be based on unit objectives.

    B. Derived scores will be used to rank student achievement.

    C. Standardized scores are effective of national performance samples.

    D. All of the above

40. For which of the following purposes is a norm-referenced test LEAST appropriate?
(Rigorous) (Skill 2.3)

    A. Screening

    B. Individual program planning

    C. Program evaluation

    D. Making placement decisions

41. Criterion-referenced tests can provide information about:
(Rigorous) (Skill 2.3)

    A. Whether a student has mastered prerequisite skills

    B. Whether a student is ready to proceed to the next level of instruction

    C. Which instructional materials might be helpful in covering program objectives

    D. All of the above

42. **Which of the following purposes of testing calls for an informal test?**
(Average Rigor) (Skill 2.3)

    A. Screening a group of children to determine their readiness for the first reader

    B. Analyzing the responses of a student with a disability to various presentations of content material to see which strategy works.

    C. Evaluating the effectiveness of a fourth-grade math program at the end of its first year of use in a specific school

    D. Determining the general level of intellectual functioning of a class of fifth graders

43. **Which of the following is not a true statement about informal tests?**
(Average Rigor) (Skill 2.3)

    A. Informal tests are useful in comparing students to others of their age or grade level.

    B. The correlation between curriculum and test criteria is much higher in informal tests.

    C. Informal tests are useful in evaluating an individual's response to instruction.

    D. Informal tests are used to diagnose a student's particular strengths and weaknesses for purposes of planning individual programs.

44. **For which situation might a teacher be apt to select a formal test?**
(Rigorous) (Skill 2.3)

    A. A pretest for studying world religions

    B. A weekly spelling test

    C. To compare student progress with that of peers of same age or grade level on a national basis

    D. To determine which content objectives outlined on the student's IEP were mastered

45. **The Key Math Diagnostic Arithmetic Test is an individually administered test of math skills. It is comprised of fourteen subtests, which are classified into the major math areas of content, operations, and applications for which subtest scores are reported. The test manual describes the population sample upon which the test was normed and reports data pertaining to reliability and validity. In addition, for each item in the test, a behavioral objective is presented. From the description, it can be determined that this achievement test is:**
(Rigorous) (Skill 2.3)

    A. Individually administered

    B. Criterion-referenced

    C. Diagnostic

    D. All of the above

46. **The best measures of a student's functional capabilities and entry-level skills are:**
(Rigorous) (Skill 2.3)

    A. Norm-referenced tests

    B. Teacher-made post-tests

    C. Standardized IQ tests

    D. Criterion-referenced measures

47. **One of your students receives a percentile rank of 45 on a standardized test. This indicates that the student's score:**
(Rigorous) (Skill 2.4)

    A. Consisted of 45 correct answers

    B. Was at the point above which 45% of the other scores fell

    C. Was at the point below which 45% of the other scores fell

    D. Was below passing

48. **Children who write poorly might be given tests that allow oral responses, unless the purpose for giving the test is to:**
(Easy) (Skill 2.5)

    A. Assess handwriting skills

    B. Test for organization of thoughts

    C. Answer questions pertaining to math reasoning

    D. Assess rote memory

49. **Alternative assessments include all of the following EXCEPT:**
(Average Rigor) (Skill 2.5)

    A. Portfolios

    B. Interviews

    C. Textbook chapter tests

    D. Student choice of assessment format

50. **Which of the following is an example of an alternative assessment?**
(Rigorous) (Skill 2.5)

    A. Testing skills in a "real world" setting in several settings

    B. Pre-test of student knowledge of fractions before beginning wood shop

    C. Answering an essay question that allows for creative thought

    D. A compilation of a series of tests in a portfolio

51. **Acculturation refers to the individual's:**
(Rigorous) (Skill 2.6)

    A. Gender

    B. Experiential background

    C. Social class

    D. Ethnic background

52. **To which aspect does fair assessment relate?**
(Easy) (Skill 2.6)

   A. Representation

   B. Acculturation

   C. Language

   D. All of the above

53. **A test that measures students' skill development in academic content areas is classified as an _____ test.**
(Average Rigor) (Skill 3.1)

   A. Achievement

   B. Aptitude

   C. Adaptive

   D. Intelligence

54. **Which of the following is an example of tactile perception?**
(Average Rigor) (Skill 3.2)

   A. Making an angel in the snow with one's body

   B. Running a specified course

   C. Identifying a rough surface with eyes closed

   D. Demonstrating aerobic exercises

55. **Which of the following activities best exemplifies a kinesthetic exercise in developing body awareness?**
(Rigorous) (Skill 3.2)

   A. Touching materials of different textures

   B. Playing a song/movement game like "Looby Loo"

   C. Identifying geometric shapes being drawn on one's back

   D. Making a shadow-box project

56. **Which of the following teaching activities is LEAST likely to enhance observational learning in students with special needs?**
(Easy) (Skill 3.2)

   A. A verbal description of the task to be performed, followed by having the children immediately attempt to perform the instructed behavior

   B. A demonstration of the behavior, followed by an immediate opportunity for the children to imitate the behavior

   C. A simultaneous demonstration and explanation of the behavior, followed by ample opportunity for the children to rehearse the instructed behavior

   D. Physically guiding the children through the behavior to be imitated, while verbally explaining the behavior

57. The _____ modality is most frequently used in the learning process.
(Average Rigor) (Skill 3.2)

   A. Auditory

   B. Visual

   C. Tactile

   D. All of the Above

58. _____ is a method used to increase student engaged learning time by having students teach other students.
(Easy) (Skill 3.2)

   A. Collaborative learning

   B. Engaged learning time

   C. Allocated learning time

   D. Teacher consultation

59. Some environmental elements that influence the effectiveness of learning styles include all EXCEPT:
(Easy) (Skill 3.2)

   A. Light

   B. Temperature

   C. Design

   D. Motivation

60. In order for a student to function independently in the learning environment, which of the following must be true?
(Average Rigor) (Skill 3.2)

   A. The learner must understand the nature of the content.

   B. The student must be able to do the assigned task.

   C. The teacher must communicate performance criteria to the learner.

   D. All of the above

61. What can a teacher plan that will allow him/her to avoid adverse situations with students?
(Rigorous) (Skill 3.2)

   A. Instructional techniques

   B. Instructional materials and formats

   C. Physical setting and the Environment

   D. All of the above

62. **John learns best through the auditory channel, so his teacher wants to reinforce his listening skills. Through which of the following types of equipment would instruction be most effectively presented?**
(Easy) (Skill 3.2)

A. Overhead projector

B. Cassette player

C. Microcomputer

D. Opaque projector

63. **When teaching a student who is predominantly auditory to read, it is best to:**
(Rigorous) (Skill 3.2)

A. Stress sight vocabulary

B. Stress phonetic analysis

C. Stress the shape and configuration of the word

D. Stress rapid reading

64. **If a student is predominantly a visual learner, he may learn more effectively by:**
(Easy) (Skill 3.2)

A. Reading aloud while studying

B. Listening to a cassette tape

C. Watching a filmstrip

D. Using body movement

65. **A prerequisite skill is:**
(Average Rigor) (Skill 3.3)

A. The lowest order skill in a hierarchy of skills needed to perform a specific task

B. A skill that must be demonstrated before instruction on a specific task can begin

C. A tool for accomplishing task analysis

D. The smallest component of any skill

66. **Presentation of tasks can be altered to match the student's rate of learning by:**
(Rigorous) (Skill 3.3)

A. Describing how much of a topic is presented in one day and how much practice is assigned according to the student's abilities and learning style

B. Using task analysis, assign a certain number of skills to be mastered in a specific amount of time

C. Introducing a new task only when the student has demonstrated mastery of the previous task in the learning hierarchy

D. Both A and C

67. **All of the following are suggestions for altering the presentation of tasks to match the student's rate of learning EXCEPT:**
(Average Rigor) (Skill 3.3)

   A. Teach in several shorter segments of time rather than a single lengthy session.

   B. Continue to teach a task until the lesson is completed in order to provide more time on task.

   C. Watch for nonverbal cues that indicate students are becoming confused, bored, or restless.

   D. Avoid giving students an inappropriate amount of written work.

68. **Which of the following is a good example of a generalization?**
(Rigorous) (Skill 3.3)

   A. Jim has learned to add and is now ready to subtract.

   B. Sarah adds sets of units to obtain a product.

   C. Bill recognizes a vocabulary word on a billboard when traveling.

   D. Jane can spell the word "net" backwards to get the word "ten."

69. **The effective teacher varies her instructional presentations and response requirements depending upon:**
(Easy) (Skill 3.3)

   A. Student needs

   B. The task at hand

   C. The learning situation

   D. All of the above

70. **For which stage of learning would computer software be utilized that allows for continued drill and practice of a skill to achieve accuracy and speed?**
(Average Rigor) (Skill 3.3)

   A. Acquisition

   B. Proficiency

   C. Maintenance

   D. Generalization

71. **Alan has failed repeatedly in his academic work. He needs continuous feedback in order to experience small, incremental achievements. What type of instructional material would best meet this need?**
(Rigorous) (Skill 3.4)

   A. Programmed materials

   B. Audiotapes

   C. Materials with no writing required

   D. Worksheets

72. After purchasing what seemed to be a very attractive new math kit for use with her SLD (specific learning disabled) students, Ms. Davis discovered her students could not use the kit unless she read the math problems and instructions to them, as the readability level was higher than the majority of the students' functional reading capabilities. Which criterion of the materials selection did Ms. Davis most likely fail to consider when selecting this math kit? *(Average Rigor) (Skill 3.4)*

    A. Durability

    B. Relevance

    C. Component parts

    D. Price

73. Which of the following questions most directly evaluates the utility of instructional material? *(Rigorous) (Skill 3.4)*

    A. Is the cost within budgetary means?

    B. Can the materials withstand handling by students?

    C. Are the materials organized in a useful manner?

    D. Are the needs of the students met by the use of the materials?

74. A money bingo game was designed by Ms. Johnson for use with her middle grade students. Cards were constructed with different combinations of coins pasted on each of the nine spaces. Ms. Johnson called out various amounts of change (e.g., 30 cents), and students were instructed to cover the coin combinations on their cards, which equaled the amount of change (e.g., two dimes and two nickels, three dimes, and so on). The student who had the first bingo was required to add the coins in each of the spaces covered and tell the amounts before being declared the winner. Five of Ms. Johnson's sixth graders played the game during the ten-minute free activity time following math the first day the game was constructed. Which of the following attributes are present in this game in this situation? *(Average Rigor) (Skill 3.4)*

    A. Accompanied by simple, uncomplicated rules

    B. Of brief duration, permitting replay

    C. Age appropriateness

    D. All of the above

75. According to the three tier RTI model described by the Florida Center for Reading Research's (FCRR), students who need a moderate amount of help in one of the five critical areas of reading instruction in a general education class would receive additional reading instruction through the:
(Average Rigor) (Skill 5.7)

    A. Core reading program

    B. Intensive Intervention program

    C. Modified Reading program

    D. Supplemental reading program

76. Modifications of course material may take the form of:
(Average Rigor) (Skill 3.5)

    A. Simplifying texts

    B. Parallel curriculum

    C. Taped textbooks

    D. All of the above

77. At which level of mathematics instruction will a child need to spend the most instructional and exploratory time in order to successfully master objectives?
(Average Rigor) (Skill 3.11)

    A. Symbolic Level

    B. Concept Level

    C. Mastery Level

    D. Connecting Level

78. Which is a less than ideal example of collaboration in successful inclusion?
(Rigorous) (Skill 3.6)

    A. Special education teachers are part of the instructional team in a regular classroom.

    B. Special education teachers assist regular education teachers in the classroom.

    C. Teaming approaches are used for problem solving and program implementation.

    D. Regular teachers, special education teachers, and other specialists or support teachers co-teach.

79. Janice requires occupational therapy and speech therapy services. She is your student. What must you do to insure her services are met?
(Rigorous) (Skill 3.6)

    A. Watch the services being rendered.

    B. Schedule collaboratively.

    C. Ask for services to be given in a push-in model.

    D. Ask them to train you to give the service.

80. **What can you do to create a good working environment with a classroom assistant?**
    (Rigorous) (Skill 3.6)

    A. Plan lessons with the assistant.

    B. Write a contract that clearly defines his/her responsibilities in the classroom.

    C. Remove previously given responsibilities.

    D. All of the above

81. **A paraprofessional has been assigned to assist you in the classroom. What action on the part of the teacher would lead to a poor working relationship?**
    (Average Rigor) (Skill 3.6)

    A. Having the paraprofessional lead a small group

    B. Telling the paraprofessional what you expect him/her to do

    C. Defining classroom behavior management as your responsibility alone

    D. Taking an active role in his/her evaluation

82. **Mrs. Freud is a consultant teacher. She has two students with Mr. Ricardo. Mrs. Freud should:**
    (Average Rigor) (Skill 3.6)

    A. Co-teach

    B. Spend two days a week in the classroom helping out.

    C. Discuss lessons with the teacher and suggest modifications before class.

    D. Pull her students out for instructional modifications.

83. **In which way is a computer like an effective teacher?**
    (Average Rigor) (Skill 3.7)

    A. Provides immediate feedback

    B. Sets the pace at the rate of the average student

    C. Produces records of errors made only

    D. Programs to skill levels at which students at respective chronological ages should be working

84. **A Behavioral Intervention Plan (BIP):**
    (Rigorous) (Skill 4.1)

    A. Should be written by a team.

    B. Should be reviewed annually.

    C. Should be written by the teacher who is primarily responsible for the student.

    D. Should consider placement.

85. **Bill talks out in class an average of 15 times an hour. Other youngsters sometimes talk out, but Bill does so at a higher:**
    (Easy) (Skill 4.2)

    A. Rate

    B. Intensity

    C. Volume

    D. Degree

86. **Which category of behaviors would most likely be found on a behavior rating scale?**
    (Easy) (Skill 4.3)

    A. Disruptive, acting out

    B. Shy, withdrawn

    C. Aggressive (physical or verbal)

    D. All of the above

87. **In establishing your behavior management plan with the students, it is best to:**
    (Average Rigor) (Skill 4.3)

    A. Have rules written and in place on day one.

    B. Hand out a copy of the rules to the students on day one.

    C. Have separate rules for each class on day one.

    D. Have students involved in creating the rules on day one.

88. **Bob shows behavior problems like lack of attention, being out of his seat, and talking out. His teacher has kept data on these behaviors and has found that Bob is showing much better self-control since he has been self-managing himself through a behavior modification program. The most appropriate placement recommendation for Bob at this time is probably:**
    (Easy) (Skill 4.4)

    A. Any available part-time special education program

    B. The regular classroom solely

    C. A behavior disorders resource room for one period a day

    D. A specific learning disabilities resource room for one period a day

89. **A Behavior Intervention Plan (BIP) is based on the behaviorist assumption that many problem behaviors are:**
(Average Rigor) (Skill 4.4)

    A. Predictable

    B. Observed

    C. Conditioned

    D. Learned

90. **Procedures employed to decrease targeted behaviors include:**
(Rigorous) (Skill 4.4)

    A. Punishment

    B. Negative reinforcement

    C. Shaping

    D. Both A and B

91. **Target behaviors must be:**
(Easy) (Skill 4.4)

    A. Observable

    B. Measurable

    C. Definable

    D. All of the above

92. **The most important step in writing a Functional Behavioral Assessment (FBA) is:**
(Rigorous) (Skill 4.4)

    A. Establish a replacement behavior.

    B. Establish levels of interventions.

    C. Establish antecedents related or causative to the behavior.

    D. Establish assessment periods of FBA effectiveness.

93. **Which description best characterizes primary reinforcers of an edible nature?**
(Average Rigor) (Skill 4.5)

    A. Natural

    B. Unconditioned

    C. Innately motivating

    D. All of the above

94. **Mrs. Chang is trying to prevent satiation from occurring so that her reinforcers will be effective, as she is using a continuous reinforcement schedule. Which of the following ideas would be LEAST effective in preventing satiation?** *(Rigorous) (Skill 4.5)*

    A. Use only one type of edible rather than a variety.

    B. Ask for ten vocabulary words rather than twenty.

    C. Give pieces of cereal, bits of fruit, or M&Ms rather than large portions of edibles.

    D. Administer a peanut then a sip of water.

95. **Which tangible reinforcer would Mr. Whiting find to be MOST effective with teenagers?** *(Easy) (Skill 4.5)*

    A. Plastic whistle

    B. Winnie-the-Pooh book

    C. Poster of a current rock star

    D. Toy ring

96. **A positive reinforcer is generally effective if it is desired by the student and is:** *(Easy) (Skill 4.5)*

    A. Worthwhile in size

    B. Given immediately after the desired behavior

    C. Given only upon the occurrence of the target behavior

    D. All of the above

97. **Dispensing school supplies is a component associated with which type of reinforcement system?** *(Average Rigor) (Skill 4.5)*

    A. Activity reinforcement

    B. Tangible reinforcement

    C. Token reinforcement

    D. Both B and C

98. **Which type of reinforcement system is most easily generalized into other settings?** *(Average Rigor) (Skill 4.5)*

    A. Social reinforcement

    B. Activity reinforcement

    C. Tangible reinforcement

    D. Token reinforcement

99. **The Carrow Elicited Language Inventory is a test designed to give the examiner diagnostic information about a child's expressive grammatical competence. Which of the following language components is being assessed?**
(Rigorous) (Skill 5.1)

A. Phonology

B. Morphology

C. Syntax

D. Both B and C

100. **In the Grammatic Closure subtest of the Illinois Test of Psycholinguistic Abilities, the child is presented with a picture representing statements such as the following: "Here is one die; here are two ____." This test is essentially a test of:**
(Rigorous) (Skill 5.1)

A. Phonology

B. Syntax

C. Morphology

D. Semantics

101. **Five-year-old Tom continues to substitute the "w" sound for the "r" sound when pronouncing words; therefore, he often distorts words, e.g., "wabbit" for "rabbit" and "wat" for "rat." His articulation disorder is basically a problem in:**
(Average Rigor) (Skill 5.1)

A. Phonology

B. Morphology

C. Syntax

D. Semantics

102. **Which of the following is untrue about the ending /er/ ?**
(Rigorous) (Skill 5.1)

A. It is an example of a free morpheme.

B. It represents one of the smallest units of meaning within a word.

C. It is called an inflectional ending.

D. When added to a word, it connotes a comparative status.

103. **Which component of language involves language content rather than the form of language?**
(Rigorous) (Skill 5.1)

A. Phonology

B. Morphology

C. Semantics

D. Syntax

104. The social skills of students in intellectual disability programs are likely to be appropriate for children of their mental age, rather than chronological age. This means that the teacher will need to do all of the following EXCEPT:
(Easy) (Skill 5.2)

    A. Model desired behavior.

    B. Provide clear instructions.

    C. Expect age-appropriate behaviors.

    D. Adjust the physical environment when necessary.

105. Which of the following is a language disorder?
(Average Rigor) (Skill 5.2)

    A. Articulation problems

    B. Stuttering

    C. Aphasia

    D. Excessive Nasality

106. Which of the following is a speech disorder?
(Average Rigor) (Skill 5.2)

    A. Disfluency

    B. Aphasia

    C. Delayed language

    D. Comprehension difficulties

107. Which of the following is an example of cross-modal perception involving integrating visual stimuli to an auditory verbal process?
(Rigorous) (Skill 5.3)

    A. Following spoken directions

    B. Describing a picture

    C. Finding certain objects in pictures

    D. Both B and C

108. Matthew's conversational speech is adequate, but when he tries to speak before a group of more than two listeners, his speech becomes mumbling and halting. Which of the following activities would be LEAST helpful in strengthening Matthew's self-expression skills?
(Rigorous) (Skill 5.3)

    A. Having him participate in show-and-tell time

    B. Asking him comprehension questions about a story that was read to the class

    C. Having him recite a poem in front of the class, with two other children

    D. Asking him to tell a joke to the rest of the class

109. All of the modes listed below are primary categories of Augmentative Alternative Communication EXCEPT:
(Easy) (Skill 5.4)

A. Wheelchairs

B. Graphical communication boards

C. Eye gaze techniques

D. Sign language

110. A functional curriculum includes:
(Average Rigor) (Skill 6.1)

A. Regents curriculum

B. Life skills

C. Remedial academics

D. Vocational placement

111. Donna has been labeled "learning disabled" since second grade and has developed a fear of not being able to keep up with her peers. She has just entered middle school with a poor self-concept and often acts out to cover up her fear of failure. What is the most appropriate action her teacher can take when Donna exhibits minor inappropriate behavior?
(Rigorous) (Skill 6.1)

A. Ignore the behavior unless it is too dangerous or distracting.

B. Praise her for her correct behavior and responses.

C. Discuss the inappropriate behavior tactfully and in private.

D. All of the above.

112. Which of the following is the first step you should take to prepare to teach preparation for social situations?
(Average Rigor) (Skill 6.1)

A. Allow students to plan events.

B. Lecture.

C. Anticipate possible problems.

D. Take your students to the anticipated setting.

113. Children with disabilities are LEAST likely to improve their social-interpersonal skills by:
(Rigorous) (Skill 6.1)

A. Developing sensitivity to other people

B. Making behavioral choices in social situations

C. Developing social maturity

D. Talking with their sister or brother

114. When you need to evaluate a student's work ethics, you should give what assessment?
(Rigorous) (Skill 6.2)

A. Naturalistic

B. Dynamic

C. Performance-based

D. Criterion-referenced

115. One of the most important goals of the special education teacher is to foster and create with the student:
(Easy) (Skill 6.3)

A. Handwriting skills

B. Self-advocacy

C. An increased level of reading

D. Logical reasoning

116. In career education, specific training and preparation required for the world of work occurs during the phase of:
(Average Rigor) (Skill 7.1)

A. Career awareness

B. Career exploration

C. Career preparation

D. Daily living and personal-social interaction

117. The transition activities that have to be addressed, unless the IEP team finds them uncalled for, are:
(Average Rigor) (Skill 7.2)

A. Instruction

B. Community experiences

C. The development of objectives related to employment and other post-school areas

D. All of the above

118. The most important member of the transition team is the:
(Easy) (Skill 7.3)

A. Parent

B. Student

C. Secondary personnel

D. Postsecondary personnel

119. **Vocational training programs are based on all of the following ideas EXCEPT:**
(Average Rigor) (Skill 7.4)

   A. Students obtain career training from elementary through high school.

   B. Students acquire specific training in job skills prior to exiting school.

   C. Students need specific training and supervision in applying skills learned in school to requirements in job situations.

   D. Students obtain needed instruction and field-based experiences that help them to be able to work in specific occupations.

120. **What is MOST descriptive of vocational training in special education?**
(Easy) (Skill 7.4)

   A. Trains students in intellectual disabilities solely.

   B. Segregates students with and without disabilities in vocational training programs.

   C. Only includes students capable of moderate supervision.

   D. Instruction focuses upon self-help skills, social-interpersonal skills, motor skills, rudimentary academic skills, simple occupational skills, and lifetime leisure and occupational skills.

ANSWER KEY

1.	C	31.	A	61.	D	91.	D
2.	C	32.	D	62.	B	92.	C
3.	A	33.	B	63.	B	93.	D
4.	D	34.	B	64.	C	94.	A
5.	A	35.	C	65.	B	95.	C
6.	C	36.	B	66.	D	96.	D
7.	B	37.	D	67.	B	97.	A
8.	D	38.	D	68.	C	98.	A
9.	D	39.	A	69.	D	99.	C
10.	B	40.	B	70.	B	100.	C
11.	D	41.	A	71.	A	101.	A
12.	A	42.	B	72.	B	102.	A
13.	A	43.	A	73.	C	103.	C
14.	C	44.	C	74.	D	104.	C
15.	A	45.	D	75.	D	105.	C
16.	A	46.	D	76.	D	106.	A
17.	B	47.	C	77.	B	107.	B
18.	A	48.	A	78.	B	108.	B
19.	D	49.	C	79.	B	109.	A
20.	C	50.	A	80.	A	110.	B
21.	A	51.	B	81.	C	111.	D
22.	C	52.	D	82.	C	112.	C
23.	C	53.	A	83.	A	113.	D
24.	B	54.	C	84.	A	114.	A
25.	D	55.	B	85.	A	115.	B
26.	D	56.	A	86.	D	116.	C
27.	A	57.	D	87.	D	117.	D
28.	D	58.	A	88.	B	118.	B
29.	D	59.	D	89.	D	119.	A
30.	D	60.	D	90.	A	120.	D

RIGOR TABLE

	Easy 20%	Average Rigor 40%	Rigorous 40%
Question #	11, 12, 17, 22, 28, 38, 48, 52, 56, 58, 59, 62, 64, 69, 85, 86, 88, 91, 95, 96, 104, 109, 115, 118, 120	6, 8, 9, 13, 14, 15, 16, 18, 23, 24, 25, 26, 27, 29, 30, 33, 34, 35, 36, 39, 42, 43, 49, 53, 54, 57, 60, 65, 67, 70, 72, 74, 75, 76, 77, 81, 82, 83, 87, 89, 93, 97, 98, 101, 105, 106, 110, 112, 116, 117, 119	1, 2, 3, 4, 5, 7, 10, 19, 20, 21, 31, 32, 37, 40, 41, 44, 45, 46, 47, 50, 51, 55, 61, 63, 66, 68,71, 73, 78, 79, 80, 84, 90, 92, 94, 99, 100, 102, 103, 107, 108, 111, 113, 114

Rationales with Sample Questions

1. **The Individuals with Disabilities Education Act (IDEA) was signed into law in and later reauthorized through a second revision in what years?**
    (Rigorous) (Skill 1.1)

    A. 1975 and 2004
    B. 1980 and 1990
    C. 1990 and 2004
    D. 1995 and 2001

Answer: C. 1990 and 2004
IDEA, Public Law 101-476, is a consolidation and reauthorization of all prior special education mandates, with amendments. It was signed into law by President Bush on October 30, 1990. Revision of IDEA occurred in 2004, and IDEA was re-authorized as the Individuals with Disabilities Education Improvement Act of 2004 (IDEIA 2004). IDEIA 2004 is commonly referred to as IDEA 2004 and was effective on July 1, 2005.

2. **How was the training of special education teachers changed by the No Child Left Behind Act of 2002?**
    (Rigorous) (Skill 1.1)

    A. It required all special education teachers to be certified in reading and math.
    B. It required all special education teachers to take the same coursework as general education teachers.
    C. If a special education teacher is teaching a core subject, he or she must meet the standard of a highly-qualified teacher in that subject.
    D. All of the above

Answer: C. If a special education teacher is teaching a core subject, he or she must meet the standard of a highly-qualified teacher in that subject.
In order for special education teachers to be a student's sole teacher of a core subject, they must meet the professional criteria of NCLB. They must be *highly qualified*, that is certified or licensed in their area of special education, and show proof of a specific level of professional development in the core subjects that they teach. As special education teachers receive specific education in the core subject they teach, they will be better prepared to teach to the same level of learning standards as the general education teacher.

3.   **The No Child Left Behind Act (NCLB) affected students with Limited English Proficiency (LEP) by:**
     (Rigorous) (Skill 1.1)

      A. Requiring these students to demonstrate English Language Proficiency before a High School Diploma is granted.
      B. Providing allowances for schools not to require them to take and pass state Reading Exams (RCTs) if the students were enrolled in U.S. schools for less than a year.
      C. Providing allowances for these students to opt out of state math tests if the students were enrolled in a U.S. school for less than one year.
      D. Both B and C

Answer: A. Requiring these students to demonstrate English Language Proficiency before a High School Diploma is granted.
The No Child Left Behind Act (NCLB) requires these students to demonstrate English Language Proficiency before a High School Diploma is granted.

4.   **Which of the following is a specific change of language in the IDEA?**
     (Rigorous) (Skill 1.1)

      A. The term "Disorder" changed to "Disability."
      B. The term "Children" changed to "Children and Youth."
      C. The term "Handicapped" changed to "Impairments."
      D. The term "Handicapped" changed to "With Disabilities."

Answer: D. The term "Handicapped" changed to "With Disabilities."
"Children" became "individuals," highlighting the fact that some students with special needs were adolescents, not just "children." The word "handicapped" was changed to "with disabilities," denoting the difference between limitations imposed by society (handicap) and an inability to do certain things (disability). "With disabilities" also demonstrates that the person is thought of first, and the disabling condition is but one of the characteristics of the individual.

5. **Which component changed with the reauthorization of the Education for all Handicapped Children Act of 1975 (EHA) 1990 EHA Amendment?**
   (Rigorous) (Skill 1.1)

   A. Specific terminology
   B. Due process protections
   C. Non-discriminatory reevaluation procedures
   D. Individual education plans

Answer: A. Specific terminology
See Skill 1.1 Question # 6.

6. **The definition of assistive technology devices was amended in the IDEA reauthorization of 2004 to exclude what?**
   (Average Rigor) (Skill 1.1)

   A. iPods and other hand-held devices
   B. Computer enhanced technology
   C. Surgically implanted devices
   D. Braille and/or special learning aids

Answer: C. Surgically implanted devices
The definition of assistive technology devices was amended to exclude devices that are surgically implanted (i.e. cochlear implants) and clarified that students with assistive technology devices shall not be prevented from having special education services. Assistive technology devices may need to be monitored by school personnel, but schools are not responsible for the implantation or replacement of such devices surgically.

7. **Which is untrue about the Americans with disabilities Act (ADA)?**
   (Rigorous) (Skill 1.1)

   A. It was signed into law by President Bush the same year as IDEA.
   B. It reauthorized the discretionary programs of EHA.
   C. It gives protection to all people on the basis of race, sex, national origin, and religion.
   D. It guarantees equal opportunities to persons with disabilities in employment, public accommodations, transportation, government services, and telecommunications.

Answer: B. It reauthorized the discretionary programs of EHA.
EHA is the precursor of IDEA, the Individuals with Disabilities Education Act. ADA, however, is Public Law 101 – 336, the Americans with disabilities Act, which gives civil rights protection to all individuals with disabilities in private sector employment, all public services, public accommodations, transportation and telecommunications. It was patterned after the Rehabilitation Act of 1973.

8. Requirements for evaluations were changed in IDEA 2004 to reflect that no 'single' assessment or measurement tool can be used to determine special education qualification, furthering that there was a disproportionate representation of what types of students?
    (Average Rigor) (Skill 1.1)

    A. Disabled
    B. Foreign
    C. Gifted
    D. Minority and bilingual

Answer: D. Minority and bilingual
IDEA 2004 recognized that there exists a disproportionate representation of minorities and bilingual students and that pre-service interventions that are *scientifically based on early reading programs, positive behavioral interventions and support,* and early intervening services may prevent some of those children from needing special education services. In addition, it recognized that students whose native language is not English do not have a language disability. They simply need to learn English.

9. What determines whether a person is entitled to protection under Section 504?
    (Average Rigor) (Skill 1.1)

    A. The individual must meet the definition of a person with a disability.
    B. The person must be able to meet the requirements of a particular program in spite of his or her disability.
    C. The school, business, or other facility must be the recipient of federal funding assistance.
    D. All of the above

Answer: D. All of the above
To be entitled to protection under Section 504, an individual must meet the definition of a person with a disability, which is: any person who (i) has a physical or mental impairment which substantially limits one or more of that person's major life activities, (ii) has a record of such impairment, or (iii) is regarded as having such an impairment. Major life activities are: caring for oneself, performing manual tasks, walking, seeing, hearing, speaking, breathing, learning, and working. The person must also be "otherwise qualified," which means that the person must be able to meet the requirements of a particular program in spite of the disability. The person must also be afforded "reasonable accommodations" by recipients of federal financial assistance.

10. **Effective transition was included in:**
    (Rigorous) (Skill 1.1)

    A. President Bush's 1990 State of the Union Message
    B. Public Law 101-476
    C. Public Law 95-207
    D. Both A and B

Answer: B. Public Law 101-476
With the enactment of P. L. 101-476 (IDEA), transition services became a right.

11. **The Free Appropriate Public Education (FAPE) describes Special Education and related services as?**
    (Easy) (Skill 1.2)

    A. Public expenditure and standard to the state educational agency.
    B. Provided in conformity with each student's individualized education program, if the program is developed to meet requirements of the law.
    C. Including preschool, elementary, and/or secondary education in the state involved.
    D. All of the above

Answer: D. All of the above
FAPE states that special education and related services are provided at public expense; meet the standards of the state educational agency; include preschool, elementary, and/or secondary education in the state involved; and are provided in conformity with each student's IEP if the program is developed to meet requirements of the law.

12. **Jane is a third grader. Mrs. Smith, her teacher, noted that Jane was having difficulty with math and reading assignments. The results from recent diagnostic tests showed a strong sight vocabulary and strength in computational skills, but a weakness in comprehending what she read. This weakness was apparent in mathematical word problems as well. The multi-disciplinary team recommended placement in a special education resource room for learning disabilities two periods each school day. For the remainder of the school day, her placement will be:**
    (Easy) (Skill 1.2)

    A. In the regular classroom
    B. At a special school
    C. In a self-contained classroom
    D. In a resource room for intellectual disabilities

Answer: A. In the regular classroom

The resource room is a special room inside the school environment where the child goes to be taught by a teacher who is certified in the area of disability. We hope the accommodations and services provided in the resource room will help her to catch up and perform with her peers in the regular classroom.

13. **Which of the following must be provided in a written notice to parents when proposing a child's educational placement?**
    (Average Rigor) (Skill 1.2)

    A. A list of parental due process safeguards
    B. A list of current test scores
    C. A list of persons responsible for the child's education
    D. A list of academic subjects the child has passed

Answer: A. A list of parental due process safeguards
Written notice must be provided to parents prior to a proposal or refusal to initiate or make a change in the child's identification, evaluation, or educational placement. Notices must contain:

- A listing of parental due process safeguards
- A description and a rationale for the chosen action
- A detailed listing of components (e.g., tests, records, reports) that were the basis for the decision
- Assurance that the language and content of the notices were understood by the parents

14. **Zero Reject requires all children with disabilities be provided with what?**
    (Average Rigor) (Skill 1.2)

    A. Total exclusion of functional exclusion
    B. Adherence to the annual local education agency (LEA) reporting
    C. Free, appropriate public education
    D. Both B and C

Answer: C. Free, appropriate public education
The principle of zero reject requires that all children with disabilities be provided with a free, appropriate public education, and the LEA reporting procedure locates, identifies, and evaluates children with disabilities within a given jurisdiction to ensure their attendance in public school.

15. **Students who receive special services in a regular classroom with consultation generally have academic and/or social-interpersonal performance deficits at which level of severity?**
(Easy) (Skill 1.2)

A. Mild
B. Moderate
C. Severe
D. Profound

Answer: A. Mild
The majority of students receiving special services are enrolled primarily in regular classes. Those with mild learning and behavior problems exhibit academic and/or social interpersonal deficits that are often evident only in a school-related setting. These students appear no different to their peers, physically.

16. **IEPs continue to have multiple sections; one section, present levels, now addresses what?**
(Average Rigor) (Skill 1.3)

A. Academic achievement and functional performance
B. English as a second language
C. Functional performance
D. Academic achievement

Answer: A. Academic achievement and functional performance
Individualized Education Plans (IEPS) continue to have multiple sections. One section, present levels, now addresses academic achievement and functional performance. Annual IEP goals must now address the same areas.

17. **What is true about IDEA? In order to be eligible, a student must:**
(Easy) (Skill 1.4)

A. Have a medical disability
B. Have a disability that fits into one of the categories listed in the law
C. Attend a private school
D. Be a slow learner

Answer: B. Have a disability that fits into one of the categories listed in the law
IDEA is a legal instrument; thus, it is defined by law. Every aspect in the operation of IDEA is laid out in law.

18. **Changes in requirements for Current Levels of performance require:** *(Average Rigor) (Skill 1.4)*

    A. student voice in each Present Level of Performance.
    B. CSE chair must tell parents when child has unrealistic goals.
    C. Parent/Guardian must attend either by phone conference or in person.
    D. Teachers must write post adult outcomes assigning a student to a specific field.

Answer: A. student voice in each Present Level of Performance
Idea's new Indicator 13 is changing the way IEPs are written. The federal government is requiring changes in IEPs to create an easier way to collect statistics on student success at reaching post school goals. While many of the requirements have been used for years, compliance is now being measured by the items listed below.

Present Levels of Performance: Student voice must be included in each Present Level of Performance. This means that Academic, Social, Physical, Management, etc. must include one student voice statement either in the strengths or needs or both. For example, "John reads fluently on a 3rd grade level. He is able to add and subtract two digit numbers. He has difficulty with grouping and multiplying. *John states that he would rather read than do math.*"

Student voice can express either his/her strengths, preferences, and/or interests. When the child begins to do vocational assessments, student voice should be related to transition to post-school activities of his/her choice. In addition, Present Levels of Performance must indicate why a student's post adult goals are realistic, or why they are not.

19. **Developmental Disabilities:** *(Rigorous) (Skill 1.4)*

    A. Is the categorical name for intellectual disabilities in IDEA
    B. Includes congenital conditions, such as severe Spina Bifida, deafness, blindness, or profound intellectual disability
    C. Includes children who contract diseases, such as polio or meningitis, and who are left in an incapacitated functional state
    D. Both B and C

Answer: D. Both B and C
Developmental disabilities include congenital conditions and children who contract diseases and are left in an incapacitated functional state.

20. **Which of the following goals reflects new IDEA requirements?**
    (Rigorous) (Skill 1.3)

    A. Janet wants to be a doctor.
    B. Frank intends to go to The Culinary Institute.
    C. Janet will go to college.
    D. Carmel currently lives independently on her own.

Answer: C. Janet will go to college.
Post adult outcome must now be written with a "student will" statement.

21. **The definition for "Other Health Impaired (OHI)" in IDEA:**
    (Rigorous) (Skill 1.4)

    A. Is the definition that accepts heart conditions
    B. Includes deafness, blindness, or profound intellectual disability
    C. Includes Autism and PDD
    D. Includes cochlear implants

Answer: A. Is the definition that accepts heart conditions
This is the definition that accepts heart conditions. OHI includes a variety of reasons and diagnoses, including heart conditions.

22. **Which is an educational characteristic common to students with mild intellectual learning and behavioral disabilities?**
    (Easy) (Skill 1.5)

    A. Show interest in schoolwork
    B. Have intact listening skills
    C. Require modification in classroom instruction
    D. Respond better to passive than to active learning tasks

Answer: C. Require modification in classroom instruction
Some of the characteristics of students with mild learning and behavioral disabilities are as follows: Lack of interest in schoolwork; prefer concrete rather than abstract lessons; weak listening skills; low achievement; limited verbal and/or writing skills; respond better to active rather than passive learning tasks; have areas of talent or ability often overlooked by teachers; prefer to receive special help in regular classroom; higher dropout rate than regular education students; achieve in accordance with teacher expectations; require modification in classroom instruction; and are easily distracted.

23. **In general, characteristics of students with learning disabilities include:** *(Average Rigor) (Skill 1.5)*

    A. A low level of performance in a majority of academic skill areas
    B. Limited cognitive ability
    C. A discrepancy between achievement and potential
    D. A uniform pattern of academic development

Answer: C. A discrepancy between achievement and potential
The individual with a specific learning disability exhibits a discrepancy between achievement and potential.

24. **Michael's teacher complains that he is constantly out of his seat. She also reports that he has trouble paying attention to what is going on in class for more than a couple of minutes at a time. He appears to be trying, but his writing is often illegible, containing many reversals. Although he seems to want to please, he is very impulsive and stays in trouble with his teacher. He is failing reading, and his math grades, though somewhat better, are still below average. Michael's psychometric evaluation should include assessment for:** *(Average Rigor)(Skill 1.5)*

    A. Mild intellectual disability
    B. Specific learning disabilities
    C. Mild behavior disorders
    D. Hearing impairment

Answer: B. Specific learning disabilities
Some of the characteristics of persons with learning disabilities are:

- Hyperactivity: a rate of motor activity higher than normal
- Perceptual difficulties: visual, auditory, and haptic perceptual problems
- Perceptual-motor impairments: poor integration of visual and motor systems, often affecting fine motor coordination
- Disorders of memory and thinking: memory deficits, trouble with problem-solving, concept formation and association, poor awareness of own metacognitive skills (learning strategies)
- Impulsiveness: acts before considering consequences, poor impulse control, often followed by remorselessness
- Academic problems in reading, math, writing or spelling; significant discrepancies in ability levels

25. **Joey is in a mainstreamed preschool program. One of the means his teacher uses in determining growth in adaptive skills is that of observation. Some questions about Joey's behavior that she might ask include:**
(Average Rigor) (Skill 1.5)

    A. Is he able to hold a cup?
    B. Can he call the name of any of his toys?
    C. Can he reach for an object and grasp it?
    D. All of the above

Answer: D. All of the above
Here are some characteristics of individuals with intellectual disabilities:

- IQ of 70 or below
- Limited cognitive ability; delayed academic achievement, particularly in language-related subjects
- Deficits in memory, which often relate to poor initial perception, or inability to apply stored information to relevant situations
- Impaired formulation of learning strategies
- Difficulty in attending to relevant aspects of stimuli: slowness in reaction time or in employing alternate strategies
- Deficits in many adaptive behavior skills

26. **Which of the following statements about children with an emotional/behavioral disorder is true?**
(Average Rigor) (Skill 1.5)

    A. They have very high IQs.
    B. They display poor social skills.
    C. They are poor academic achievers.
    D. Both B and C

Answer: D. Both B and C
Children who exhibit mild behavioral disorders are characterized by:

- Average or above average scores on intelligence tests
- Poor academic achievement; learned helplessness
- Unsatisfactory interpersonal relationships
- Immaturity; attention seeking
- Aggressive, acting-out behavior: (hitting, fighting, teasing, yelling, refusing to comply with requests, excessive attention seeking, poor anger control, temper tantrums, hostile reactions, defiant use of language) OR Anxious, withdrawn behavior: (infantile behavior, social isolation, few friends, withdrawal into fantasy, fears, hypochondria, unhappiness, crying)

27. **Which behavior would be expected at the mild level of emotional/behavioral disorders?**
    (Average Rigor) (Skill 1.5)

    A. Attention seeking
    B. Inappropriate affect
    C. Self-Injurious
    D. Poor sense of identity

Answer: A. Attention seeking
See rationale to question 34.

28. **Autism is a condition characterized by:**
    (Easy) (Skill 1.5)

    A. Distorted relationships with others
    B. Perceptual anomalies
    C. Self-stimulation
    D. All of the above

Answer: D. All of the above
In IDEA, the 1990 Amendment to the Education for All Handicapped Children Act, autism was classified as a separate exceptionality category. It is thought to be caused by a neurological or biochemical dysfunction. It generally becomes evident before age 3. The condition occurs in about 4 of every 10,000 persons. Smith and Luckasson, 1992, describe it as a severe language disorder that affects thinking, communication, and behavior. They list the following characteristics:

- **Absent or distorted relationships with people**—inability to relate with people except as objects, inability to express affection, or ability to build and maintain only distant, suspicious, or bizarre relationships.
- **Extreme or peculiar problems in communication**—absence of verbal language or language that is not functional, such as echolalia (parroting what one hears), misuse of pronouns (e.g., he for you or I for her), neologisms (made-up meaningless words or sentences), talk that bears little or no resemblance to reality.
- **Self-stimulation**—repetitive stereotyped behavior that seems to have no purposes other than providing sensory stimulation. This may take a wide variety of forms, such as swishing saliva, twirling objects, patting one's cheeks, flapping one's arms, staring, etc.
- **Self-injury**—repeated physical self-abuse, such as biting, scratching, or poking oneself, head banging, etc.
- **Perceptual anomalies**—unusual responses or absence of response to stimuli that seem to indicate sensory impairment or unusual sensitivity.

29. **As a separate exceptionality category in IDEA, autism:**
(Average Rigor) (Skill 1.5)

A. Includes emotional/behavioral disorders as defined in federal regulations
B. Adversely affects educational performance
C. Is thought to be a form of mental illness
D. Is a developmental disability that affects verbal and non-verbal communication

Answer: D. Is a developmental disability that affects verbal and non-verbal communication
See rationale to question 36.

30. **The CST coordinates and participates in due diligence through what process?**
(Average Rigor) (Skill 1.6)

A. Child study team meets for the first time without parents.
B. Teachers take child learning concerns to the school counselor.
C. School counselor contacts parents for permission to perform screening assessments.
D. All of the above

Answer: D. All of the above
The CST coordinates and participates in due diligence through a process that includes teachers' or parents' concerns about academic or functional development and goes to the counselor who then obtains permission for screening assessments of child's skills, and the results determine need. If needed, the child study team meets without parents first.

31. **Which of the following examples would be considered of highest priority when determining the need for the delivery of appropriate special education and related services?**
(Rigorous) (Skill 1.6)

   A. An eight-year-old boy is repeating first grade for the second time and exhibits problems with toileting, gross motor functions, and remembering number and letter symbols. His regular classroom teacher claims the referral forms are too time-consuming and refuses to complete them. He also refuses to make accommodations because he feels every child should be treated alike.
   B. A six-year-old girl who has been diagnosed as autistic is placed in a special education class within the local school. Her mother wants her to attend residential school next year even though the girl is showing progress.
   C. A ten-year-old girl with a profound intellectual disability who is receiving education services in a state institution.
   D. A twelve-year-old boy with mild disabilities who was placed in a behavior disorders program but displays obvious perceptual deficits (e.g., reversal of letters and symbols and inability to discriminate sounds). He originally was thought to have a learning disability but did not meet state criteria for this exceptionality category based on results of standard scores. He has always had problems with attending to a task and is now beginning to get into trouble during seatwork time. His teacher feels that he will eventually become a real behavior problem. He receives social skills training in the resource room one period a day.

Answer: A. An eight-year-old boy is repeating first grade for the second time and exhibits problems with toileting, gross motor functions, and remembering number and letter symbols. His regular classroom teacher claims the referral forms are too time-consuming and refuses to complete them. He also refuses to make accommodations because he feels every child should be treated alike.
No modifications are being made, so the child is not receiving any services whatsoever. Note also, that the teacher in this scenario is in violation of the law.

32. **When a student is identified as being at-risk academically or socially what does Federal law hope for first?**
    (Rigorous) (Skill 1.6)

    A. Move the child quickly to assessment.
    B. Place the child in special education as soon as possible.
    C. Observe the child to determine what is wrong.
    D. Perform remedial intervention in the classroom.

Answer: D. Perform remedial intervention in the classroom.
Once a student is identified as being at-risk academically or socially, remedial interventions are attempted within the regular classroom. Federal legislation requires that sincere efforts be made to help the child learn in the regular classroom.

33. **What do the 9th and 10th Amendments to the U.S. Constitution state about education?**
    (Average Rigor) (Skill 1.8)

    A. That education belongs to the people
    B. That education is an unstated power vested in the states
    C. That elected officials mandate education
    D. That education is free

Answer: B. That education is an unstated power vested in the states
The 9th and 10th Amendments state that education is an unstated power vested in the states.

34. **The IDEA states that child assessment is?**
    (Average Rigor) (Skill 2.1)

    A. At intervals with teacher discretion
    B. Continuous on a regular basis
    C. Left to the counselor
    D. Conducted annually

Answer: B. Continuous on a regular basis
Assessments in Special Education are continuous and occur on a regular basis.

35. **Safeguards against bias and discrimination in the assessment of children include:**
    (Average Rigor) (Skill 2.2)

    A. The testing of a child in Standard English
    B. The requirement for the use of one standardized test
    C. The use of evaluative materials in the child's native language or other mode of communication
    D. All testing performed by a certified, licensed psychologist

Answer: C. The use of evaluative materials in the child's native language or other mode of communication
The law requires that the child be evaluated in his native language or mode of communication. The idea that a licensed psychologist evaluates the child does not meet the criteria if it is not done in the child's normal mode of communication.

36. **Which is characteristic of group tests?**
    (Average Rigor) (Skill 2.3)

    A. Directions are always read to students.
    B. The examiner monitors several students at the same time.
    C. The teacher must follow a standardized procedure.
    D. Diagnostic information cannot be gathered.

Answer: B. The examiner monitors several students at the same time.
The group test variable simply refers to the manner of presentation of the test. A group test is given to more than one student at a time and the teacher monitors all the students taking the test simultaneously. Group assessments can be formal or informal, standardized or not, criterion or norm referenced. Individual assessments can be found in all these types, as well.

37. **For which of the following uses are standardized individual tests MOST appropriate?**
    (Rigorous) (Skill 2.3)

    A. Screening students to determine possible need for special education services
    B. Evaluation of special education curricula
    C. Tracking of gifted students
    D. Evaluation of a student for eligibility and placement, or individualized program planning, in special education

Answer: D. Evaluation of a student for eligibility and placement, or individualized program planning, in special education
See previous question. Standardized tests are useful for these decisions, because they are very objective and can provide a wide range of data, from comparison with grade peers (

a norm-referenced test), to mastery of certain skills (criterion referenced test), to pinpointing specific areas of strength or weakness (intelligence tests or psychological tests).

38. **Which of the following is an advantage of giving informal, individual rather than standardized group tests?**
(Easy) (Skill 2.3)

   A. Questions can be modified to reveal a specific student's strategies or misconceptions..
   B. The test administrator can clarify or rephrase questions.
   C. They can be inserted into the class quickly on an as needed basis.
   D. All of the above

Answer: D. All of the above
Standardized group tests are administered to a group in a specifically prescribed manner, with strict rules to keep procedures, scoring, and interpretation of results uniform in all cases. Such tests allow comparisons to be made across populations, ages, or grades. *Informal* assessments have less objective measures, and may include anecdotes or observations that may or may not be quantified, interviews, informal questioning during a task, etc. An example of an informal *individually* administered assessment might be watching a student sort objects to see what attribute is most important to the student, or questioning a student to see what he or she found confusing about a task. All of the answers listed are advantages of giving informal individual rather than standardized group tests. Since standardized tests require rigid adherence to a precise format and presentation, they do not have the flexibility needed to modify questions to follow an individual student's strategies or needs as they work.

39. **Mrs. Stokes has been teaching her third grade students about mammals during a recent science unit. Which of the following would be true of a criterion-referenced test she might administer at the conclusion of the unit?**
(Average Rigor) (Skill 2.3)

   A. It will be based on unit objectives.
   B. Derived scores will be used to rank student achievement.
   C. Standardized scores are effective of national performance samples.
   D. All of the above

Answer: A. It will be based on unit objectives.
Criterion-referenced tests measure the progress made by individuals in mastering specific skills. The content is based on a specific set of objectives rather than on the general curriculum. Criterion-referenced tests provide measurements pertaining to the information a given student needs to know and the skills that student needs to master.

40. **For which of the following purposes is a norm-referenced test LEAST appropriate?**
(Rigorous) (Skill 2.3)

   A. Screening
   B. Individual program planning
   C. Program evaluation
   D. Making placement decisions

Answer: B. Individual program planning
Norm-referenced tests provide a means of comparing a student's performance to the performance typically expected of others the same age or grade but should not be used for individual program planning. Norm-referenced tests have a large advantage over criterion-referenced tests when used for screening or program evaluation. Norm-referenced tests provide a means of comparing a student's performance to the performance typically expected of others of his age or grade

41. **Criterion-referenced tests can provide information about:**
(Rigorous) (Skill 2.3)

   A. Whether a student has mastered prerequisite skills
   B. Whether a student is ready to proceed to the next level of instruction
   C. Which instructional materials might be helpful in covering program objectives
   D. All of the above

Answer: A. Whether a student has mastered prerequisite skills
In criterion-referenced testing, the emphasis is on assessing specific and relevant behaviors that have been mastered. Items on criterion-referenced tests are often linked directly to specific instructional objectives.

42. **Which of the following purposes of testing calls for an informal test?**
(Average Rigor) (Skill 2.3)

   A. Screening a group of children to determine their readiness for the first reader.
   B. Analyzing the responses of a student with a disability to various presentations of content material to see which strategy works for him.
   C. Evaluating the effectiveness of a fourth grade math program at the end of its first year of use in a specific school.
   D. Determining the general level of intellectual functioning of a class of fifth graders.

Answer: B. Analyzing the responses of a student with a disability to various presentations of content material to see which strategy works for him.
Formal tests, such as standardized tests or textbook quizzes are objective tests that include primarily questions for which there is only one correct answer. Some are teacher

prepared, but many are commercially prepared and frequently standardized. To analyze the response of a student to different types of instructional presentation informal methods such as observation and questioning are more useful.

43. **Which of the following is not a true statement about informal tests?**
    (Average Rigor) (Skill 2.3)

    A. Informal tests are useful in comparing students to others of their age or grade level.
    B. The correlation between curriculum and test criteria is much higher in informal tests.
    C. Informal tests are useful in evaluating an individual's response to instruction.
    D. Informal tests are used to diagnose a student's particular strengths and weaknesses for purpose of planning individual programs.

Answer: A. Informal tests are useful in comparing students to others of their age or grade.
Informal tests do NOT allow comparison among students of the same age or grade. Norm referenced tests are standardized tests that compare a student's responses to those of a large population of the same age or grade. Informal tests are not useful in comparing students to others in the population because they are neither standardized nor normed. Informal tests are often teacher made and usually criterion referenced. They are useful for a variety of diagnostic and instructional planning purposes.

44. **For which situation might a teacher be apt to select a formal test?**
    (Rigorous) (Skill 2.3)

    A. A pretest for studying world religions
    B. A weekly spelling test
    C. To compare student progress with that of peers of same age or grade level on a national basis
    D. To determine which content objectives outlined on the student's IEP were mastered

Answer: C. To compare student progress with that of peers of same age or grade level on a national basis
See previous question.

45. **The Key Math Diagnostic Arithmetic Test is an individually administered test of math skills. It is comprised of fourteen subtests, which are classified into the major math areas of content, operations, and applications for which subtest scores are reported. The test manual describes the population sample upon which the test was normed and reports data pertaining to reliability and validity. In addition, for each item in the test, a behavioral objective is presented. From the description, it can be determined that this achievement test is:**
(Rigorous) (Skill 2.3)

    A. Individually administered
    B. Criterion-referenced
    C. Diagnostic
    D. All of the above

Answer: D. All of the above
The test has a limited content designed to measure to what extent the student has mastered specific areas in math. The expressions "individually administered" and "diagnostic" appear in the description of the test.

46. **The best measures of a student's functional capabilities and entry- level skills are:**
(Rigorous) (Skill 2.3)

    A. Norm-referenced tests
    B. Teacher-made post-tests
    C. Standardized IQ tests
    D. Criterion-referenced measures

Answer: D. Criterion-referenced measures
Criterion-referenced measures are useful for assessment of a student's functional capabilities and entry-level skills. Unlike norm referenced tests, which compare an individual with others of the same grade or age level, criterion-referenced tests, measure the level of functions and skills of the individual.

47. **One of your students receives a percentile rank of 45 on a standardized test. This indicates that the student's score:**
(Rigorous) (Skill 2.4)

    A. Consisted of 45 correct answers
    B. Was at the point above which 45% of the other scores fell
    C. Was at the point below which 45% of the other scores fell
    D. Was below passing

Answer: C. Was at the point below which 45% of the other scores fell

Percentile scores indicate how well the student did compared to the other students tested. A percentile rank of 45 indicates that the student's score was at the point below which 45% of the other scores fell.

48. **Children who write poorly might be given tests that allow oral responses, that is unless the purpose for giving the test is to:**
    (Easy) (Skill 2.5)

    A. Assess handwriting skills
    B. Test for organization of thoughts
    C. Answer questions pertaining to math reasoning
    D. Assess rote memory

Answer: A. Assess handwriting skills
It is necessary to have the child write if we are assessing his skill in that domain.

49. **Alternative assessments include all of the following EXCEPT:**
    (Average Rigor) (Skill 2.5)

    A. Portfolios
    B. Interviews
    C. Textbook chapter tests
    D. Student choice of assessment format

Answer: C. Textbook chapter tests
Textbook chapter tests are formal, usually multiple choice tests with one fixed, correct answer. Portfolios, interviews, and student choices in assessment format are alternative assessments with flexible formats and alternative, individually based, criteria.

50. **Which of the following is an example of an alternative assessment?**
    (Rigorous) (Skill 2.5)

    A. Testing skills in a "real world" setting in several settings
    B. Pre-test of student knowledge of fractions before beginning wood shop
    C. Answering an essay question that allows for creative thought
    D. A compilation of a series of tests in a portfolio

Answer: A. Testing skills in a "real world" setting in several settings
Naturalistic assessment is a form of alternative assessment that requires testing in actual application settings of life skills. The skill of using money correctly could be correctly assessed in this method by taking the student shopping in different settings.

51. **Acculturation refers to the individual's:**
    (Rigorous) (Skill 2.6)

    A. Gender
    B. Experiential background
    C. Social class
    D. Ethnic background

Answer: B. Experiential background
A person's culture has little to do with gender, social class, or ethnicity. A person is the product of his experiences. Acculturation is defined as: differences in experiential background.

52. **To which aspect does fair assessment relate?**
    (Easy) (Skill 2.6)

    A. Representation
    B. Acculturation
    C. Language
    D. All of the above

Answer: D. All of the above
All three aspects are necessary and vital for assessment to be fair.

53. **A test that measures students' skill development in academic content areas is classified as an _____ test.**
    (Average Rigor) (Skill 3.1)

    A. Achievement
    B. Aptitude
    C. Adaptive
    D. Intelligence

Answer: A. Achievement
Achievement tests directly assess students' skill development in academic content areas. They measure the degree to which a student has benefited from education and/or life experiences compared to others of the same age or grade level. They may be used as diagnostic tests to find strengths and weaknesses of students. They may also be used for screening, placement, progress evaluation, and curricular effectiveness.

54. **Which of the following is an example of tactile perception?**
(Average Rigor) (Skill 3.2)

A. Making an angel in the snow with one's body
B. Running a specified course
C. Identifying a rough surface with eyes closed
D. Demonstrating aerobic exercises

Answer: C. Identifying a rough surface with eyes closed
Tactile perception indicates the use of touch is being employed. Tactile surfaces are tangible and concrete.

55. **Which of the following activities best exemplifies a kinesthetic exercise in developing body awareness?**
(Rigorous) (Skill 3.2)

A. Touching materials of different textures
B. Playing a song and movement game like "Looby Loo"
C. Identifying geometric shapes being drawn on one's back
D. Making a shadow-box project

Answer: B. Playing a game like "Looby Loo"
Kinesthetic means having to do with body movement.

56. **Which of the following teaching activities is LEAST likely to enhance observational learning in students with special needs?**
(Easy) (Skill 3.2)

A. A verbal description of the task to be performed, followed by having the children immediately attempt to perform the instructed behavior
B. A demonstration of the behavior, followed by an immediate opportunity for the children to imitate the behavior
C. A simultaneous demonstration and explanation of the behavior, followed by ample opportunity for the children to rehearse the instructed behavior
D. Physically guiding the children through the behavior to be imitated, while verbally explaining the behavior

Answer: A. A verbal description of the task to be performed, followed by having the children immediately attempt to perform the instructed behavior
Students are given verbal instructions only. The children are not given a chance to observe or see the behavior so that they can imitate it. Some of the students may have hearing deficiencies. Others may need visual or kinesthetic cues to help them understand what is wanted of them.

57. The _____ modality is most frequently used in the learning process.
(Average Rigor) (Skill 3.2)

    A. Auditory
    B. Visual
    C. Tactile
    D. All of the Above

Answer: D. All of the above
The auditory, visual, and tactile modalities are the ones frequently used in the learning process. We learn through an integration of these modalities (multi-sensory approach).

58. _____ is a method used to increase student engaged learning time by having students teach other students.
(Easy) (Skill 3.2)

    A. Collaborative learning
    B. Engaged learning time
    C. Allocated learning time
    D. Teacher consultation

Answer: A. Collaborative learning
Collaborative learning is a method for increasing student learning time by having students teach other students.

59. Some environmental elements that influence the effectiveness of learning styles include all EXCEPT:
(Easy) (Skill 3.2)

    A. Light
    B. Temperature
    C. Design
    D. Motivation

Answer: D. Motivation
Individual learning styles are influenced by environmental, emotional, sociological, and physical elements. Environmental elements include sound, light, temperature, and design. Emotional elements include motivation, persistence, responsibility, and structure. Motivation is not an environmental element.

60. **In order for a student to function independently in the learning environment, which of the following must be true?**
(Average Rigor) (Skill 3.2)

   A. The learner must understand the nature of the content.
   B. The student must be able to do the assigned task.
   C. The teacher must communicate performance criteria to the learner.
   D. All of the above

Answer: D. All of the above
Together with the above, the child must be able to ask for and obtain assistance if necessary.

61. **What can a teacher plan that will allow him/her to avoid adverse situations with students?**
(Rigorous) (Skill 3.2)

   A. Instructional techniques
   B. Instructional materials and formats
   C. Physical setting and environment
   D. All of the above

Answer: D. All of the above
It is the teacher's responsibility to select instructional practices that reflect students' individual learning needs and to incorporate a wide range of learning strategies and specialized materials to meet those needs. Students display preferences for certain learning styles, and these differences are also factors in the teacher's choice of presentation and materials. Physical settings, instructional arrangements, materials available, and presentation techniques, are all factors under the teacher's control and can be manipulated to meet student needs.

62. **John learns best through the auditory channel, so his teacher wants to reinforce his listening skills. Through which of the following types of equipment would instruction be most effectively presented?**
(Easy) (Skill 3.2)

   A. Overhead projector
   B. Cassette player
   C. Microcomputer
   D. Opaque projector

Answer: B. Cassette player
An audio cassette player would help sharpen and further develop his listening skills, as he is an auditory learner.

63. **When teaching a student who is predominantly auditory to read, it is best to:**
(Rigorous) (Skill 3.2)

    A. Stress sight vocabulary
    B. Stress phonetic analysis
    C. Stress the shape and configuration of the word
    D. Stress rapid reading

Answer: B. Stress the phonetic analysis
Sensory modalities are one of the physical elements that affect learning style. Some students learn best through their visual sense (sight), others through their auditory sense (hearing), and still others by doing, touching, and moving (tactile-kinesthetic). Auditory learners generally listen to people, follow verbal directions, and enjoy hearing records, cassette tapes, and stories. Phonics has to do with sound, an auditory stimulus. Since phonics involves attaching sounds to letters, visual stimuli, the child will need to integrate the two modalities. An auditory learner will start with the sounds, then move to visual cues.

64. **If a student is predominantly a visual learner, he may learn more effectively by:**
(Easy) (Skill 3.2)

    A. Reading aloud while studying
    B. Listening to a cassette tape
    C. Watching a filmstrip
    D. Using body movement

Answer: C. Watching a filmstrip
Visual learners use their sense of sight, which is the sense being used to watch a filmstrip.

65. **A prerequisite skill is:**
(Average Rigor) (Skill 3.3)

    A. The lowest order skill in a hierarchy of skills needed to perform a specific task
    B. A skill that must be demonstrated before instruction on a specific task can begin
    C. A tool for accomplishing task analysis
    D. The smallest component of any skill

Answer: B. A skill that must be demonstrated before instruction on a specific task can begin
This is an enabling skill that a student needs in order to perform an objective successfully.

66. **Presentation of tasks can be altered to match the student's rate of learning by:** *(Rigorous) (Skill 3.3)*

   A. Describing how much of a topic is presented in one day and how much practice is assigned according to the student's abilities and learning style
   B. Using task analysis, assign a certain number of skills to be mastered in a specific amount of time
   C. Introducing a new task only when the student has demonstrated mastery of the previous task in the learning hierarchy
   D. Both A and C

Answer: D. Both A and C
Pacing is the term used for altering of tasks to match the student's rate of learning. This can be done in two ways: altering the subject content and the rate at which tasks are presented.

67. **All of the following are suggestions for altering the presentation of tasks to match the student's rate of learning EXCEPT:** *(Average Rigor) (Skill 3.3)*

   A. Teach in several shorter segments of time rather than a single lengthy session.
   B. Continue to teach a task until the lesson is completed in order to provide more time on task.
   C. Watch for nonverbal cues that indicate students are becoming confused, bored, or restless.
   D. Avoid giving students an inappropriate amount of written work.

Answer: B. Continue to teach a task until the lesson is completed in order to provide more time on task.
This action taken does not alter the subject content; neither does it alter the rate at which tasks are presented.

68. Which of the following is a good example of a generalization?
**   *(Rigorous) (Skill 3.3)***

    A. Jim has learned to add and is now ready to subtract.
    B. Sarah adds sets of units to obtain a product.
    C. Bill recognizes a vocabulary word on a billboard when traveling.
    D. Jane can spell the word "net" backwards to get the word "ten."

Answer: C. Bill recognizes a vocabulary word on a billboard when traveling.
Generalization is the occurrence of a learned behavior in the presence of a stimulus other than the one that produced the initial response. It is the expansion of a student's performance beyond the initial setting. Students must be able to expand or transfer what is learned to other settings (e.g., reading to math word problems, resource room to regular classroom). Generalization may be enhanced by the following:

*   Use many examples in teaching to deepen application of learned skills.
*   Use consistency in initial teaching situations and later introduce variety in format, procedure, and use of examples.
*   Have the same information presented by different teachers, in different settings, and under varying conditions.
*   Include a continuous reinforcement schedule at first, later changing to delayed and intermittent schedules as instruction progresses.
*   Teach students to record instances of generalization and to reward themselves at that time.
*   Associate naturally occurring stimuli when possible.

69. The effective teacher varies her instructional presentations and response
**   requirements depending upon:**
**   *(Easy) (Skill 3.3)***

    A. Student needs
    B. The task at hand
    C. The learning situation
    D. All of the above

Answer: D. All of the above
An effective teacher examines student needs, the task at hand, and the learning situation when developing instructional presentations and response requirements.

70. **For which stage of learning would computer software be utilized that allows for continued drill and practice of a skill to achieve accuracy and speed?**
(Average Rigor) (Skill 3.3)

    A. Acquisition
    B. Proficiency
    C. Maintenance
    D. Generalization

Answer: B. Proficiency
The four stages of learning are as follows:

- *Acquisition:* Introduction of a new skill
- *Maintenance:* Continued practice without further instruction
- *Proficiency:* Practice under supervision to achieve accuracy and speed
- *Generalization:* Application of the new skills in new settings and situations

71. **Alan has failed repeatedly in his academic work. He needs continuous feedback in order to experience small, incremental achievements. What type of instructional material would best meet this need?**
(Rigorous) (Skill 3.4)

    A. Programmed materials
    B. Audiotapes
    C. Materials with no writing required
    D. Worksheets

Answer: A. Programmed materials
Programmed materials are best suited, as Alan would be able to chart his progress as he achieves each goal. He can monitor himself and take responsibility for his successes.

72. After purchasing what seemed to be a very attractive new math kit for use with her SLD (specific learning disabled) students, Ms. Davis discovered her students could not use the kit unless she read the math problems and instructions to them, as the readability level was higher than the majority of the students' functional reading capabilities. Which criterion of the materials selection did Ms. Davis most likely fail to consider when selecting this math kit?
(Average Rigor) (Skill 3.4)

   A. Durability
   B. Relevance
   C. Component parts
   D. Price

Answer: B. Relevance
Relevance is the only cognitive factor listed. Since her students were severely learning disabled, she almost certainly would have considered the kit's durability and component parts. She did not have to consider price, as that would be taken care of by the district. To be fully relevant to a population, the material must be *accessible* to the population, and the reading level of the material made it inaccessible to her students.

73. Which of the following questions most directly evaluates the utility of instructional material?
(Rigorous) (Skill 3.4)

   A. Is the cost within budgetary means?
   B. Can the materials withstand handling by students?
   C. Are the materials organized in a useful manner?
   D. Are the needs of the students met by the use of the materials?

Answer: C. Are the materials organized in a useful manner?
It is a question of utility or usefulness.

74. A money bingo game was designed by Ms. Johnson for use with her middle grade students. Cards were constructed with different combinations of coins pasted on each of the nine spaces. Ms. Johnson called out various amounts of change (e.g., 30 cents), and students were instructed to cover the coin combinations on their cards, which equaled the amount of change (e.g., two dimes and two nickels, three dimes, and so on). The student who had the first bingo was required to add the coins in each of the spaces covered and tell the amounts before being declared the winner. Five of Ms. Johnson's sixth graders played the game during the ten-minute free activity time following math the first day the game was constructed. Which of the following attributes are present in this game in this situation?
(Average Rigor) (Skill 3.4)

A. Accompanied by simple, uncomplicated rules
B. Of brief duration, permitting replay
C. Age appropriateness
D. All of the above

Answer: D. All of the above
Games and puzzles should also be colorful and appealing, of relevance to individual students, and appropriate for learners at different skill levels in order to sustain interest and motivational value.

75. According to the three tier RTI model described by the Florida Center for Reading Research's (FCRR), students who need a moderate amount of help in one of the five critical areas of reading instruction in a general education class would receive additional reading instruction through the:
(Average Rigor) (Skill 5.7)

A. Core reading program
B. Intensive Intervention program
C. Modified Reading program
D. Supplemental reading program

Answer: D. Supplemental Reading Program.
Supplemental intervention programs provide help in one of the five critical areas of reading instruction: phonemic awareness, phonics, fluency, vocabulary, or comprehension. Children who have moderate needs will be in a second "tier" of assistance and will receive additional reading instruction each day. The intent is that these programs can be used to differentiate reading instruction in a general education setting, either through small group or individual work with the teacher or through additional staff assistance. The core reading program is the main program through which most children successfully achieve reading goals. Children who are two or more years behind grade level and who need much smaller group instruction or individual instruction on a much more intensive level, are in "tier 3," the *Intensive Intervention Program.*

76. **Modifications of course material may take the form of:**
(Average Rigor) (Skill 3.5)

   A. Simplifying texts
   B. Parallel curriculum
   C. Taped textbooks
   D. All of the above

Answer: D. All of the above
Materials, usually textbooks, are frequently modified because of reading level. The goal of modification is to present the material in a manner that the student can more readily understand, while preserving the basic ideas and content.

77. **At which level of mathematics instruction will a child need to spend the most instructional and exploratory time in order to successfully master objectives?**
(Average Rigor) (Skill 3.11)

   A. Symbolic Level
   B. Concept Level
   C. Mastery Level
   D. Connecting Level

Answer: B. Concept Level.
In order to internalize the concept, the child needs repeated and varied interaction with manipulatives at the concept level. It is important that, wherever possible, the child be led to *discover* the concept rather than having it stated by the teacher, then trying to memorize it. Following this stage, the child can begin to apply labels and representations *along with the manipulatives.* This stage forms a bridge, or *connecting level* to the last stage, the *symbolic level* when the child has internalized the concepts behind the symbols and can manipulate them to learn more without the support of more concrete scaffolding.

78. **Which is a less than ideal example of collaboration in successful inclusion?**
(Rigorous) (Skill 3.6)

   A. Special education teachers are part of the instructional team in a regular classroom.
   B. Special education teachers assist regular education teachers in the classroom.
   C. Teaming approaches are used for problem solving and program implementation.
   D. Regular teachers, special education teachers, and other specialists or support teachers co-teach.

Answer: B. Special education teachers assist regular education teachers in the classroom.
In a special education setting, the special education teacher should be the lead teacher.

79. **Janice requires occupational therapy and speech therapy services. She is your student. What must you do to insure her services are met?**
(Rigorous) (Skill 3.6)

   A. Watch the services being rendered.
   B. Schedule collaboratively.
   C. Ask for services to be given in a push-in model.
   D. Ask them to train you to give the service.

Answer: B. Schedule collaboratively.
Collaborative scheduling of students to receive services is both your responsibility and that of the service provider. Scheduling together allows for both your convenience and that of the service provider. It also will provide you with an opportunity to make sure the student does not miss important information.

80. **What can you do to create a good working environment with a classroom assistant?**
(Rigorous) (Skill 3.6)

   A. Plan lessons with the assistant.
   B. Write a contract that clearly defines his/her responsibilities in the classroom.
   C. Remove previously given responsibilities.
   D. All of the above

Answer: A. Plan lessons with the assistant.
Planning with your classroom assistant shows that you respect his/her input and allows you to see where he/she feels confident.

81. **A paraprofessional has been assigned to assist you in the classroom. What action on the part of the teacher would lead to a poor working relationship?**
(Average Rigor) (Skill 3.6)

   A. Having the paraprofessional lead a small group
   B. Telling the paraprofessional what you expect him/her to do
   C. Defining classroom behavior management as your responsibility alone
   D. Taking an active role in his/her evaluation

Answer: C. Defining classroom behavior management as your responsibility alone
When you do not allow another adult in the room to enforce the class rules, you create an environment where the other adult is seen as someone not to be respected. No one wants to be in a work environment where they do not feel respected.

82. **Mrs. Freud is a consultant teacher. She has two students with Mr. Ricardo. Mrs. Freud should:**
    (Average Rigor) (Skill 3.6)

    A. Co-teach
    B. Spend two days a week in the classroom helping out.
    C. Discuss lessons with the teacher and suggest modifications before class.
    D. Pull her students out for instructional modifications.

Answer: C. Discuss lessons with the teacher and suggest modifications before class.
Consultant teaching provides the fewest interventions possible for the academic success of the academic child. Pushing in or pulling out are not essential components. However, an occasional observation as a classroom observer who does not single out any students may also be helpful in providing modifications for the student.

83. **In which way is a computer like an effective teacher?**
    (Average Rigor) (Skill 3.7)

    A. Provides immediate feedback
    B. Sets the pace at the rate of the average student
    C. Produces records of errors made only
    D. Programs to skill levels at which students at respective chronological ages should be working

Answer: A. Provides immediate feedback
The computer is a good tool for providing immediate feedback to the student. Immediate feedback increases motivation and lessens the risk that the student will practice the wrong answers.

84. **A Behavioral Intervention Plan (BIP):**
    (Rigorous) (Skill 4.4)

    A. Should be written by a team.
    B. Should be reviewed annually.
    C. Should be written by the teacher who is primarily responsible for the student.
    D. Should consider placement.

Answer: A. Should be written by a team.
IDEA 2004 establishes that the BIP is a team intervention. Writing BIPs without a team approach does not allow the behavior to truly be addressed as a team.

85. **Bill talks out in class an average of 15 times an hour. Other youngsters sometimes talk out, but Bill does so as a higher:**
(Easy) (Skill 4.2)

   A. Rate
   B. Intensity
   C. Volume
   D. Degree

Answer: A. Rate
Rate or frequency is the number of times the behavior is displayed in a given period.

86. **Which category of behaviors would most likely be found on a behavior rating scale?**
(Easy) (Skill 4.3)

   A. Disruptive, acting out
   B. Shy, withdrawn
   C. Aggressive (physical or verbal)
   D. All of the above

Answer: D. All of the above
These are all possible problem behaviors that can adversely impact the student or the class; thus, they may be found on behavior rating scales.

87. **In establishing your behavior management plan with the students, it is best to:**
(Average Rigor) (Skill 4.3)

   A. Have rules written and in place on day one.
   B. Hand out a copy of the rules to the students on day one.
   C. Have separate rules for each class on day one.
   D. Have students involved in creating the rules on day one.

Answer: D. Have students involved in creating the rules on day one.
Rules are easier to follow when you not only know the reason they are in place, but you also took part in creating them. It may be good to have a few rules pre-written and then to discuss if they cover all the rules the students have created. If not, it is possible you may want to modify your set of pre-written rules.

88. Bob shows behavior problems like lack of attention, being out of his seat, and talking out. His teacher has kept data on these behaviors and has found that Bob is showing much better self-control since he has been self-managing himself through a behavior modification program. The most appropriate placement recommendation for Bob at this time is probably:
(Easy) (Skill 4.4)

   A. Any available part-time special education program
   B. The regular classroom solely
   C. A behavior disorders resource room for one period a day
   D. A specific learning disabilities resource room for one period a day

Answer: B. The regular classroom solely
Bob is able to manage himself and is very likely to behave like the other children in the regular classroom. The classroom is the least restrictive environment.

89. A Behavior Intervention Plan (BIP) is based on the behaviorist assumption that many problem behaviors are:
(Average Rigor) (Skill 4.4)

   A. Predictable
   B. Observed
   C. Conditioned
   D. Learned

Answer: D. Learned
Behavior modification is based on the premise that most behavior, regardless of its appropriateness, has been learned, and therefore, can be changed.

90. Procedures employed to decrease targeted behaviors include:
(Rigorous) (Skill 4.4)

   A. Punishment
   B. Negative reinforcement
   C. Shaping
   D. Both A and B

Answer: A. Punishment
Punishment and extinction may be used to decrease target behaviors.

91. **Target behaviors must be:**
(Easy) (Skill 4.4)

   A. Observable
   B. Measurable
   C. Definable
   D. All of the above

Answer: D. All of the above
Behaviors must be observable, measurable, and definable in order to be assessed and changed.

92. **The most important step in writing a Functional Behavioral Assessment (FBA) is:**
(Rigorous) (Skill 4.4)

   A. Establish a replacement behavior.
   B. Establish levels of interventions.
   C. Establish antecedents related or causative to the behavior.
   D. Establish assessment periods of FBA effectiveness.

Answer: C. Establish antecedents related or causative to the behavior.
An FBA will only be successful if antecedents are recognized. Avoidance of situations and training/cultivating of replacement behaviors then become possible.

93. **Which description best characterizes primary reinforcers of an edible nature?**
(Average Rigor) (Skill 4.5)

   A. Natural
   B. Unconditioned
   C. Innately motivating
   D. All of the above

Answer: D. All of the above
Primary reinforcers are those stimuli that are of biological importance to an individual. They are natural, unlearned, unconditioned, and innately motivating. The most common and appropriate reinforcer used in the classroom is food.

94. **Mrs. Chang is trying to prevent satiation from occurring so that her reinforcers will be effective, as she is using a continuous reinforcement schedule. Which of the following ideas would be LEAST effective in preventing satiation?**
(Rigorous) (Skill 4.5)

    A. Use only one type of edible rather than a variety.
    B. Ask for ten vocabulary words rather than twenty.
    C. Give pieces of cereal, bits of fruit, or M&Ms rather than large portions of edibles.
    D. Administer a peanut then a sip of water.

Answer: A. Use only one type of edible rather than a variety.
Here are some suggestions for preventing satiation:

- Vary reinforcers with instructional tasks.
- Shorten the instructional sessions, and presentation of reinforcers will be decreased.
- Alternate reinforcers (e.g., food, then juice).
- Decrease the size of edibles presented.
- Have an array of edibles available.

95. **Which tangible reinforcer would Mr. Whiting find to be MOST effective with teenagers?**
(Easy) (Skill 4.5)

    A. Plastic whistle
    B. Winnie-the-Pooh book
    C. Poster of a current rock star
    D. Toy ring

Answer: C. Poster of a current rock star
This tops the list of things that teenagers crave. It is the most desirable.

96. **A positive reinforcer is generally effective if it is desired by the student and is:**
(Easy) (Skill 4.5)

    A. Worthwhile in size
    B. Given immediately after the desired behavior
    C. Given only upon the occurrence of the target behavior
    D. All of the above

Answer: D. All of the above
Timing and quality of the reinforcer are key to encouraging the individual to continue the targeted behavior.

97. **Dispensing school supplies is a component associated with which type of reinforcement system?**
(Average Rigor) (Skill 4.5)

A. Activity reinforcement
B. Tangible reinforcement
C. Token reinforcement
D. Both B and C

Answer: A. Activity reinforcement
The Premack Principle states that any activity in which a student voluntarily participates on a frequent basis can be used as a reinforcer for any activity in which the student seldom participates. Running errands, decorating bulletin boards, leading group activities, passing out books or papers, collecting materials, or operating equipment all provide activity reinforcement.

98. **Which type of reinforcement system is most easily generalized into other settings?**
(Average Rigor) (Skill 4.5)

A. Social reinforcement
B. Activity reinforcement
C. Tangible reinforcement
D. Token reinforcement

Answer: A. Social reinforcement
There are many advantages to social reinforcement. It is easy to use, takes little of the teacher's time or effort, and is available in any setting. It is always positive, unlikely to satiate, and can be generalized to most situations.

99. **The Carrow Elicited Language Inventory is a test designed to give the examiner diagnostic information about a child's expressive grammatical competence. Which of the following language components is being assessed?** *(Rigorous) (Skill 5.1)*

   A. Phonology
   B. Morphology
   C. Syntax
   D. Both B and C

Answer: C. Syntax
   - Morphology and syntax refer to understanding grammatical structure of language in the receptive channel and using the grammatical structure of language in the expressive channel.
   - Assessment of morphology refers to linguistic structure of words.
   - Assessment of syntax includes grammatical usage of word classes, word order, and transformational rules for the variance of word order in constructing sentences.

100. **In the Grammatic Closure subtest of the Illinois Test of Psycholinguistic Abilities, the child is presented with a picture representing statements such as the following: "Here is one die; here are two ____." This test is essentially a test of:**
   (Rigorous) (Skill 5.1)

   A. Phonology
   B. Syntax
   C. Morphology
   D. Semantics

Answer: C. Morphology
Morphology refers to the rules governing the structure of words and how to put morphemes together to make words. "Dice" is the irregular plural form of "Die." Changing the ending to -ce is using a morphological structure. Syntax is a system of rules for sentence formation, not word formation.

101. **Five-year-old Tom continues to substitute the "w" sound for the "r" sound when pronouncing words; therefore, he often distorts words, e.g., "wabbit" for "rabbit" and "wat" for "rat." His articulation disorder is basically a problem in:**
(Average Rigor) (Skill 5.1)

    A. Phonology
    B. Morphology
    C. Syntax
    D. Semantics

Answer: A. Phonology
  - Phonology: The study of significant units of speech sounds
  - Morphology: The study of the smallest units of language that convey meaning
  - Syntax: A system of rules for making grammatically-correct sentences
  - Semantics: The study of the relationships between words and grammatical forms in a language and their underlying meaning

102. **Which of the following is untrue about the ending /er/ ?**
(Rigorous) (Skill 5.1)

    A. It is an example of a free morpheme.
    B. It represents one of the smallest units of meaning within a word.
    C. It is called an inflectional ending.
    D. When added to a word, it connotes a comparative status.

Answer: A. It is an example of a free morpheme.
A morpheme is the smallest unit of meaningful language. A free morpheme has meaning that can stand alone as a word. The ending /er/ on its own, has no meaning. It is a bound morpheme, and is affixed to a free morpheme to alter its meaning.

103. **Which component of language involves language content rather than the form of language?**
(Rigorous) (Skill 5.1)

    A. Phonology
    B. Morphology
    C. Semantics
    D. Syntax

Answer: C. Semantics
Semantics is the study of the relationships between words and grammatical forms in a language and their underlying meaning.

104. The social skills of students in intellectual disability programs are likely to be appropriate for children of their mental age, rather than chronological age. This means that the teacher will need to do all of the following EXCEPT: *(Easy) (Skill 5.2)*

  A. Model desired behavior.
  B. Provide clear instructions.
  C. Expect age-appropriate behaviors.
  D. Adjust the physical environment when necessary.

Answer: C. Expect age-appropriate behaviors
Age appropriate means mental age appropriate, not chronological age appropriate.

105. Which of the following is a language disorder? *(Average Rigor) (Skill 5.2)*

  A. Articulation problems
  B. Stuttering
  C. Aphasia
  D. Excessive Nasality

Answer: C. Aphasia
Language disorders are often considered just one category of speech disorder. The problem is really different, with its own origins and causes. Persons with language disorders exhibit one or more of the following traits:

- Difficulty in comprehending questions, commands, or statements (receptive language problems)
- Inability to adequately express their own thoughts (expressive language problems)
- Language that is below the level expected for the child's chronological age (delayed language)
- Interrupted language development (dysphasia)
- Qualitatively different language
- Total absence of language

106. Which of the following is a speech disorder?
(Average Rigor) (Skill 5.2)

    A. Disfluency
    B. Aphasia
    C. Delayed language
    D. Comprehension difficulties

Answer: A. Disfluency
Persons with speech disorders exhibit one or more of the following traits:

- Unintelligible speech or speech that is difficult to understand, and articulation disorders (distortions, omissions, substitutions)
- Speech-flow disorders (sequence, duration, rate, rhythm, fluency)
- Unusual voice quality (nasality, breathiness, hoarseness, pitch, intensity, quality disorders)
- Obvious emotional discomfort when trying to communicate (stuttering, cluttering)
- Damage to nerves or brain centers which control muscles used in speech (dysarthria).

107. Which of the following is an example of cross-modal perception involving integrating visual stimuli to an auditory verbal process?
(Rigorous) (Skill 5.3)

    A. Following spoken directions
    B. Describing a picture
    C. Finding certain objects in pictures
    D. Both B and C

Answer: B. Describing a picture
We see (visual modality) the picture and use words (auditory modality) to describe it.

108. Matthew's conversational speech is adequate, but when he tries to speak before a group of more than two listeners, his speech becomes mumbling and halting. Which of the following activities would be LEAST helpful in strengthening Matthew's self-expression skills?
(Rigorous) (Skill 5.3)

    A. Having him participate in show-and-tell time
    B. Asking him comprehension questions about a story that was read to the class
    C. Having him recite a poem in front of the class, with two other children
    D. Asking him to tell a joke to the rest of the class

Answer: B. Asking him comprehension questions about a story that was read to class.

Answering the teacher's questions emphasizes speaking in front of one other person (the teacher) and does not expand his comfort zone to a larger group. The other activities require him to speak in front of more people.

109. **All of the modes listed below are primary categories of Augmentative Alternative Communication EXCEPT:**
(Easy) (Skill 5.4)

    A. Wheelchairs
    B. Graphical communication boards
    C. Eye gaze techniques
    D. Sign language

Answer: A. Wheelchairs
The primary purpose of a wheelchair is mobility, not communication.

110. **A functional curriculum includes:**
(Average Rigor) (Skill 6.1)

    A. Regents curriculum
    B. Life skills
    C. Remedial academics
    D. Vocational placement

Answer: B. Life skills
While a, c and, d may be utilized in the functional curriculum, the curriculum may not be considered functional without addressing life skills.

111. **Donna has been labeled "learning disabled" since second grade and has developed a fear of not being able to keep up with her peers. She has just entered middle school with a poor self-concept and often acts out to cover up her fear of failure. What is the most appropriate action her teacher can take when Donna exhibits minor inappropriate behavior?**
(Rigorous) (Skill 6.1)

    A. Ignore the behavior unless it is too dangerous or distracting.
    B. Praise her for her correct behavior and responses.
    C. Discuss the inappropriate behavior tactfully and in private.
    D. All of the above.

Answer: D. All of the above
All three of the actions listed will help correct the minor inappropriate behavior, while at the same time helping to improve the child's self-concept.

112. **Which of the following is the first step you should take to prepare to teach preparation for social situations?**
(Average Rigor) (Skill 6.1)

   A. Allow students to plan events.
   B. Lecture.
   C. Anticipate possible problems.
   D. Take your students to the anticipated setting.

Answer: C. Anticipate possible problems.
Look at all the things that could go wrong first. Chances are that if you are not prepared, an embarrassing situation could occur.

113. **Children with disabilities are LEAST likely to improve their social-interpersonal skills by:**
(Rigorous) (Skill 6.1)

   A. Developing sensitivity to other people
   B. Making behavioral choices in social situations
   C. Developing social maturity
   D. Talking with their sister or brother

Answer: D. Talking with their sister or brother
The social skills of the child are known in the family and seen as "normal" for him/her. Regular conversation with a family member would be the least conducive to improving social skills. Remember, the purpose in building social-interpersonal skills is to improve a person's ability to maintain interdependent relationships between persons.

114. **When you need to evaluate a student's work ethics, you should give what assessment?**
(Rigorous) (Skill 6.2)

   A. Naturalistic
   B. Dynamic
   C. Performance-based
   D. Criterion-referenced

Answer: A. Naturalistic
Work ethics are social skills. Social skills are best evaluated over time in their natural surroundings.

115. **One of the most important goals of the special education teacher is to foster and create with the student:**
(Easy) (Skill 6.3)

   A. Handwriting skills
   B. Self-advocacy
   C. An increased level of reading
   D. Logical reasoning

Answer: B. Self-advocacy
When a student achieves the ability to recognize his/her deficits and knows how to correctly advocate for his/her needs, the child has learned one of the most important life skills.

116. **In career education, specific training and preparation required for the world of work occurs during the phase of:**
(Average Rigor) (Skill 7.1)

   A. Career awareness
   B. Career exploration
   C. Career preparation
   D. Daily living and personal-social interaction

Answer: C. Career preparation
Curricular aspects of career education include:

   - *career awareness:* diversity of available jobs
   - *career exploration:* skills needed for occupational groups
   - *career preparation:* specific training and preparation required for the world of work

117. **The transition activities that have to be addressed, unless the IEP team finds them uncalled for, are:**
(Average Rigor) (Skill 7.2)

   A. Instruction
   B. Community experiences
   C. The development of objectives related to employment and other post-school areas
   D. All of the above

Answer: D. All of the above
Transition services will be different for each student, but all three aspects must be addressed. Transition services must take into account the student's interests and

preferences. Evaluation of career interests, aptitudes, skills, and training may be considered.

118. **The most important member of the transition team is the:**
(Easy) (Skill 7.3)

   A. Parent
   B. Student
   C. Secondary personnel
   D. Postsecondary personnel

Answer: B. Student
Transition planning is a student-centered event that necessitates a collaborative endeavor. Responsibilities are shared by the student, parents, secondary personnel, and postsecondary personnel, who are all members of the transition team; however, it is important that the student play a key role in transition planning. This will entail asking the student to identify preferences and interests and to attend meetings on transition planning. The degree of success experienced by the student in postsecondary educational settings depends on the student's degree of motivation, independence, self-direction, self-advocacy, and academic abilities developed in high school. Student participation in transition activities should be implemented as early as possible and no later than age 16.

119. **Vocational training programs are based on all of the following ideas EXCEPT:**
(Average Rigor) (Skill 7.4)

   A. Students obtain career training from elementary through high school.
   B. Students acquire specific training in job skills prior to exiting school.
   C. Students need specific training and supervision in applying skills learned in school to requirements in job situations.
   D. Students obtain needed instruction and field-based experiences that help them to be able to work in specific occupations.

Answer: A. Students obtain career training from elementary through high school.
Vocational education programs or transition programs prepare students for entry into the labor force. They are usually incorporated into the work-study at the high school or post-secondary levels, and are focused on job skills, job opportunities, skill requirements for specific jobs, personal qualifications in relation to job requirements, work habits, money management, and academic skills needed for specific jobs.

120. **What is MOST descriptive of vocational training in special education?**
(Easy) (Skill 7.4)

    A. Trains students in intellectual disabilities solely.
    B. Segregates students with and without disabilities in vocational training programs.
    C. Only includes students capable of moderate supervision.
    D. Instruction focuses upon self-help skills, social-interpersonal skills, motor skills, rudimentary academic skills, simple occupational skills, and lifetime leisure and occupational skills

Answer: D. Instruction focuses upon self-help skills, social-interpersonal skills, motor skills, rudimentary academic skills, simple occupational skills, and lifetime leisure and occupational skills.

Persons with disabilities are mainstreamed with non-disabled students where possible. Special sites provide training for those persons with more severe disabilities who are unable to be successfully taught in an integrated setting. Specially-trained vocational counselors monitor and supervise student work sites.

References

Ager, C.L. & Cole, C.L. (1991). A review of cognitive-behavioral interventions for children and adolescents with behavioral disorders. *Behavioral Disorders,* 16(4), 260-275.

Aiken, L.R. (1985). *Psychological testing and assessment* (5th ed.). Boston: Allyn and Bacon.

Alberto, P.A. & Trouthman, A.C. (1990). *Applied behavior analysis for teachers: Influencing student performance.* Columbus, Ohio: Charles E. Merrill.

Algozzine, B. (1990). *Behavior problem management: Educator's resource service.* Gaithersburg, MD: Aspen Publishers.

Algozzine, B., Ruhl, K., & Ramsey, R. (1991). *Behaviorally disordered: Assessment for identification and instruction CED mini-library.* Renson, VA: The Council for Exceptional Children.

Ambron, S.R. (1981). *Child development* (3rd ed.). New York: Holt, Rinehart and Winston.

Anerson, V., & Black, L. (Eds.). (1987, Winter). National news: U.S. Department of Education releases special report (Editorial). *GLRS Journal* [Georgia Learning Resources System].

Anguili, R. (1987, Winter). The 1986 amendment to the Education of the Handicapped Act. *Confederation* [A quarterly publication of the Georgia Federation Council for Exceptional Children].

Ashlock, R.B. (1976). *Error patterns in computation: A semi-programmed approach* (2nd ed.). Columbus, Ohio: Charles E. Merrill.

Association of Retarded Citizens of Georgia (1987). *1986-87 Government report.* College Park, GA: Author.

Ausubel, D.P. & Sullivan, E.V. (1970). *Theory and problems of child development.* New York: Grune & Stratton.

Banks, J.A., & McGee Banks, C.A. (1993). *Multicultural education* (2nd ed.). Boston: Allyn and Bacon.

Baratta-Lorton, Mary. *Mathematics Their Way.* Menlo Park, Ca: Addison-Wesley, 1978.

Barrett, T.C. (Ed.). (1967). *The evaluation of children's reading achievement. in perspectives in reading, No. 8.* Newark, Delaware: International Reading Association.

Bartoli, J.S. (1989). An ecological response to Cole's interactivity alternative. *Journal of Learning Disabilities*, 22 (5), 292-297.

Basile-Jackson, J. (1982) *The exceptional child in the regular classroom.* Augusta, GA: East Georgia Center, Georgia Learning Resources System.

Bauer, A.M., & Shea, T.M. (1989). *Teaching exceptional students in your classroom.* Boston: Allyn and Bacon.

Bentley, E.L. Jr. (1980). *Questioning skills* (Videocassette & manual series). Northbrook, IL: Hubbard Scientific Company. (Project STRETCH [Strategies to Train Regular Educators to Teach Children with Handicaps], Module 1, ISBN 0-8331-1906-0).

Berdine, W.H., & Blackhurst, A.E. (1985). *An introduction to special education.* (2nd ed.) Boston: Little, Brown and Company.

Biemiller, Andrew. (2003). "Vocabulary: Needed If More Children Are To Read Well". *Reading Psychology.* 24, no. 3-4: 323-35.

Blake, K. (1976). *The mentally retarded: An educational psychology.* Englewood Cliff, NJ: Prentice-Hall.

Blevins, Wiley. *Phonemic Awareness Activities for Early Reading Success: Easy, Playful Activities That Prepare Children for Phonics Instruction.* New York: Scholastic, 1997.

Bloom, B.S. (1956). *Taxonomy of Educational Objectives, Handbook I: The Cognitive Domain.* New York: David McKay Co. Inc.

Bohline, D.S. (1985). *Intellectual and affective characteristics of attention deficit disordered children.* Journal of Learning Disabilities, 18 (10),604-608.

Bond, Linda A. *Norm-Referenced Testing and Criterion-Referenced Testing: The Differences in Purpose, Content, and Interpretation of Results.* Oak Brook, IL: North Central Regional Educational Laboratory, 1995. ERIC Document 402327.

Boone, R. (1983). Legislation and litigation. In R.E. Schmid, & L. Negata (Eds.). *Contemporary Issues in Special Education.* New York: McGraw Hill.

Brantlinger, E.A., & Guskin, S.L. (1988). Implications of social and cultural differences for special education. In Meten, E.L. Vergason, G.A., & Whelan, R.J. *Effective Instructional Strategies for Exceptional Children.* Denver, CO: Love Publishing.

Brewton, B. (1990). Preliminary identification of the socially maladjusted. In Georgia Psycho-educational Network, Monograph #1. *An Educational Perspective On:*

Emotional Disturbance and Social Maladjustment. Atlanta, GA Psychoeducational Network.

Brodesky, Amy R., et al. *Planning Strategies for Students with Special Needs: A Professional Development Activity.* Teaching Children Mathematics, 11 (October 2004): 146-54.

Brolin, D.E., & Kokaska, C.J. (1979). *Career education for handicapped children approach.* Renton, VA: The Council for Exceptional Children.

Brolin, D.E. (Ed). (1989). *Life centered career education: A competency based approach.* Reston, VA: The Council for Exceptional Children.

Brown, J.W., Lewis, R.B., & Harcleroad, F.F. (1983). *AV instruction: Technology, media, and methods* (6TH ed.). New York: McGraw-Hill.

Bryan, T.H., & Bryan, J.H. (1986). *Understanding learning disabilities* (3rd ed.). Palo Alto, CA: Mayfield.

Brown, Roger, and Hanlon, Camille. "Derivational Complexity and Order of Acquisition in Child Speech," In Hayes, J. r., ed. *Cognition and the Development of Language.* New York: Wiley, 1970.

Bryen, D.N. (1982). *Inquiries into child language.* Boston: Allyn & Bacon.

Bucher, B.D. (1987). *Winning them over.* New York: Times Books.

Burns, Paul C., Roe, Betty D., and Smith, Sandy, H. (2002) *Teaching Reading in Today's Elementary Schools.* Boston: Houghton Mifflin Co.

Burns, M. Susan, et al. *Prekindergarten Benchmarks for Language and Literacy: Progress Made and Challenges to Be Met.* NIEER Working Papers. ERIC Document 479991.

Bush, W.L., & Waugh, K.W. (1982). *Diagnosing learning problems* (3rd ed.). Columbus, OH: Charles E. Merrill.

Campbell, P. (1986). *Special needs report* [Newsletter]. 1(1), 1-3.

Carbo, M., & Dunn, K. (1986). *Teaching students to read through their individual learning styles.* Englewood Cliffs, NJ: Prentice Hall.

Cartwright, G.P., & Cartwright, C.A., & Ward, M.E. (1984). *Educating special learners* (2nd ed.). Belmont, CA: Wadsworth.

Cejka, J.M. (Consultant), & Needham, F. (Senior Editor). (1976). *Approaches to mainstreaming.* (Filmstrip and cassette kit, units 1 & 2). Boston: Teaching Resources Corporation. (Catalog Nos. 09-210 & 09-220).

Chalfant, J. C. (1985). *Identifying learning disabled students: A summary of the national task force report.* Learning Disabilities Focus, 1, 9-20.

Charles, C.M. (1976). *Individualizing instructions.* St Louis: The C.V. Mosby Company.

Chrispeels, J.H. (1991). *District leadership in parent involvement: Policies and actions in San Diego.* Phi Delta Kappa, 71, 367-371.

Clarizio, H.F. (1987). Differentiating characteristics. In Georgia Psychoeducational Network, Monograph #1, *An educational perspective on: Emotional disturbance and social maladjustment.* Atlanta, GA: Psychoeducational Network.

Clay, Marie (1975). *The Early Detection of Reading Difficulties.* London: Heinemann.

Clay, Marie M. (1995) *An Observation Survey: Of Early Literacy Achievement.* Auckland, N.Z.: Heinemann.

Clarizio, H.F. & McCoy, G.F. (1983). *Behavior disorders in children* (3rd ed.). New York: Harper & Row.

Coles, G.S. (1989). *Excerpts from the learning mystique: A critical look at disabilities.* Journal of Learning Disabilities, 22 (5), 267-278.

Collins, E. (1980). *Grouping and special students.* (Videocassette & manual series). Northbrook, IL: Hubbard Scientific Company. (Project STRETCH [Strategies to Train Regular Educators to Teach Children with Handicaps], Module 17, ISBN 0-8331-1922-2).

Craig, E., & Craig, L. (1990). *Reading In the Content Areas.* (Videocassette & manual series). Northbrook, IL: Hubbard Scientific Company. (Project STRETCH [Strategies to Train Regular Educators to Teach Children with Handicaps], Module 13, ISBN 0-8331-1918-4).

Compton, C., (1984). *A Guide to 75 Tests for Special Education.* Belmont, CA., Pitman Learning.

Cooper, J. David, and Nancy D. Kiger. *Literacy Assessment: Helping Teachers Plan Instruction.* Boston: Houghton Mifflin Co., 2008.

Council for Exceptional Children. (1976). *Introducing P.L. 94-142.* [Filmstrip-cassette kit manual]. Reston, VA: Author.

Council for Exceptional Children. (1987). *The Council for Exceptional Children's Fall 1987. Catalog of Products and Services.* Renton, VA: Author.

Council for Exceptional Children Delegate Assembly. (1983). *Council for Exceptional Children Code of Ethics* (Adopted April 1983). Reston, VA: Author.

Cunnigham, P. M., and Hall, D. (1994). *Making Words.* Torrence, CA: Good Apple Publishing.

Czajka, J.L. (1984). *Digest of Data on Person With Disabilities* (Mathematics Policy Research, Inc.). Washington, D.C.: U.S. Government Printing Office.

Dell, H.D. (1972). *Individualizing Instruction: Materials and Classroom Procedures.* Chicago: Science Research Associates.

Demonbreun, C., & Morris, J. *Classroom Management* [Videocassette & Manual series]. Northbrook, IL: Hubbard Scientific Company. Project STRETCH (Strategies to Train Regular Educators to Teach Children with Handicaps]. Module 5, ISBN 0-8331-1910-9).

Deno, E. (1970). "Special Education as Developmental Capital." *Exceptional Children* 37 (3), 229-37.

Department of Education. *Education for the Handicapped Law Reports.* Supplement 45 (1981), p. 102: 52. Washington, D.C.: U.S. Government Printing Office.

Department of Health, Education, and Welfare, Office of Education. (1977, August 23). *Education of Handicapped Children.* Federal Register, 42, (163).

Diana vs. State Board of Education, Civil No. 70-37 R.F.P. (N.D.Cal. January, 1970).

Digangi, S.A., Perryman, P., & Rutherford, R.B., Jr. (1990). Juvenile Offenders in the 90's A Descriptive Analysis. *Perceptions, 25*(4), 5-8.

Division of Educational Services, Special Education Programs (1986). *Fifteenth Annual Report to Congress on Implementation of the Education of the Handicapped Act.* Washington, D.C.: U.S. Government Printing Office.

Doyle, B.A. (1978). Math Readiness Skills. Paper presented at National Association of School Psychologists, New York. K.J. (1978). *Teaching Students Through Their Individual Learning Styles.*

Drummond, R.J. (2000). *Appraisal Procedures for Counselors and Helping Professionals.* (4th ed.) Englewood Cliffs, NJ: Merrill/Prentice Hall.

Duke, N. K., Bennett-Armistead, V. S., & Roberts, E. M. (2002). "Incorporating Information text in the Primary Grades." In C. Roller (Ed.), *Comprehensive Reading Instruction across Grade Levels* (pp. 40-54). Newark, DE: International Reading association.

Duke, N. K., Bennett-Armistead, V. S., & Roberts, E. M. (2003). "Bridging the Gap Between Learning to Read and Reading to Learn." In D. M. Barone & L. M.

Morrow (Eds.), *Literacy and Young Children: Research-Based Practices* (pp. 226-242). New York: Guilford Press.

Dunn, R.S., & Dunn, K.J. (1978). *Teaching Students Through Their Individual Learning Styles: A Practical Approach.* Reston, VA: Reston.

Ehri, L. (1999). Phases if Development in Learning to Read Words. In J. Oakhill & R. Beard (Eds.), *Reading Development and the Teaching of reading: A Psychological Perspective,* 79-108. Oxford, UK: Blackwell Publishers.

Ehri, L. C., and S. McCormick. (1998). "Phases of Word Learning: Implications for Instruction with Delayed and Disabled Readers". *Reading and Writing Quarterly.* 14, no. 2: 135-164.

Ehri, Linnea C., and Alison G. Soffer. (1999). "Graphophonemic Awareness: Development in Elementary Students". *Scientific Studies of Reading.* 3, no. 1: 1-30

Ekwall, E.E., & Shanker, J.L. 1983). *Diagnosis and Remediation of the Disabled Reader* (2nd ed.) Boston: Allyn and Bacon.

Epstein, M.H., Patton, J.R., Polloway, E.A., & Foley, R. (1989). Mild retardation: Student characteristics and services. *Education and Training of the Mentally Retarded,* 24, 7-16.

Firth, E.E. & Reynolds, I. (1983). Slide tape shows: A creative activity for the gifted students. *Teaching Exceptional Children.* 15(3), 151-153.

Frymier, J., & Gansneder, B. (1989). *The Phi Delta Kappa Study of Students at Risk.* Phi Delta Kappa. 71(2) 142-146.

Fuchs, D., & Deno, S.L. 1992). Effects of curriculum within curriculum-based measurement. *Exceptional Children 58* (232-242).

Fuchs, D., & Fuchs, L.S. (1989). Effects of examiner familiarity on Black, Caucasian, and Hispanic Children. A Meta-Analysis. *Exceptional Children.* 55, 303-308.

Fuchs, L.S., & Shinn, M.R. (1989). Writing CBM IEP objectives. In M.R. Shinn, *Curriculum-based Measurement: Assessing Special Students.* New York: Guilford Press.

Gage, N.L. (1990). *Dealing With the Dropout Problems?* Phi Delta Kappa. 72(4), 280-285.

Gallagher, P.A. (1988). *Teaching Students with Behavior Disorders: Techniques and Activities for Classroom Instruction* (2nd ed.). Denver, CO: Love Publishing.

Gearheart, B.R. (1980). *Special Education for the 80s.* St. Louis, MO: The C.V. Cosby Company.

Gearhart, B.R. & Weishahn, M.W. (1986). *The Handicapped Student in the Regular Classroom* (2nd ed.). St Louis, MO: The C.V. Mosby Company.

Gearhart, B.R. (1985). *Learning Disabilities: Educational Strategies* (4th ed.). St. Louis: Times Mirror/ Mosby College of Publishing.

Georgia Department of Education, Program for Exceptional Children. (1986). *Mild Mentally Handicapped* (Vol. II), Atlanta, GA: Office of Instructional Services, Division of Special Programs, and Program for Exceptional Children. Resource Manuals for Program for Exceptional Children.

Georgia Department of Human Resources, Division of Rehabilitation Services. (1987, February). Request for Proposal [Memorandum]. Atlanta, GA: Author.

Georgia Psychoeducational Network (1990). *An Educational Perspective on: Emotional Disturbance and Social Maladjustment.* Monograph #1. Atlanta, GA Psychoeducational Network.

Geren, K. (1979). *Complete Special Education Handbook.* West Nyack, NY: Parker.

Gillet, P.K. (1988). Career Development. Robinson, G.A., Patton, J.R., Polloway, E.A., & Sargent, L.R. (eds.). *Best Practices in Mild Mental Disabilities.* Reston, VA: The Division on Mental Retardation of the Council for Exceptional Children.

Gleason, J.B. (1993). *The Development of Language* (3rd ed.). New York: Macmillan Publishing.

Good, T.L., & BROPHY, J.E. (1978). *Looking into Classrooms* (2nd Ed.). New York: Harper & Row.

Hall, M.A. (1979). Language-Centered Reading: Premises and Recommendations. *Language Arts, 56* 664-670.

Hallahan, D.P. & Kauffman, J.M. (1988). *Exceptional Children: Introduction to Special Education.* (4th Ed.). Englewood Cliffs, NJ; Prentice-Hall.

Hallahan, D.P. & Kauffman, J.M. (1994). *Exceptional Children: Introduction to Special Education* 6th ed.). Boston: Allyn and Bacon.

Hammill, D.D., & Bartel, N.R. (1982). *Teaching Children With Learning and Behavior Problems* (3rd ed.). Boston: Allyn and Bacon.

Hammill, D.D., & Bartel, N.R. (1986). *Teaching Students with Learning and Behavior Problems* (4th ed.). Boston and Bacon.

Hamill, D.D., & Brown, L. & Bryant, B. (1989) *A Consumer's Guide to Tests in Print.* Austin, TX: Pro-Ed.

Haney, J.B. & Ullmer, E.J. ((1970). *Educational Media and the Teacher.* Dubuque, IA: Wm. C. Brown Company.

Hardman, M.L., Drew, C.J., Egan, M.W., & Wolf, B. (1984). *Human Exceptionality: Society, School, and Family.* Boston: Allyn and Bacon.

Hardman, M.L., Drew, C.J., Egan, M.W., & Worlf, B. (1990). *Human Exceptionality* (3rd ed.). Boston: Allyn and Bacon.

Hargrove, L.J., & Poteet, J.A. (1984). *Assessment in Special Education.* Englewood Cliffs, NJ: Prentice-Hall.

Haring, N.G., & Bateman, B. (1977). *Teaching the Learning Disabled Child.* Englewood Cliffs, NJ: Prentice-Hall.

Harris, K.R., & Pressley, M. (1991). The Nature of Cognitive Strategy Instruction: Interactive strategy instruction. *Exceptional Children, 57,* 392-401.

Hart, T., & Cadora, M.J. (1980). *The Exceptional Child: Label the Behavior* [Videocassette & manual series], Northbrook, IL: Hubbard Scientific Company. (Project STRETCH [Strategies to Train Regular Educators to Teach Children with Handicaps], Module 12, ISBN 0-8331-1917-6).

HART, V. (1981) *Mainstreaming Children with Special Needs.* New York: Longman.

Hatfield, Mary M., Edwards, Nancy Tanner, Bitter, Gary, and Morrow, Jean. *Mathematics Methods for Elementary and Middle School Students.* John Wiley and Sons, Inc.: 2005

Henley, M., Ramsey, R.S., & Algozzine, B. (1993). *Characteristics of and Strategies for Teaching Students with Mild Disabilities.* Boston: Allyn and Bacon.

Hewett, F.M., & Forness, S.R. (1984). *Education of Exceptional Learners.* (3rd ed.). Boston: Allyn and Bacon.

Howe, C.E. (1981) *Administration of Special Education.* Denver: Love.

Human Services Research Institute (1985). *Summary of Data on Handicapped Children and Youth.* (Digest). Washington, D.C.: U.S. Government Printing Office.

Hunt, Nancy, and Kathleen J. Marshall. *Exceptional Children and Youth: An Introduction to Special Education.* Boston: Houghton Mifflin Co, 2005.

International Reading Association. (1997). *The Role of Phonics in reading Instruction: a Positional Statement of the International Reading Association.* Newark, DE: Author (Brochure)

International Reading Association. (1981). *Resolution on Misuse of Grade Equivalents.* Newark, DE: Author.

Johnson, D.W. (1972) *Reaching Out: Interpersonal Effectiveness and Self-Actualization.* Englewood Cliffs, NJ: Prentice-Hall.

Johnson, Dale D, and Pearson, P. David. (1984). *Teaching Reading Vocabulary.* New York: Holt, Rinehart and Winston.

Johnson, D.W. (1978) H*uman Relations and Your Career: A Guide to Interpersonal Skills.* Englewood Cliffs, NJ: Prentice-Hall.

Johnson, D.W., & Johnson, R.T. (1990). *Social Skills for Successful Group Work. Educational Leadership. 47* (4) 29-33.

Johnson, S.W., & Morasky, R.L. *Learning Disabilities* (2nd ed.) Boston: Allyn and Bacon.

Jones, F.H. (1987). *Positive Classroom Discipline.* New York: McGraw-Hill Book Company.

Jones, V.F., & Jones, L. S. (1986). *Comprehensive Classroom Management: Creating Positive Learning Environments.* (2nd ed.). Boston: Allyn and Bacon.

Jones, V.F. & Jones, L.S. (1981). *Responsible Classroom Discipline: Creating Positive Learning Environments and Solving Problems.* Boston: Allyn and Bacon.

Kauffman, J.M. (1981) *Characteristics of Children's Behavior Disorders.* (2nd ed.). Columbus, OH: Charles E. Merrill.

Kauffman, J.M. (1989). *Characteristics of Behavior Disorders of Children and Youth.* (4th ed.). Columbus, OH: Merrill Publishing.

Kem, M., & Nelson, M. (1983). *Strategies for Managing Behavior Problems in the Classroom.* Columbus, OH: Charles E. Merrill.

Kerr, M.M., & Nelson, M. (1983) *Strategies for Managing Behavior Problems in the Classroom.* Columbus, OH: Charles E. Merrill.

Kirk, S.A., & Gallagher, J.J. (1986). *Educating Exceptional Children* (5th ed.). Boston: Houghton Mifflin.

Kohfeldt, J. (1976). Blueprints for construction. *Focus on Exceptional Children. 8* (5), 1-14.

Kokaska, C.J., & Brolin, D.E. (1985). *Career Education for Handicapped Individuals* (2nd ed.). Columbus, OH: Charles E. Merrill.

Lambie, R.A. (1980). A systematic approach for changing materials, instruction, and assignments to meet individual needs. *Focus on Exceptional Children,* 13(1), 1-12.

Larson, S.C., & Poplin, M.S. (1980). *Methods for Educating the Handicapped: An Individualized Education Program Approach.* Boston: Allyn and Bacon.

Lerner, J. (1976) *Children with Learning Disabilities.* (2ⁿᵈ ed.). Boston: Houghton Mifflin.

Lerner, J. (1989). *Learning Disabilities,: Theories, Diagnosis and Teaching Strategies* (3ʳᵈ ed.). Boston: Houghton Mifflin.

Levenkron, S. (1991). *Obsessive-Compulsive Disorders.* New York: Warner Books.

Lewis, R.B., & Doorlag, D.H. (1991). *Teaching Special Students in the Mainstream.* (3ʳᵈ ed.). New York: Merrill.

Lindsley, O. R. (1990). Precision Teaching: By Teachers for Children. *Teaching Exceptional Children, 22.* (3), 10-15.

Linddberg, L., & Swedlow, R. (1985). *Young Children Exploring and Learning.* Boston: Allyn and Bacon.

Linn, R.L., Gronlund, N.E., & Gronlund, N.E. (1995). *Measurement and Assessment in Teaching.* Upper Saddle River, NJ: Merrill.

Long, N.J., Morse, W.C., & Newman, R.G. (1980). *Conflict in the Classroom: The Education of Emotionally Disturbed Children.* Belmont, CA: Wadsworth.

Losen, S.M., & Losen, J.G. (1985). *The Special Education Team.* Boston: Allyn and Bacon.

Lovitt, T.C. (1989). *Introduction to Learning Disabilities.* Boston: Allyn and Bacon.

Lund, N.J., & Duchan, J.F. (1988)/ *Assessing Children's Language in Naturalist Contexts.* Englewood Cliffs, NJ: Prentice Hall

Male, M. (1994) *Technology for Inclusion: Meeting the Special Needs of all Children.* (2ⁿᵈ ed.). Boston: Allyn and Bacon.

Mandelbaum, L.H. (1989). Reading. In G.A. Robinson, J.R., Patton, E.A., Polloway, & L.R. Sargent (eds.). *Best Practices in Mild Mental Retardation.* Reston, VA: The Division of Mental Retardation, Council for Exceptional Children.

Mannix. D. (1993). *Social Skills for Special Children.* West Nyack, NY: The Center for Applied Research in Education.

Marshall, et al. vs. Georgia U.S. District Court for the Southern District of Georgia. C.V. 482-233. June 28, 1984.

Marshall, E.K., Kurtz, P.D., & Associates. *Interpersonal Helping Skills.* San Francisco, CA: Jossey-Bass Publications.

Marston, D.B. (1989) A curriculum-based measurement approach to assessing academic performance: What it is and why do it. In M. Shinn (Ed.). *Curriculum-Based Measurement: Assessing Special Children.* New York: Guilford Press.

McDowell, R.L., Adamson, G.W., & Wood, F.H. (1982). *Teaching Emotionally Disturbed Children.* Boston: Little, Brown and Company.

MCGINNIS, E., GOLDSTEIN, A.P. (1990). *Skill Streaming in Early Childhood: Teaching prosocial skills to the preschool and kindergarten child.* Champaign, IL: Research Press.

Mcloughlin, J.A., & Lewis, R.B. (1986). *Assessing Special Students* (3rd ed.). Columbus, OH: Charles E. Merrill.

Mercer, C.D. (1987). *Students with Learning Disabilities.* (3rd. ed.). Merrill Publishing.

Mercer, C.D., & Mercer, A.R. (1985). *Teaching Children with Learning Problems* (2nd ed.). Columbus, OH: Charles E. Merrill.

Meyen, E.L., Vergason, G.A., & Whelan, R.J. (Eds.). (1988). *Effective Instructional Strategies for Exceptional Children.* Denver, CO: Love Publishing.

Miller, L.K. (1980). *Principles of Everyday Behavior Analysis* (2nd ed.). Monterey, CA: Brooks/Cole Publishing Company.

Mills Vs. The Board of Education of The District of Columbia, 348 F. Supp. 866 (D.C. 1972).

Mitchell, J.N. & Irwin, P.A. (1992) "Using a process-oriented retelling profile." In Gambrell, L.B. & Walker, B.J., *Holistic comprehension: Linking instruction and assessment,* Pre-Convention Institute, International Reading Association, Orlando, Florida

Mopsick, S.L. & Agard, J.A. (Eds.) (1980). Cambridge, MA: Abbott Associates.

Morsink, Catherine V. (1984). *Teaching special needs students in regular classrooms.* Boston: Little, Brown.

Morris, C.G. (1985). *Psychology: An Introduction* (5th Ed.). Englewood Cliffs, Nj: Prentice-Hall.

Morris, J. (1980). *Behavior Modification.* [Videocassette And Manual Series]. Northbrook, Il: Hubbard Scientific Company. (Project Stretch [Strategies To

Train Regular Educators To Teach Children With Handicaps,] Module 16, Metropolitan Cooperative Educational Service Agency.).

Morris, J. & Demonbreun, C. (1980). *Learning Styles* [Videocassettes & Manual Series]. Northbrook, Il: Hubbard Scientific Company. (Project Stretch [Strategies To Train Regular Educators To Teach Children With Handicaps], Module 15, Isbn 0-8331-1920-6).

Morris, R.J. (1985). *Behavior Modification With Exceptional Children: Principles And Practices.* Glenview, Il: Scott, Foresman And Company.

Morsink, C.V. (1984). *Teaching Special Needs Students In Regular Classrooms.* Boston: Little, Brown And Company.

Morsink, C.V., Thomas, C.C., & Correa, V.L. (1991). *Interactive Teaming, Consultation And Collaboration In Special Programs.* New York: Macmillan Publishing.

Mullsewhite, C.R. (1986). *Adaptive Play For Special Needs Children: Strategies To Enhance Communication And Learning.* San Diego: College Hill Press.

Nagy, William E. (1988) *Teaching Vocabulary to Improve Reading Comprehension.* ERIC Clearinghouse on Reading and Communication Skills.

National Council of Teachers of Mathematics. *Principles and Standards for School mathematics.* Reston, VA: NCTM, 2000

National Reading Panel. *Teaching Children To Read: An Evidence-Based Assessment of the Scientific Research Literature on Reading and Its Implications for Reading Instruction:* Reports of the Subgroups. ERIC Document 444127

North Central Georgia Learning Resources System/Child Serve. (1985). *Strategies Handbook For Classroom Teachers.* Ellijay, Ga.

Patton, J.R., Cronin, M.E., Polloway, E.A., Hutchinson, D., & Robinson, G.A. (1988). Curricular Considerations: A Life Skills Orientation. In Robinson, G.A., Patton, J.R., Polloway, E.A., & Sargent, L.R. (Eds.). *Best Practices In Mental Disabilities.* Des Moines, Ia: Iowa Department Of Education, Bureau Of Special Education.

Patton, J.R., Kauggman, J.M., Blackbourn, J.M., & Brown, B.G. (1991). *Exceptional Children In Focus* (5th Ed.). New York: Macmillan.

Paul, J.L. (Ed.). (1981). *Understanding And Working With Parents Of Children with Special Needs.* New York: Holt, Rinehart and Winston.

Paul, J.L. & Epanchin, B.C. (1991). *Educating Emotionally Disturbed Children And Youth: Theories And Practices For Teachers.* (2nd Ed.). New York: MacMillan. PENNSYLVANIA ASSOCIATION FOR RETARDED CHILDREN VS. COMMONWEALTH OF PENNSYLVANIA, 334 F. Supp. 1257 (E.D., PA., 1971), 343 F. Supp. 279 (L.D. PA., 19972).

Perfetti, C. A., Beck, I., Bell, L., & Hughes, C. (1987). "Phonemic Knowledge and Learning to read are reciprocal: A Longitudinal Study of First Grade Children." *Merrill-Palmer Quarterly, 33,* 283-319.

Phillips, V., & Mccullough, L. (1990). Consultation Based Programming: Instituting The Collaborative Work Ethic. *Exceptional Children. 56* (4), 291-304.

Podemski, R.S., Price, B.K., Smith, T.E.C., & Marsh, G.E., Il (1984). *Comprehensive Administration Of Special Education.* Rockville, Md: Aspen Systems Corporation.

Polloway, E.A., & Patton, J.R. (1989). *Strategies For Teaching Learners With Special Needs.* (5th Ed.). New York: Merrill.

Polloway, E.A., Patton, J.R., Payne, J.S., & Payne, R.A. 1989). *Strategies For Teaching Learners With Special Needs,* 4th Ed.). Columbus, Oh: Merrill Publishing.

Pugach, M.C., & Johnson, L.J. (1989a). The Challenge Of Implementing Collaboration Between General And Special Education. *Exceptional Children, 56* (3), 232-235.

Pugach, M.C., & Johnson, L.J. (1989b). Pre-Referral Interventions: Progress, Problems, And Challenges. *Exceptional Children, 56* (3), 217-226.

Radabaugh, M.T., & Yukish, J.F. (1982). *Curriculum And Methods For The Mildly Handicapped.* Boston: Allyn And Bacon.

Ramsey, R.S. (1981). Perceptions Of Disturbed And Disturbing Behavioral Characteristics By School Personnel. (Doctoral Dissertation, University Of Florida) Dissertation Abstracts International, 42(49), Da8203709.

Ramsey, R.S. (1986). Taking The Practicum Beyond The Public School Door. *Journal Of Adolescence.* 21(83), 547-552.

Ramsey, R.S., (1988). *Preparatory Guide For Special Education Teacher Competency Tests.* Boston: Allyn And Bacon, Inc.

Ramsey, R.S., Dixon, M.J., & Smith, G.G.B. (1986) *Eyes On The Special Education: Professional Knowledge Teacher Competency Test.* Albany, Ga: Southwest Georgia Learning Resources System Center.

Ramsey R.W., & Ramsey, R.S. (1978). Educating The Emotionally Handicapped Child In The Public School Setting. *Journal Of Adolescence. 13*(52), 537-541.

Reid, D.K. (1988). *Teaching the Learning Disabled: A Cognitive Developmental Approach.* Boston: Allyn & Bacon.

Reinheart, H.R. (1980). *Children I Conflict: Educational Strategies For The Emotionally Disturbed And Behaviorally Disordered.* (2nd Ed.). St Louis, Mo: The C.V. Mosby Company.

Rigg, Pat, and Virginia G. Allen, eds. *When They Don't All Speak English: Integrating the ESL Student into the Regular Classroom.* Urbana, IL: National Council of Teachers of English, 1989.

Robinson, G.A., Patton, J.R., Polloway, E.A., & Sargent, L.R. (Eds.). (1989a). *Best Practices In Mental Disabilities.* Des Moines, IA Iowa Department Of Education, Bureau Of Special Education.

Robinson, G.A., Patton, J.R., Polloway, E.A., & Sargent, L.R. (Eds.). (1989b). *Best Practices In Mental Disabilities.* Renton, VA: The Division On Mental Retardation Of The Council For Exceptional Children.

Rothstein, L.F. (1995). *Special Education Law* (2nd Ed.). New York: Longman Publishers.

Sabatino, D.A., Sabation, A.C., & Mann, L. (1983). *Management: A Handbook Of Tactics, Strategies, And Programs.* Aspen Systems Corporation.

Salvia, J., & Ysseldyke, J.E. (1985). *Assessment In Special Education* (3rd. Ed.). Boston: Houghton Mifflin.

Salvia J., & Ysseldyke, J.E. (1991). *Assessment* (5th Ed.). Boston: Houghton Mifflin.

Salvia, J. & Ysseldyke, J.E. (1995) *Assessment* (6th Ed.). Boston: Houghton Mifflin.

Sattler, J.M. (1982). *Assessment Of Children's Intelligence And Special Abilities* (2nd Ed.). Boston: Allyn And Bacon.

Schloss, P.J., Harriman, N., & Pfiefer, K. (In Press). Application Of A Sequential Prompt Reduction Technique To The Independent Composition Performance Of Behaviorally Disordered Youth. *Behavioral Disorders.*

Schloss, P.J.., & Sedlak, R.A.(1986). *Instructional Methods For Students With Learning And Behavior Problems.* Boston: Allyn And Bacon.

Schmuck, R.A., & Schmuck, P.A. (1971). *Group Processes In The Classroom.* Dubuque, Ia: William C. Brown Company.

Schubert, D.G. (1978). Your Teaching - The Tape Recorder. *Reading Improvement, 15*(1), 78-80.

Schulz, J.B., Carpenter, C.D., & Turnbull, A.P. (1991). *Mainstreaming Exceptional Students: A Guide For Classroom Teachers.* Boston: Allyn And Bacon.

Semmel, M.I., Abernathy, T.V., Butera G., & Lesar, S. (1991). Teacher Perception Of The Regular Education Initiative. *Exceptional Children, 58* (1), 3-23.

Shea, T.M., & Bauer, A.M. (1985). *Parents And Teachers Of Exceptional Students: A Handbook For Involvement.* Boston: Allyn And Bacon.

Silvaroli, Nicholas, and Warren Wheelock. (2004) *Classroom Reading Inventory.* Boston: McGraw-Hill.

Simeonsson, R.J. (1986). *Psychological And Development Assessment Of Special Children.* Boston: Allyn And Bacon.

Smith, C.R. (1991). *Learning Disabilities: The Interaction Of Learner, Task, And Setting.* Boston: Little, Brown, And Company.

Smith, D.D., & Luckasson, R. (1992). *Introduction to Special Education: Teaching In An Age Of Challenge.* Boston: Allyn And Bacon.

Smith, J.E., & Patton, J.M. (1989). *A Resource Module On Adverse Causes Of Mild Mental Retardation.* (Prepared For The President's Committee On Mental Retardation).

Smith, Richard John, and Thomas C. Barrett. *Teaching reading in the middle grades.* Reading, Mass.: Addison-Wesley, 1974.

Smith, T.E.C., Finn, D.M., & Dowdy, C.A. (1993). *Teaching Students With Mild Disabilities.* Fort Worth, Tx: Harcourt Brace Jovanovich College Publishers.

Smith-Davis, J. (1989a April). *A National Perspective On Special Education.* Keynote Presentation At The Glrs/College/University Forum, Macon, Ga.

Stephens, T.M. (1976). *Directive Teaching Of Children With Learning And Behavioral Disorders.* Columbus, Oh Charles E. Merrill.

Sternburg, R.J. (1990). *Thinking Styles: Key To Understanding Performance.* Phi Delta Kappa, 71(5), 366-371.

Stiggins, R.J. (1997). *Student-Centered Classroom Assessment.* Upper Saddle River, NJ: Merrill.

Strickland, Dorothy S., and Shannon Riley-Ayers. *Early Literacy: Policy and Practice in the Preschool Years.* New Brunswick, N.J.: National Institute for Early Education Research, 2006.

Sulzer, B., & Mayer, G.R. (1972). *Behavior Modification Procedures For School Personnel.* Hinsdale, Il: Dryden.

Taberski, Sharon. *On Solid Ground: Strategies for Teaching Reading K-3*. Westport, CT: Heinemann, 2000.

Tateyama-Sniezek, K.M. (1990.) Cooperative Learning: Does It Improve The Academic Achievement Of Students With Handicaps? *Exceptional Children, 57*(2), 426-427.

Thiagarajan, S. (1976). Designing Instructional Games For Handicapped Learners. *Focus On Exceptional Children.* 7(9), 1-11.

Thomas, O. (1980). *Individualized Instruction* [Videocassette & Manual Series]. Northbrook, Il: Hubbard Scientific Company. (Project Stretch [Strategies To Train Regular Educators To Teach Children With Handicaps]. Module 14, Isbn 0-8331-1919-2).

Thomas, O. (1980). *Spelling* [Videocassette & Manual Series]. (Project Stretch [Strategies To Train Regular Educators To Teach Children With Handicaps]. Module 10, Isbn 0-83311915-X).

Thornton, C.A., Tucker, B.F., Dossey, J.A., & Bazik, E.F. (1983). *Teaching Mathematics To Children With Special Needs.* Menlo Park, Ca: Addison-Wesley.

Tomlinson, Carol A. *How to Differentiate Instruction in Mixed-Ability Classrooms.* Alexandria, Va.: Association for Supervision and Curriculum Development, 1995.

Torgesen, J. K., and Bryant, B. R. (1993). *Test of Phonological Awareness*. Austin, Texas: PRO-ED.

Torgesen, Joseph K. (2007). *Using an RTI model to Guide Early Reading Instruction: Effects on Identification Rates for Students with Learning Disabilities.* Florida State University: Florida Center for reading Research.

Turkel, S.R., & Podel, D.M. (1984). Computer-Assisted Learning For Mildly Handicapped Students. *Teaching Exceptional Children.* 16(4), 258-262.

Turnbull, A.P., Strickland, B.B., & Brantley, J.C. (1978). *Developing Individualized Education Programs.* Columbus, Oh: Charles E. Merrill.

U.S. Department Of Education. (1993). *To Assure The Free Appropriate Public Education Of All Children With Disabilities. (Fifteenth Annual Report To Congress On The Implementation Of The Individuals With Disabilities Education Act.).* Washington, D.C.

Venn, John. (2004). *Assessing Students With Special Needs*. Upper Saddle River, N.J.: Pearson/Merrill/Prentice Hall.

Walker, J.E., & Shea, T.M. (1991). *Behavior Management: A Practical Approach For Educators.* New York: Macmillan.

Wallace, G., & Kauffman, J.M. (1978). *Teaching Children With Learning Problems.* Columbus, Oh: Charles E. Merrill.

Warger, Cynthia. *Helping Students With Disabilities Participate In Standards-Based Mathematics Curriculum.* Arlington, Va: Eric Clearinghouse On Disabilities And Gifted Education, 2002. Eric Document 468579

Wehman, P., & Mclaughlin, P.J. (1981). *Program Development In Special Education.* New York: Mcgraw-Hill.

Weintraub, F.J. (1987, March). [Interview].

Wesson, C.L. (1991). Curriculum-Based Measurement And Two Models Of Follow-Up Consultation. *Exceptional Children.* 57(3), 246-256.

West, R.P., Young, K.R., & Spooner, F. (1990). Precision Teaching: An Introduction. *Teaching Exceptional Children.* 22(3), 4-9.

Wheeler, J. (1987). *Transitioning Persons With Moderate And Severe Disabilities From School To Adulthood: What Makes It Work?* Materials Development Center, School Of Education, And Human Services. University Of Wisconsin-Stout.

Whiting, J., & Aultman, L. (1990). *Workshop For Parents.* (Workshop Materials). Albany, Ga: Southwest Georgia Learning Resources System Center.

Wiederholt, J.L., Hammill, D.D., & Brown, V.L. (1983). *The Resource Room Teacher: A Guide To Effective Practices* (2nd Ed.). Boston: Allyn And Bacon.

Wiig, E.H., & Semel, E.M. (1984). *Language Assessment And Intervention For The Learning Disabled.* (2nd Ed.). Columbus, Oh: Charles E. Merrill.

Wolfgang, C.H., & Glickman, C.D.(1986). *Solving Discipline Problems: Strategies For Classroom Teachers* (2nd Ed.). Boston: Allyn And Bacon.

Wood, Barbara S.(1976). *Children and Communication: Verbal and Nonverbal Language.* Englewood Cliffs, NJ:Prentice-hall.

Woods, Mary Lynn, and Alden J. Moe. (1995) *Analytical Reading Inventory: Assessing Reading Strategies for Literature/Story, Science, and Social Studies. For Use with All Students Including Gifted and Remedial. Fifth Edition.* Old Tappan, NJ: Simon & Schuster.

Ysselkyke, J.E., Algozzine, B., (1990). *Introduction To Special Education* (2nd Ed.). Boston: Houghton Mifflin.

Ysseldyke, J.E., Algozzine, B., & Thurlow, M.L. (1992). *Critical Issues In Special Education* (2nd Ed.). Boston: Houghton Mifflin Company.

Yssedlyke, J.E., Thurlow, M.L., Wotruba, J.W., Nania, Pa.A (1990). Instructional Arrangements: Perceptions From General Education. *Teaching Exceptional Children, 22*(4), 4-8.

Zargona, N., Vaughn, S., 7 Mcintosh, R. (1991). Social Skills Interventions And Children With Behavior Problems: A Review. *Behavior Disorders, 16*(4), 260-275.

Zigmond, N., & Baker, J. (1990). Mainstream Experiences For Learning Disabled Students (Project Meld): Preliminary Report. *Exceptional Children, 57*(2), 176-185.

Zirpoli, T.J., & Melloy, K.J. (1993). *Behavior Management.* New York: Merrill.

Additional updated citations to add to the reference list:

ACT. (2013). Readiness matters: The impact of college readiness on college persistence and degree completion. In ACT (Ed.), *ACT Research and Policy: Policy Report*. ACT. Retrieved from

http://www.act.org/research/policymakers/pdf/ReadinessMatters.pdf

Bandura, A. (1994). Self-efficacy. *Encyclopedia of Human Behavior*. New York: Academic Press.

Bausmith, J. M., & Barry, C. (2011). Revisiting professional learning communities to increase college readiness: The importance of pedagogical content knowledge. *Educational Researcher, 40*(4), 175-178.

Berry, M. (2002). Healthy school environment and enhanced school performance: The case of Charles Young Elementary School, Washington, DC, *The Carpet and Rug Institute,* 1-27.

Casilas, A., Allen, J., Kuo, Y., Pappas, S., Hanson, M., & Robbins, S. (2011). *Development and validation of ENGAGE, grades 6-9*. Iowa City, IA: ACT Research Report Series. Retrieved from

http://files.eric.ed.gov/fulltext/ED542015.pdf

College Board. (2013, September 26). *Stagnant 2013 SAT results are a call to action for the College Board*. Retrieved from

http://press.collegeboard.org/releases/2013/stagnant-2013-sat-results-require-action

Dobler, E., Johnson, D., & Wolsey, T. (2013). *Teaching the language arts: Forward thinking in today's classrooms*. (1st ed.) : Holcomb Hathaway.

Fullan, M. (2011). Intrinsic motivation. *Leadership Excellence, 28*(12), 6-7.

Fullan, M. (1995). The school as a learning organization: Distant dreams. *Theory Into Practice, 34*(4), 230.

Fullan, M. (2001). *Leading in a culture of change.* San Francisco: Jossey-Bass.

Goleman, D. (2004). What makes a leader? *Harvard Business Review, 82*(1), 82- 91.

Goleman, D., Boyatzis, R.E., McKee, A. (2004). *Primal leadership, learning to lead with emotional intelligence.* (1 ed.). Boston: Harvard Business Press.

Goleman, D., Boyatzis, R., & McKee, A. (2004). *Primal leadership: Learning to lead with emotional intelligence.* Boston: Harvard Business Review Press.

Graham, S., MacArthur, C. A., & Fitzgerald, J. (Eds.). (2013). *Best practices in writing instruction.* Guilford Press.

Kitchen, M. (2012). Facilitating small groups: How to encourage student learning. *Clinical Teacher 9*(1), 3-8.

Kouzes, J., & Posner, B. (2012). *The leadership challenge.* (5th ed.). San Francisco: Jossey-Bass.

Lacey-Castelot, S. (2013). *Note-taking technology for students with LD and ADHD.* Retrieved from http://www.smartkidswithld.org/guide-to-action/at-tool-kit/note-taking-technology-for-students-with-ld-and-adhd

Leonard, J. (2013). Maximizing college readiness for all through parental support. *School Community Journal, 23*(1), 183-202.

Marshall, J., & Peters, M. (1985). Evaluation and education: The ideal learning community. *Policy Sciences, 18*(3), 263-288.

National Governors Association Center for Best Practices and Council of Chief State School Officers, (2012).*Common core state standards initiative*. Retrieved from website: http://www.corestandards.org/

Palestini, R. (2003). The human touch. Lanham, Maryland: Scarecrow Press, Inc.

Pattakos, A. (2009). The search for meaning in education. *Interbeing, 3*(2), 31-32.

Periathiruvadi, S., & Rinn, A. N. (2012). Technology in gifted education: A review of best practices and empirical research. *Journal Of Research On Technology In Education, 45*(2), 153-169.

Ramani, G., Siegler, R. & Hitti, A. (2012). Taking it to the classroom: Number board games as a small group learning activity. *Journal of Educational Psychology, 104*(3), 661-672.

Santos, A. (2009). Going green: The impact on higher education institutions. *Journal Of International Business Research,* 895-100.

Smilkstein, R. (2003). *We're born to learn: Using the brain's natural learning process to create today's curriculum*. Thousand Oaks, CA: Corwin Press.

Interested in dual certification?

XAMonline offers over 25 FTCE study guides which are aligned to current standards and provide a comprehensive review of the core test content. Want certification success on your first exam? Trust XAMonline's study guides to help you succeed!

FTCE Series:

- **Educational Media Specialist PK-12**
  978-1-58197-578-9
- **Middle Grades General Science 5-9**
  978-1-60787-008-1
- **Middle Grades Social Science 5-9**
  978-1-60787-010-4
- **Exceptional Education Ed. K-12**
  978-1-60787-473-7
- **Guidance and Counseling PK-12**
  978-1-58197-586-4
- **Prekindergarten/Primary PK-3**
  978-1-60787-386-0
- **FELE Florida Education Leadership**
  978-1-60787-001-2
- **Elementary Education K–6**
  978-1-60787-506-2
- **Middle Grades English 5-9**
  978-1-58197-597-0
- **Physical Education K-12**
  978-1-58197-616-8

- **General Knowledge Test**
  978-1-60787-533-8
- **Mathematics 6–12**
  978-1-60787-505-5
- **Professional Education**
  978-1-60787-574-1
- **Social Science 6–12**
  978-1-60787-503-1
- **English 6-12**
  978-1-60787-463-8
- **ESOL K–12**
  978-1-60787-530-7
- **Biology 6-12**
  978-1-58197-689-2
- **Chemistry 6-12**
  978-1-58197-046-3
- **Physics 6-12**
  978-1-58197-044-9
- **Reading K-12**
  978-1-58197-659-5

Don't see your test? Visit our website: www.xamonline.com

XAMonline.com

CPSIA information can be obtained
at www.ICGtesting.com
Printed in the USA
LVOW05s2122151117
556474LV00028B/168/P